AI
RISING

AI RISING

INDIA'S ARTIFICIAL INTELLIGENCE GROWTH STORY

Leslie D'Monte and Jayanth N. Kolla

JAICO PUBLISHING HOUSE

Ahmedabad Bangalore Chennai
Delhi Hyderabad Kolkata Mumbai

Published by Jaico Publishing House
A-2 Jash Chambers, 7-A Sir Phirozshah Mehta Road
Fort, Mumbai - 400 001
jaicopub@jaicobooks.com
www.jaicobooks.com

AI RISING
ISBN 978-93-93559-84-5

First Jaico Impression: 2023

Page design and layout by Inosoft Systems, Delhi

This book has been entirely written by humans.
No chapter, section, or even paragraph has been generated by
AI—maybe one of the last ones of its kind on the subject.

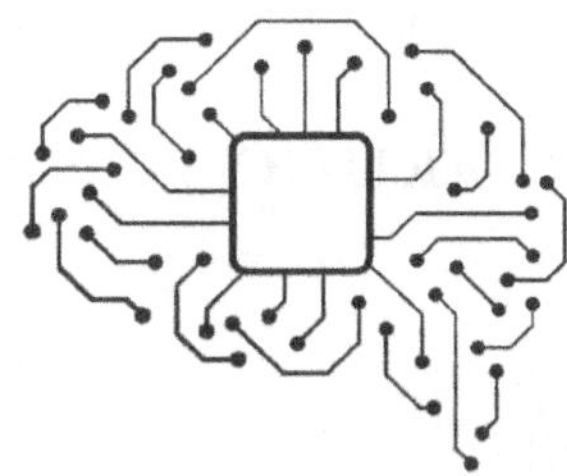

CONTENTS

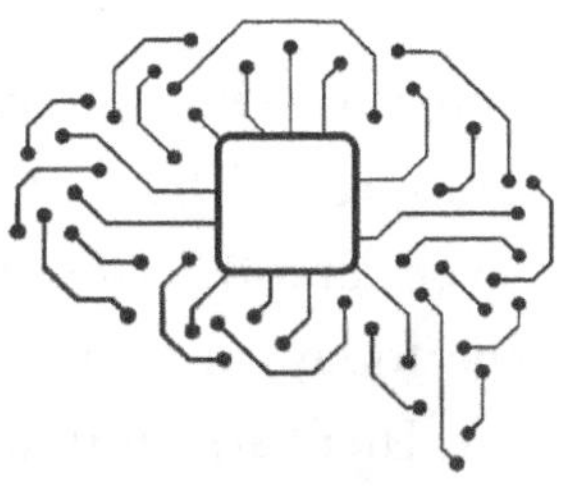

FOREWORD

Today, AI can fly an aeroplane, beat humans at the game of Go, solve protein folding, and predict the next weather storm. It touches every part of our lives. Every time you used that search engine to look for something online or had your favourite OTT platform recommend a movie you might like, it was AI at work. AI has spared you from those thousands of spam emails in your inbox and performed millions of calculations to assist you during your online shopping. It understood your voice commands and unlocked your phone by simply looking at you. Indeed! AI is at work.

In fact, it would be almost impossible to find a domain or industry today that is not in some way touched by or is not benefiting from digital technologies or AI.

SECOND SPRING OF AI

All these things did not happen overnight. AI has been in the making for a long 60+ years in the computer science research community. It has even been in computer science curricula for 30+ years. The development of modern AI came to where we are today in a series of dramatic ups and downs, which are often referred to as "AI Winters".

AI HAS ARRIVED, AND IT IS GOING TO STAY

I clearly remember my engineering school days (not that long ago) when AI was going through its second winter. It was an optional subject in our computer engineering curriculum, and to be perfectly honest, it was taught as nothing more than simple symbol manipulation techniques or rule-based semantic ontologies. Those memories of programming in Prolog and Lisp are not even remotely close to what AI looks like today. AI has taken centre stage today when it comes to computer science research and development. There are thousands of AI software libraries, platforms, and frameworks with large research communities behind them. Computing hardware and devices are also being specifically built with a core focus on AI runtime performance.

We have made a huge leap after the long second winter of AI. The recent developments in the sub-fields of AI, such as deep learning (DL) and generative AI, have given new hope and generated new possibilities. As we speak, millions of new AI models are being trained, and new architectures are being developed. Once optional, AI is now at the core of the software and computing industry.

But the AI we are talking about is still simple, task-oriented, and domain-specific. It could be an algorithm or piece of code that has learnt which movie you may like based on your preferences and your browsing (and movie-watching) history. Or a voice assistant that helps you reserve a table for dinner by calling the restaurant and booking it on your behalf. All this may sound magical and lull us into thinking that digital computing has come this far, thanks to AI.

In reality, we are still leagues away from a fully autonomous, general-purpose intelligence or a machine that can truly feel and emote. That said, AI has made great strides in the past couple of years after a long second winter, in my humble opinion. It is an exciting time, and one thing is clear: now that AI is here, it is going to stay and define the next chapter of how we live, play, learn, and work.

COFFEE IN CAMBRIDGE

I met Leslie in person for the first time in the fall of 2010. While I was doing my PhD at MIT, he was an MIT Knight Science Journalism Fellow and was visiting Cambridge for a year. From our very first meeting, our interests seemed aligned. From the future of technology to how we learn, from augmented reality to AI, we had some intriguing conversations over coffee on varied topics. Leslie's ability to bridge the gap between science and business or technology and its effects has always impressed me.

In this book, Leslie again does what he is best at. He seamlessly demystifies the buzzwords in the context of AI and presents a fresh perspective on the subject. He makes a topic as complex as AI easy to understand. I was fortunate to read the first drafts of this book, and I can firmly say that whether you are a student or a businessman, this book will delight you and help you navigate the AI terrain—what it is all about, where it is headed, and how it will help you. In the later chapters of the book, he also introduces some interesting hypotheses on why India is primed and ready to be a leader in this space. I particularly enjoyed his take on data and ethics in AI.

THE THREE *A'S* OF AI

Development in the field of AI can be broadly segmented into three categories (explained in detail later). These three A's of AI are like the three stages of maturity or intelligence levels of AI.

Automation is about encoding abstractions from provided large data sets and using them to automate simple tasks normally performed by humans. Nearly all current machine learning (ML) and early symbolic AI development fall into this category. Simple tasks such as spam detection and optical character recognition (OCR) are some examples.

The second level is Assistance, where AI can help us make sense of the world. At present, major new developments in DL and ML fall into this category, but they are mostly limited to simple text, audio, or simple visual manipulation that require supervision and lack personalisation. When you ask your voice assistant what the weather will be like this weekend, AI, and in particular NLU (natural language understanding), helps the app to understand our voice commands and assist us.

The last level is Autonomy: AI or AGI (artificial general intelligence) that could think and exist independently. This is still very much in the research domain and will require completely new approaches than the current state-of-the-art AI technologies. Yes, this is what you have seen in that sci-fi movie when AI falls in love or takes over the world. Be assured we are nowhere close to full autonomy, and those are simply imaginative movie scripts (at least, so far). Humans come with a lot of scripted behavioural wisdom. AI comes with none.

DATA AND ETHICS

They say, "AI is as good as the data." I don't disagree. But I would certainly say it is not data that AI is all about. In fact, we have had a lot of data about many things earlier too. There is more to AI than just data or the algorithms that we write to make sense of or train models on that data. The magic is in the architectural structure, the design of learning logic that makes AI powerful and beautiful. Think of our brain. We do have the concept of intelligence, and we do have memory (akin to structured data). But there is a difference between intelligence and memory. Similarly, what brings intelligence to AI is more than data.

The development of AI has been centred on this quest to mimic the human brain or brains in general. We have come a long way in this but still have far to go. As early as 1943, McCulloch and Pitts began to explore how artificial neurons can mimic the human brain. This was well before even a commercial computer existed. But it was Frank Rosenblatt's perceptron in 1958 that was modelled on the structure of the human brain. Although the perceptron demonstrated that it is possible to make an algorithm learn and associate inputs with outputs similar to how our brain learns (as per our current understanding of the brain), it, unfortunately, failed to progress further partially due to Minsky and Papert's 1969 hypothesis.

These two main schools of thought on AI have differed from each other ever since, and even to date, we have no clear common understanding of what AI is. Minsky, in *The Society of Mind*, defines AI as the science of making machines capable of performing tasks that would require intelligence if done by humans. On the other hand, some recent trends in ML/DL tend to define AI more as an ability or capability to learn rather than one that acquires new skills. But both of these explanations define intelligence in the realm of human-like skills or capabilities and, in my opinion, miss the point that for machines to be intelligent, they need not necessarily have human-like intelligence.

What I want to argue here is that our general quest to build a human-like intelligence should not come in the way of us making smarter machines or smarter systems that can empower our daily life. My coffee machine or vacuum cleaner, for instance, doesn't need to have human-like intelligence or emotions to help me make good coffee or clean my carpet better.

Also, our understanding of data comes preloaded with concerns about privacy and ethics. While this is an important topic, I believe there are ways we can handle data without compromising privacy or ethics. For example, a recent development such as homomorphic encryption—where we can do ML training and inference on encrypted data—is one indication of the future of data for AI.

AI is the next chapter of the software industry, and here's why we know India will lead in this area.

INDIA AND AI

India's leadership in the IT industry has no parallel. It will be incorrect to say that in this case, AI will follow the same route. But we can surely say that India today has the ability and foundation to lead the future of AI. When software is becoming a synonym for AI, it is almost given that India can lead this next chapter of computing as well. It will not happen automatically, and there will be a need for everyone's support—the software industry, policymakers, and, of course, end-users. The book has a whole chapter dedicated to this theme, so I will not dwell on this further.

THIS BOOK IS ABOUT

No, this book is not about how AI internally works. It is not about the mathematical foundation for ML or DL. Luckily, you will not find any intimidating equations or algorithms or guides on how to train an AI model in this book. For that, there are thousands of online articles and tutorial videos. This book is also not a guide about how one should deploy or use AI in your industry or domain.

This book is way more enlightening and engaging. In this book, Leslie and Jayanth take us on a thought journey, which I found equivalent to my coffee conversations in Cambridge with Leslie during our shared time at MIT. The book brings a sense of order and simplicity to explain how AI is at work in different domains and different industries. During my days at IIT Bombay, I worked extensively on Indian languages, so I personally found the chapter on AI and Indian languages compelling. In his usual style, Leslie also asks what that super app of AI can be. The answer is, to say the least, interesting.

I would say this book is for everyone. If you are an aspiring student of AI or an entrepreneur, this book is for you. If you are a policymaker or a decision-maker in your business, this book is for you.

BEYOND THE METAVERSE

Our human brains are different from those of every other species of animal. A spider's brain is geared to weaving webs and catching flies, a fish's brain is tuned for life in the water, and a human brain is geared to human affairs. All species' brains have been tuned to their lifestyles through millions of years of evolution. In my opinion, the AI or artificial brain that we create for a machine doesn't need to mimic the human brain or any other brain per se. Nature has always inspired us to create better technologies, and this surely applies to the current development of AI. AI has come a long way and now has become the fabric of our everyday life. It has been invisibly assisting us in everything we do. AI is already at work. We are at the dawn of the AI era, and a whole new exciting tomorrow is waiting to be created.

It took evolution 3.2 billion years to create Einstein. How long would it take AI?

Pranav Mistry
CEO, Two Platforms
and former president and CEO of Samsung Technology & Advanced Research Labs

PART-1

UNDERSTANDING ARTIFICIAL INTELLIGENCE

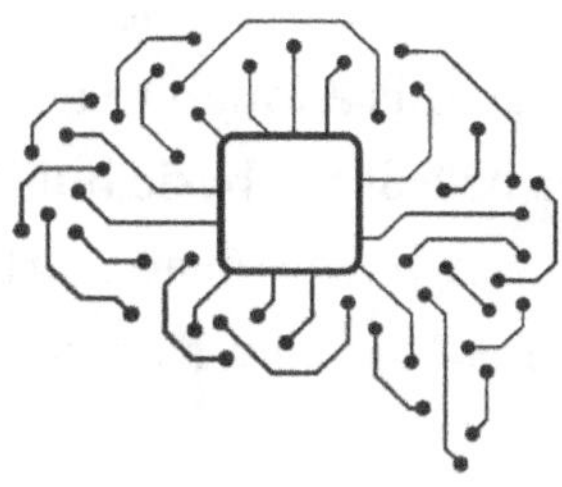

INTRODUCTION

"Education is not the learning of facts, but the training of the mind to think."

—*Albert Einstein*

In 2016, *Mint*—India's second-largest business newspaper that belongs to the HT Media group—signed a deal with the *Massachusetts Institute of Technology (MIT) Technology Review* to jointly organise its prestigious EmTech event in India. Since EmTech stands for Emerging Technologies, the event focused on technologies such as artificial intelligence (AI), machine learning (ML), deep learning (DL), the internet of things, data analytics, blockchain, 3D printing, and Industry 4.0.

As *Mint*'s national technology editor, I was elated and honoured when Sukumar Ranganathan, the then editor of the newspaper, asked me to curate EmTech India. The timing was right. Terms like "Social, Mobile, Analytics and Cloud" (SMAC) and "Bring Your Own Device" (BYOD) had matured to quite an extent. Many people were already banking online and doing banking on their smartphones too. Hence, we decided on the theme, "The Road to Digital Transformation", to reflect all these trends.

It was serendipitous that the government's Digital India campaign had been launched just nine months previously. This gave the speakers and panellists from around the world much to analyse, share, and debate at the EmTech India event, which was held in March 2016 in New Delhi.

R.S. Sharma, the then chairman of the Telecom Regulatory Authority of India (TRAI), was gracious enough to accept our invitation to be the guest of honour. "India has all the basic building blocks of Digital India ready … While we did not have a head start, we do have an advantage going forward and, thus, we can leapfrog," Sharma insisted in his keynote.[1]

I recall John Chambers, who was then the executive chairman of Cisco Systems Inc., enthusiastically pacing up and down the hall during his keynote. In his inimitable style, he pronounced, "If you want to do a startup, this is the right time." He received thunderous applause.

Another keynote speaker at the event, Una May O'Reilly, founder and principal research scientist of the ALFA Group at MIT's Computer Science and Artificial Intelligence (CSAIL) Lab, underscored the potential of AI, the importance of data-driven analytics and ML.

Their observations were bang on target. India's ecosystem now comprises digital payments, digital banking, e-commerce, smart cities, smart governance and Aadhaar—the world's largest biometric ID system—and a National Digital Health Mission too.

India, as Chambers predicted, is now a nation of thousands of startups, of which nearly 10,000 are tech startups. Of these, 44 are tech unicorns that have cumulatively generated $106 billion in value to date, resulting in direct and indirect employment of 1.4 million-plus jobs annually, according to the Indian Tech Unicorn Report 2020 by Orios Venture Partners—an early-stage venture capital fund. These unicorns, or startups, valued at over $1 billion, include MakeMyTrip, InMobi, Paytm, Byju's, Cars24, and Ola.

That said, when we compare India's tech ecosystem with that of the US and China, it is evident that there is much catching up to do. The US has more than 80,000 tech startups, while China has over 15,000 tech startups. The US and China lead in the unicorn space too. According to a March 24, 2021 report by market research firm CB Insights, the US accounts for 50 per cent of all unicorns. China comes second with 23 per cent. The UK takes a distant third spot with 5 per cent, followed by India with 4 per cent.

The good news, though, is that investors continue to believe in the India tech startup story. More importantly, they are also pumping money into artificial intelligence startups, which indicates that they believe in the ability of entrepreneurs in India to create scalable, cutting-edge startups. We will be explaining in detail what AI means and how it works and helps businesses and society over the next few chapters.

For now, though, we will work with Prof. Marvin Minsky's definition of AI as the human desire to make machines do things that would require human-like intelligence, which is an excellent starting point. Minsky knew what he was talking about. He was an AI pioneer, co-founder of the Massachusetts Institute of Technology's AI laboratory, and author of several texts concerning AI and philosophy.

But how do we fulfil this desire to make machines as intelligent as humans, or even more? This question poses a major challenge to scientists since our intelligence stems from our brains. The reason is that the human brain is very complex, and we do not fully understand how it functions. What we do know is that the human brain comprises 80–100 billion neurons that help us think and feel, of course, with assistance from numerous glial cells.

Neurons use electrical impulses and chemical signals to transmit information from one part of the brain to another and to the rest of our nervous system. The way these neurons communicate with each other by making connections is what makes each of us unique in how we think, feel, and act.

We currently do not have the technology to insert a human brain into a machine, though some university researchers are attempting this feat. Ken Hayworth is one such cognitive neuroscientist. President of the Brain Preservation Foundation, his long-term goal is to upload a human mind into a machine.

But this is easier said than done. Preserving the brain using subfreezing temperatures—a practice called cryonics—and resurrecting it when the technology is available is something you currently see only in movies like *Demolition Man*.

In our real world, Arizona-based Alcor Life Extension Foundation does offer a chance to preserve bodies indefinitely using cryonics. That's if you can shell out $2,20,000 per body. As of January 31, 2021, nearly 1,400 people have signed up to have their bodies preserved at Alcor, as per the information available on the Alcor website. The Foundation currently has 181 bodies that are being preserved, waiting for the technology to come of age.

Till such time, though, scientists are using AI applications such as ML, DL, computer vision, natural language processing (NLP), robotics, and automation to make machines intelligent.

ML, a subset of AI, provides systems with the ability to automatically learn and improve from experience without specific programming. DL is an ML technique that uses artificial neural networks (ANNs) modelled loosely on the human brain to identify patterns and classify information.

For instance, radiologists are using ML and DL to see visual patterns in X-rays and detect the risk of diseases like cancers faster and more accurately. DL is being used at airports to scan faces and identify suspicious behaviour or criminals who are using disguises. We have provided numerous examples in the following chapters to show how AI helps companies across sectors.

That investors understand the benefit of AI well can be surmised from the fact that AI startups in India attracted $836.3 million in funding in 2020, according to a report by AIM Research. The research projects double-digit growth in the next five to six years.[2]

The report points out that in 2020, most of the funding went to AI startups that utilised data science or DL technologies to develop their core digital or technology products and services across various sectors. In the same period, robotics startups received $7 million in funding. AI startups in agriculture, industrial and manufacturing, real estate, and consumer goods sectors, too, attracted cumulative funding of $23.3 million.

All these developments indicate that India has all the makings of a robust AI ecosystem, which again spells good news for companies that use AI.

Many of us think of AI as an exotic technology that is restricted to laboratories. The fact is that AI is all around us. It is already in our smartphones, cameras, and voice assistants, and it can even check our heartbeat and blood pressure. AI is being used to develop driverless vehicles, low-cost satellites, flying copters, and smart robots that work in factories; and care for the elderly, clean our rooms, move goods, serve food, and even issue parking tickets, among other things.

India has thousands of AI-powered chatbots that help humans by answering bank- and insurance-related queries. AI is also being used to help farmers in India. Google is using ML to provide flood forecasts and warnings in developing countries, having started the pilot in Patna, an Indian city.

Consider another case. The World Health Organization (WHO) estimates there are 422 million people with diabetes globally, of which India is home to 19 per cent. Diabetes can also trigger diabetic retinopathy, caused by high blood sugar levels that damage the back of the eye. Almost 35 per cent of all diabetic patients have some form of diabetic retinopathy. If left undiagnosed and untreated, this can lead to blindness.

However, a frequent problem that ophthalmologists face during mass eyecare check-ups, especially in remote areas, is the lack of skilled technicians who can capture good images that can be used to grade diabetic retinopathy. If the quality of the images is not good, the patients are asked to come back and repeat the process. This makes it a time-consuming exercise, and delays can cost a patient their vision.

With AI, the system checks the image as soon as it is clicked and prompts the technician to click another image in case it is not good enough. This enables even a technician with minimal skills to shoot usable images of the eye fundus and refer them to ophthalmologists if the patient is found to be diabetic-retinopathy positive.

Microsoft partnered with a healthcare startup, Forus Health, to solve this problem by integrating AI-based retinal imaging application programming interfaces (APIs) into the startup's 3nethra devices using its own cloud and internet of things (IoT) solutions. This enables operators of the 3nethra device to get AI-powered insights even when they are working at eye check-up camps in remote areas with no or intermittent connectivity to the cloud.

Also, consider the fact that it's the power of AI that has made the smartphone in our pocket today no longer a mere calling and texting machine. It has many other functions—a wallet, an office, an entertainment jukebox, a channel for mobile banking and government services, and a personal healthcare adviser, to name a few.

All these developments indicate that India is slowly but steadily transforming itself from a mobile-first nation to an AI-first country, which we will discuss in detail in the following chapter.

India's AI advantage stems from the fact that it has a skilled talent pool of over five million technology professionals and more than five million software developers. It also has a robust AI startup ecosystem comprising entrepreneurs, venture capitalists (VCs), and research and development (R&D) hubs. Last but not least, the government also believes that AI can benefit society.

Speaking at the Responsible AI for Social Empowerment (RAISE) 2020 summit, Prime Minister Narendra Modi pointed out that AI can play a crucial role in developing solutions in agriculture, creating next-generation urban infrastructure, as well as making disaster management systems in the country stronger. It's here that he reiterated the vision of making India a "global hub for AI". We believe the stars are perfectly aligned for India to achieve this goal.

I curated EmTech India for three successive years before we independently launched the Mint Digital Innovation Summit in 2019. AI, by now, was already the centre of attraction, even as the umbrella theme remained "Digital Transformation".

This time around, we had many AI experts from India too. My co-author, Jayanth N. Kolla—founder and principal analyst of a cutting-edge technology research and advisory firm Convergence Catalyst—was one of them.

Kolla and I share a symbiotic relationship, relying on each other for information and perspective. We continue to have long, unscheduled deliberations on technological progress and its implications.

We have often asked ourselves questions such as: What do these developments mean for a country like India and its citizens? Can India become an AI superpower, given that it is already an information technology (IT) services and biotech hub? What kind of safeguards does India need to put in place so that governments and authorities do not misuse the power of AI algorithms while implementing face recognition or using health reports to discriminate against poor patients?

But, most importantly, we asked ourselves: How will Indian businesses benefit from AI? This question is of utter importance since we have come across many businesses globally that talk about AI but do not understand whether, or why, they really need it.

For many businesses, AI is simply a sales pitch to make a product more appealing than it is—a trend that is known as "AI washing". This is the primary reason that senior executives (clubbed as CXOs) of many enterprises remain sceptical about AI and fear that the cost of implementing AI may outweigh its benefits.

They do have a point. If you cannot see how AI is solving your business problem or increasing your company's efficiency, you will think twice, even before warming up to the idea of using AI or investing time and energy in the exercise.

Keeping in mind this dilemma that CXOs share, this book demonstrates with numerous examples why AI is important and how it can be seamlessly integrated into your business. We show you how AI can solve business problems much more efficiently than traditional technology tools. Last but not least, we also show you how to examine the return on investment (ROI) from AI.

This continuing exploration is the primary reason for writing this book.

OLD, YET NEW

AI is no longer a buzzword in India. Big companies and startups have already implemented AI in some form or the other in the last six years. Industry bodies like NASSCOM, too, have sharpened their focus on the role of AI, startups and Digital India.

Premier institutions like the Indian Institutes of Technology (IITs) now offer multiple AI-related courses and have incubated hundreds of deep tech—another term for these cutting-edge technologies—startups. Further, investors love to pump money into AI-powered companies in the hope of spectacular returns.

It's hardly a surprise then that professional services firm Accenture predicts that AI can add about $1 trillion to India's economy by 2035.

Interestingly, the world had great expectations from AI in the sixties and seventies too. However, AI could not deliver the high expectations that governments had from it—such as NLP, abstract thinking, and self-recognition—mostly due to the lack of computer power.[3] This resulted in reduced funding for, and even cancellation of, AI projects—a period now referred to as the "AI Winter".

AI has found its place in the sun again around the world, as the following chapters will sufficiently demonstrate. This is primarily due to the availability of sophisticated algorithms (step-by-step rules that computers use to perform calculations or solve problems), large data sets that companies have collected from their customers over the years, and also those that have been made available by technology companies such as Google and Facebook for public use. Add to this the massive increase in computing power, funding from VCs, media coverage of AI's potential and its misuse, coupled with the unprecedented cooperation between technology companies, academics, institutions, and governments on AI projects.

We believe AI will soon join the group of core technologies such as electricity, wireless communication, and global positioning systems (GPS) that work in the background and power just about every aspect of our lives.

KEEPING ABREAST

As you may have realised by now, the AI treadmill is moving at a very rapid pace. This makes it very challenging to keep abreast of the developments. Kolla and I are fortunate that our professions allow us opportunities to meet up with and interview global chief executives and experts from cutting-edge technology companies and institutions. Both of us have also moderated tech panel discussions around the globe—all of which help us stay updated to the extent possible.

Here are some important learnings. First, AI is not a single technology. Rather, it is an umbrella term for a spectrum of tools, including ML,

DL, computer vision, robotics, and NLP—all of which help us make machines more and more intelligent.

Second, it's also important to realise that AI introduces a very high level of automation. ML, for instance, does not require explicit programming by a human. DL uses ANNs, also known as neural networks or neural nets, that simulate the human brain. Unsupervised ML can decipher patterns from humungous amounts of unstructured data and offer solutions without any human participation.

NLP, a sub-field of AI, helps machines process and understand human language in a given context to enable them to automatically perform repetitive tasks such as machine translation, summarisation, and ticket classification, among other things. We will explain more about these technologies in the book and also discuss many questions that they raise, given the fact that automation can replace many routine workers and add to the huge unemployment figures that developing countries such as India already face.

We would, however, like to reiterate that this book is not just about AI in terms of technology. It's about how AI is influencing the way we work, do business, play, and live. After all, AI tools are useful only if they address and solve a business problem. Hence, we have explained just enough about the technology for you to appreciate the whole AI ecosystem, including the business aspects and applications of AI, specifically in the Indian context.

In the first part of this book, we provide a very broad understanding of AI, which is important to grasp so that you can appreciate why AI makes businesses more efficient. The second part is completely devoted to how AI is being used in India. The third segment deals with global issues that certainly have a bearing on how AI will be used in India too. Finally, we conclude with how we believe AI will shape up in the coming years.

Thus, we first cover how the pandemic has unwittingly raised the world's digital intelligence quotient. We then establish the symbiotic relationship of AI with technologies like IoT, 3D printing, and robotics. This, as the chapters in this book will demonstrate, is true around the world, including in India.

The rise of artificial intelligence over the last 8 decades: As training computation has increased, AI systems have become more powerful

Our World in Data

The color indicates the domain of the AI system: ● Vision ● Games ● Drawing ● Language ● Other

Shown on the vertical axis is the **training computation** that was used to train the AI systems.

10 billion petaFLOP

Computation is measured in floating point operations (FLOP). One FLOP is equivalent to one addition, subtraction, multiplication, or division of two decimal numbers.

100 million petaFLOP

The data is shown on a logarithmic scale, so that from each grid-line to the next it shows a 100-fold increase in training computation.

1 million petaFLOP

10,000 petaFLOP

100 petaFLOP

1 petaFLOP = 1 quadrillion FLOP

10 trillion FLOP

Minerva: built in 2022 and trained on 2.7 billion petaFLOP
Minerva can solve complex mathematical problems at the college level.

PaLM: built in 2022 and trained on 2.5 billion petaFLOP
PaLM can generate high-quality text, explain some jokes, cause & effect, and more.

GPT-3: 2020; 314 million petaFLOP
GPT-3 can produce high-quality text that is often indistinguishable from human writing.

DALL-E: 2021; 47 million petaFLOP
DALL-E can generate high-quality images from written descriptions.

NEO: 2021; 1.1 million petaFLOP
Recommendation systems like Facebook's NEO determine what you see on your social media feed, online shopping, streaming services, and more.

AlphaGo: 2016; 1.9 million petaFLOP
AlphaGo defeated 18-time champion Lee Sedol in the ancient and highly complex board game Go. The best Go players are no longer human.

AlphaFold: 2020; 100,000 petaFLOP
AlphaFold was a major advance toward solving the protein-folding problem in biology.

MuZero: 2019; 48,000 petaFLOP
MuZero is a single system that achieved superhuman performance at Go, chess, and shogi (Japanese chess) — all without ever being told the rules.

AlexNet: 2012; 470 petaFLOP
A pivotal early "deep learning" system, or neural network with many layers that could recognize images of objects such as dogs and cars at near-human level.

NPLM

Decision tree

LSTM

LeNet-5

TD-Gammon: 1992; 18 trillion FLOP
TD-Gammon learned to play backgammon at a high level, just below the top human players of the time.

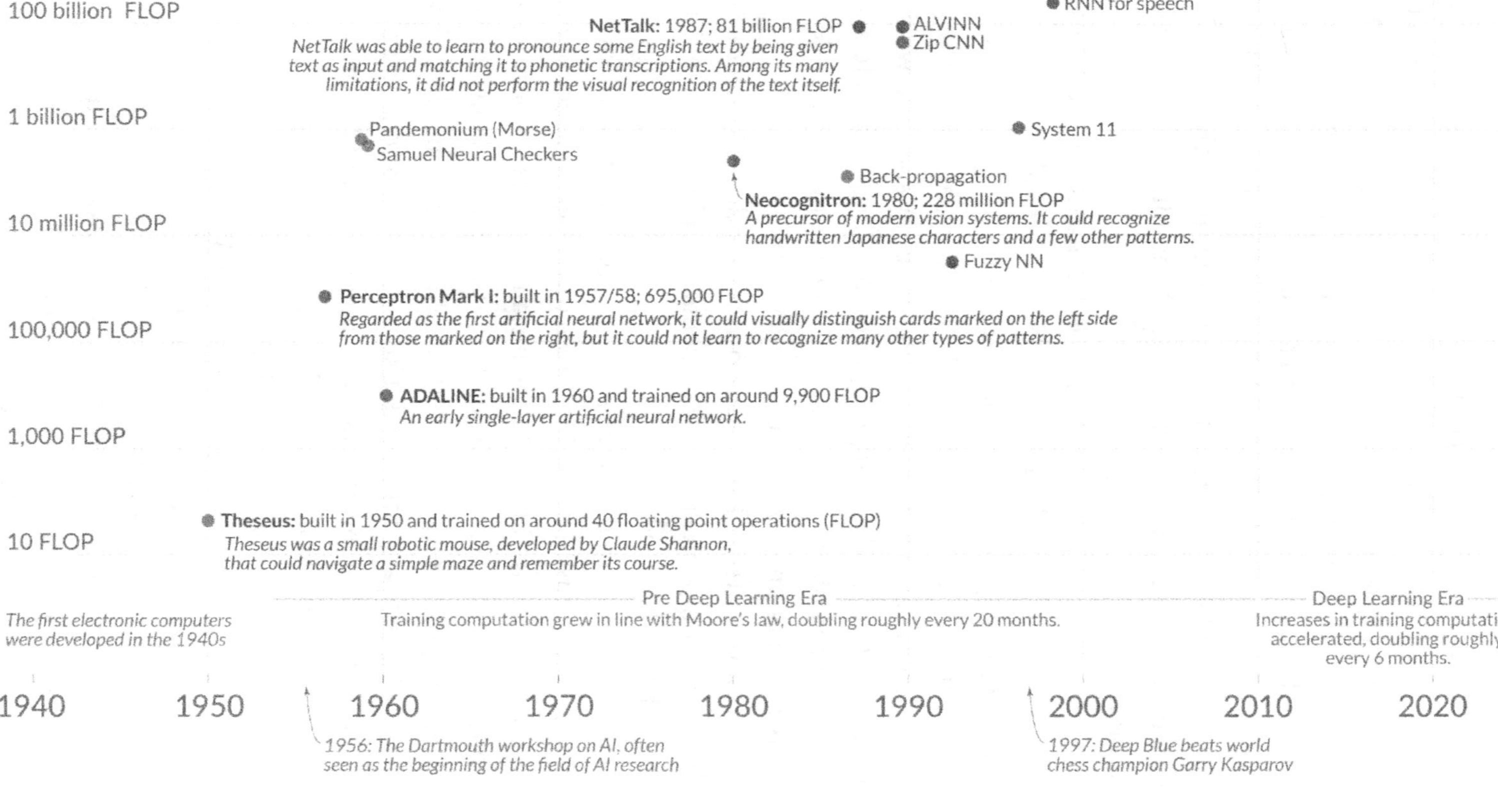

The data on training computation is taken from Sevilla et al. (2022) – Parameter, Compute, and Data Trends in Machine Learning. It is estimated by the authors and comes with some uncertainty. The authors expect the estimates to be correct within a factor of two.
OurWorldinData.org – Research and data to make progress against the world's largest problems.

We have devoted six chapters completely to the progress of AI in India and provided numerous examples of how India has built a smart digital payment ecosystem, how companies and startups are using AI, and the policies in India that currently deal with AI developments.

In the later chapters, we have explained the importance of developing "super apps" in India, presented learnings from multinational companies such as Google, Microsoft, and Amazon, and highlighted the emergence of the hybrid or phygital (physical combined with digital) model in India.

We have also devoted a couple of chapters to discussing the thorny issue of how AI and automation are redefining—and even taking away—jobs. These chapters explore the bias in AI algorithms and what policymakers are doing to fix it, which is why they largely deal with "Giving AI the human touch" and the "Future of Work". We would like to especially thank N. S. Nappinai, Supreme Court advocate and founder of Cyber Saathi, who took time out from her hectic schedule to write a whole chapter on framing an AI policy in India.

The last portion of the book explores how AI in India will evolve and the roadmap that companies and governments should chart to emulate the progress that AI has made in countries like the US and China.

We acknowledge that by the time this book is published, there will be numerous developments in this field that we would not have covered.

At the time of writing this book, for instance, AI developers were raving about the potential of Generative Pre-trained Transformer 3, or GPT-3, to produce human-like text. Put simply, an algorithm could potentially write an entire book like this in the coming years as algorithms are trained on bigger data sets, making it hard for most to believe that no human was involved in the process.

The world is already going crazy over OpenAI's artificial AI-powered chatbot, ChatGPT, which even rivalled the FIFA World Cup 2022 for social media eyeballs. Introduced to the public on November 30, 2022, for testing and feedback, netizens were overwhelmed with this smart chatbot's prowess at engaging with them while answering questions and writing code, poems, and essays, among other things.

To be sure, even the third iteration of Generative Pre-trained

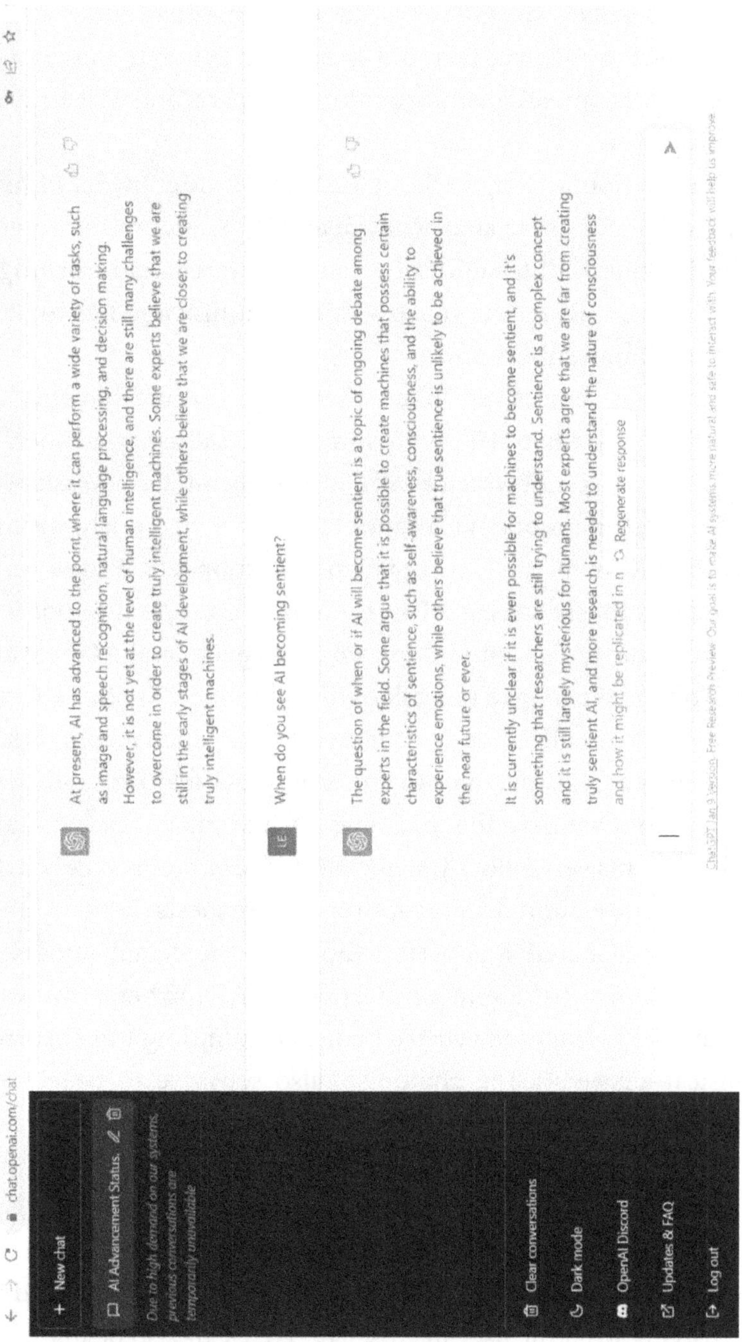
chat.openai.com/chat
+ New chat
AI Advancement Status
Due to high demand on our systems, previous conversations are temporarily unavailable
Clear conversations
Dark mode
OpenAI Discord
Updates & FAQ
Log out
At present, AI has advanced to the point where it can perform a wide variety of tasks, such as image and speech recognition, natural language processing, and decision making. However, it is not yet at the level of human intelligence, and there are still many challenges to overcome in order to create truly intelligent machines. Some experts believe that we are still in the early stages of AI development, while others believe that we are closer to creating truly intelligent machines.
LE
When do you see AI becoming sentient?
The question of when or if AI will become sentient is a topic of ongoing debate among experts in the field. Some argue that it is possible to create machines that possess certain characteristics of sentience, such as self-awareness, consciousness, and the ability to experience emotions, while others believe that true sentience is unlikely to be achieved in the near future or ever.
It is currently unclear if it is even possible for machines to become sentient, and it's something that researchers are still trying to understand. Sentience is a complex concept and it is still largely mysterious for humans. Most experts agree that we are far from creating truly sentient AI, and more research is needed to understand the nature of consciousness and how it might be replicated in n
Regenerate response
ChatGPT Jan 9 Version. Free Research Preview. Our goal is to make AI systems more natural and safe to interact with. Your feedback will help us improve.

Transformer (GPT-3) with 175 billion parameters impressed many with its potential to write human-like poems, articles, books, tweets, resumes, and even code. GPT-3 is trained to predict the next word on a large dataset of internet text, but it can also generate untruthful and toxic comments, spread misinformation and spam, and write fraudulent academic essays.

OpenAI, co-founded by Tesla, SpaceX and Twitter owner Elon Musk (who is no longer associated with OpenAI), is attempting to address these limitations with ChatGPT by using reinforcement learning from human feedback (RLHF) to make it "more truthful and less toxic" with the help of human supervisors.

People used adjectives like "amazing", "mind-blowing", and "astonishing" for ChatGPT, with some even calling it a much faster Google search—a point which I will address in a bit. Elon Musk tweeted, "ChatGPT is scary good. We are not far from dangerously strong AI." To this, Sam Altman, the CEO of OpenAI, responded, "i agree on being close to dangerously strong AI in the sense of an AI that poses e.g. a huge cybersecurity risk. and i think we could get to real AGI in the next decade, so we have to take the risk of that extremely seriously too."

The model can still be tested for free at chat.openai.com, but users will have to pay $20 per month for additional features and benefits. According to OpenAI, the dialogue format makes it possible for ChatGPT to answer follow-up questions, admit mistakes, challenge incorrect premises, and reject inappropriate requests.

It's not that ChatGPT is perfect. For one, the default models were trained on data till the end of 2021. OpenAI further acknowledges that ChatGPT "sometimes writes plausible-sounding but incorrect or nonsensical answers". The chatbot is also sensitive to tweaks to the input phrasing or attempting the same prompt multiple times. For instance, if you phrase the question differently, it will give a slightly different response. The model also overuses certain phrases, which arise from biases in the training data and over-optimization issues. Moreover, current models typically guess what the user intended rather than clarifying what the user means. ChatGPT can also be manipulated to respond to harmful prompts or questions.

In a related move, Alphabet-owned DeepMind, an AI company that Google acquired in January 2014, is also mulling the release of its chatbot called Sparrow for a "private beta" sometime in 2023. However, it has delayed the release reportedly for DeepMind to work on reinforcement learning-based features that ChatGPT lacks, such as citing sources. Similar to ChatGPT, Sparrow says it is a dialogue agent that is "useful and reduces the risk of unsafe and inappropriate answers" (https://www.deepmind.com/blog/building-safer-dialogue-agents).

Content creators and voice actors, thus, have their work cut out for them with intelligent software mimicking their writings, art, voice, and even their emotions. If OpenAI's DALL-E can generate realistic art and images from plain text prompts, and ChatGPT can write poems, articles, books and even code, Microsoft's text-to-speech AI model, VALL-E, can simulate a person's voice with just a 3-second recording. Initial results show that VALL-E can also preserve the speaker's emotional tone. According to the paper's authors, VALL-E was pre-trained on 60,000 hours of English speech data, which the paper claims is "hundreds of times larger than existing systems" (https://arxiv.org/abs/2301.02111).

But this is just the beginning. When ChatGPT was released, everyone asked, "Will ChatGPT be a search engine killer or be integrated with it?" Search engines like Bing or Google Search are fully automated and use software known as web crawlers to surf the internet regularly to locate pages that can be indexed in real-time, following which they serve the information relevant to a user query. But they do not engage with users or respond to queries in a user-friendly dialogue format like ChatGPT. Search engines may also show irrelevant links or display unwarranted ads if their algorithms think it fits your profile as defined in your settings.

Meta's BlenderBot3 is already connected to the internet, though it's not very impressive yet. And OpenAI's WebGPT prototype uses a text-based browser to submit search queries, follow links, scroll web pages, and also cite sources. And the phenomenal success of ChatGPT, which crossed 100 million users in January, forced Google to launch Bard, an AI-powered chatbot, in February. However, Microsoft countered two days later after Bard's launch with its AI chatbot-powered Bing and AI-powered Edge browser.

Now, the question is: Will Google succumb to or prevail over the onslaught of OpenAI and Microsoft? And is this a battle for AI supremacy?

To place this in perspective, OpenAI's ChatGPT is based on a transformer model called GPT-3.5, but Google pioneered transformer models, which are essentially large language models that have been trained on humongous amounts of raw text. Google's Bard, which is powered by its Language Model for Dialogue Applications (LaMDA) that a former Google engineer claimed had become sentient, was yet to be integrated with Google Search at the time of writing this book, but it's a foregone conclusion.

These developments clearly indicate that search engines and browsers will no longer be the same. Search engines, for instance, typically display a list of results in a manner that is best suited to answer a user's query. With the inclusion of a ChatGPT-like interface, users may simply ask a question instead of scouting through scores of links.

The use of such AI could also change how search engine optimization (SEO) works for websites since websites will now seek to provide the "best" answer to a query instead of focusing on where they appear in the list of Search results. AI, meanwhile, could help browsers display additional or related information or even summarize a document you're viewing automatically.

That said, "smart" platforms like ChatGPT can also provide "incorrect" and "nonsensical" answers, leading to a lot more misinformation. As an example, when Bard shared inaccurate information in a promotional video in the late hours of February 9, Alphabet Inc.—Google's parent— lost $100 billion in market value, with its shares crashing as much as 9% during regular trading. On the other hand, Microsoft's shares rose around 3% before paring gains, following the better performance of the chatbot-powered Bing coupled with the fact that it has invested billions of dollars in OpenAI, the company that built ChatGPT.

To avoid such bloopers, Microsoft says it has built-in classifiers to its AI to avoid biases when using Bing for search, but there's a clear need for the framing of AI governance policies, which will talk about in detail in the later chapters.

But what does this AI prowess mean for humans? While OpenAI's DALL-E is trained to generate images from just text, WebGPT is helping GPT-3 answer open-ended user questions with a text-based browser. OpenAI's neural (modelled on neurons in the human brain) net called Whisper enables transcription in multiple languages, as well as translation from those languages into English.

The fact is that large language models (LLMs) like GPT-3 and chatbots like ChatGPT are trained on billions of words from sources like the internet, books, and sources including Common Crawl and Wikipedia, which makes them more knowledgeable than humans.

LLMs use transformer neural networks to read many words (sentences and paragraphs too) at a time, figure out how they relate, and predict the following word. However, while LLMs such as GPT-3 and models like ChatGPT may outperform humans at some tasks, they do not understand what they read or write, unlike humans. Moreover, these models use human supervisors to make them more sensible and less toxic. Regardless, the release of GPT-4, which was expected to significantly outperform GPT-3 with its rumoured 100 trillion parameters, has only raised more questions despite OpenAI not publicly disclosing the number of parameters.

As you may have realized by now, the shift is already happening.

Such developments, however, need not overwhelm us. Most humans, for instance, can learn basic driving skills in just a day. This is not the case with AI. To build a driverless car, as an example, companies must perform millions of trials with millions of hours of practice and millions and billions of examples. Even then, they cannot ensure that there won't be any accidents.

Similarly, children effortlessly learn to speak multiple languages. Hence, even though we say that neural nets are loosely modelled on the human brain, they are nowhere close to resembling it or performing like it.

That said, AI excels at repetitive tasks and can disrupt the way we live, work, and play. American AI researcher and writer Eliezer Shlomo

Yudkowsky says, "By far, the greatest danger of artificial intelligence is that people conclude too early that they understand it."

Hence, it's important to understand how these developments are impacting our lives and prepare ourselves to tackle these issues with the appropriate skill sets and policy frameworks.

We believe this book will provide you with enough information and perspective to form your own opinion about AI and its applications in businesses, industries, and society at large. It will also help you understand and appreciate the progress that AI has made in India, regardless of whether you are a student, professional, senior executive, entrepreneur, investor or policymaker.

In the next chapter, we will explore the transition from a mobile-first to an AI-first world.

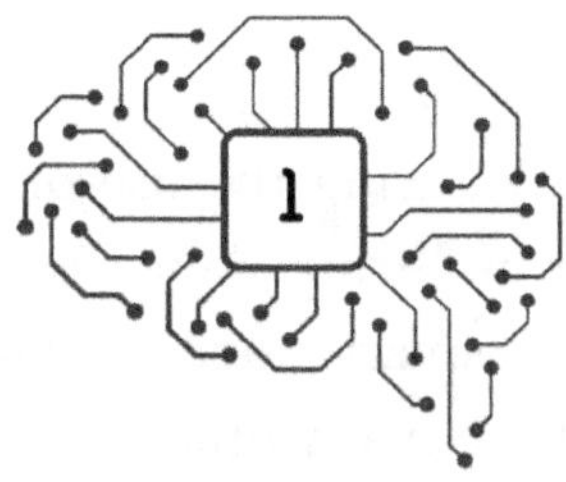

TOWARDS AN AI-FIRST WORLD

"No computer has ever been designed that is ever aware of what it's doing; but most of the time, we aren't either."
—*Marvin Minsky*

On February 1, 2021, the ongoing COVID-19 pandemic compelled the Indian Government to do the unthinkable. For the first time since India's Independence, Union Budget 2021 went paperless when Finance Minister Nirmala Sitharaman ditched the traditional "Bahi-Khata" in favour of a Made-in-India tablet. Further, all the Budget documents were made available on a mobile app too.

Most of us who do our office work on personal computers (PCs)—be they desktops, laptops or tablets—may wonder what the fuss was all about. Nevertheless, when the government uses the latest technology tools, it sends a strong signal that India is on its way to adopting digital wholeheartedly.

The fact is that over the last two decades, we have transitioned from a solely PC-centric world to one that was also being powered by cloud computing—broadly, a metaphor for the Internet. The cloud helped us complete some of our office work at home too. This made us "mobile" workers since we could transfer our documents using cloud-based email applications like Gmail and Outlook or even use cloud-based drives that help us store documents and access them from anywhere and on any device.

Things changed more dramatically with the advent of smartphones, which helped us access our office emails and documents on these devices. When companies began allowing the use of smartphones in offices, the trend became known as "Bring Your Own Device" or BYOD. The interesting part is that these smartphones are no longer mere calling and texting machines. They have many other functions—they are a wallet, an office, an entertainment jukebox, a mobile channel for banking and government services, and a personal healthcare adviser, to name a few.

Now our smartphones are becoming smarter since they are also AI-enabled. For instance, AI-powered cameras automatically improve the images you shoot, while voice assistants and the hundreds of apps that we download on them help us perform tasks such as instructing our phones in the language we speak and doing other tasks such as shopping, banking, and taking care of our health.

These are clear signs that we have already begun moving from a mobile-first world to an AI-first world where every bit of software and hardware is being made more and more intelligent with ML, DL, computer vision, NLP, and image recognition, among other technologies.

We will explain how these technologies work, but first, consider these cases. In July 2020, Tesla CEO Elon Musk said his car company would have the "basic functionality" to deliver Level 5 autonomous driving by the end of the year. A Level 5 car does not need a driver—or even a steering wheel, for that matter.

In April 2018, Musk made a similar claim, outlining his ambitious plan to build a fleet of robotaxis that would compete with the likes of Google spin-off Waymo and General Motors' Cruise.

A month earlier, Amazon had announced the acquisition of self-driving startup Zoox for $1.2 billion. Amazon has already pumped money into autonomous car firm Aurora Innovation and an electric vehicle startup, Rivian, which is also working on self-driving cars. So is Apple Inc.

These examples reveal that AI is at the core of autonomous driving, just as it powers many other game-changing innovations.

Love it or fear it, AI will remain the overarching theme of the digital transformation story for many more years. Hence, it's important to understand the nature of AI—what it can do, what it can't, how it can empower businesses of the future, how it can transform or endanger our lives, and what steps we need to take to regulate its misuse. However, to do so, we must first understand what AI means.

BUT WHAT EXACTLY IS AI?

AI, simply put, is the desire to make machines as intelligent as humans or even more. The concept dates to the 1960s. British polymath Alan Turing mooted building intelligent machines way back in 1950. His Turing Test, for instance, assesses whether a machine can think like a human or not.

That said, AI formally took shape during a 1956 workshop that was held to explore how machines could be made to simulate aspects of intelligence. The workshop was organised by John McCarthy, at the Dartmouth Summer Research Project on Artificial Intelligence, who is credited with the first use of the term AI in the proposal he co-authored for the workshop with Marvin Minsky, Nathaniel Rochester, and Claude Shannon.[1]

Today, most of the AI we see around us caters to narrow or specific areas and hence is categorised as "weak" AI or "narrow" AI. Examples include the AI chatbots, AI personal assistants and smart home assistants that we see, including Apple's Siri, Microsoft's Cortana, Google's Allo, Amazon's Alexa or Echo, and Google's Home, since they all perform a specific function—that of a helper or assistant.

Weak or narrow AI is excellent at performing linear tasks that require repetition and practice. It does not think like humans, as shown in sci-fi movies. Even completely autonomous (Level 5) driverless cars and trucks, however impressive they appear, remain stronger manifestations of a weak or narrow AI.

Narrow AI machines also do not have a moral compass. For instance, if a driverless car encounters two pedestrians jaywalking in its path, it may randomly choose to crash into either of them. A human, on the other hand, may choose to crash into a pole rather than hurt fellow

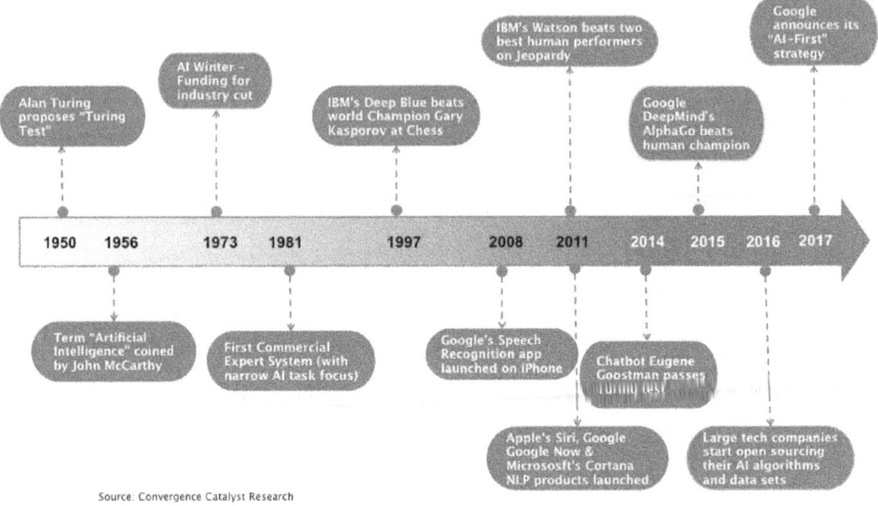

Source: Convergence Catalyst Research

humans, even if the pedestrian is on the wrong side of the law. Simply put, a driverless car does not have a brain or conscience, so it cannot think like a human or make moral decisions.

We are yet to see machines with "strong AI", also called true intelligence or artificial general intelligence (AGI). In fact, we may or may not see such machines in our lifetime, despite the talk of achieving technological singularity—the point when machines surpass humans in intelligence.

India got its first look at AI in the 1960s when Prof. H.N. Mahabala introduced an AI course at IIT Kanpur. In an interview, Prof. Mahabala recounts computers back then were "flown in and taken by bullock cart to the campus". Interestingly, it was the very same Prof. Mahabala who mentored Kris Gopalakrishnan—one of the six co-founders of India's second-largest IT services provider, Infosys Ltd.—at IIT Madras.[2]

HOW AI WORKS

AI has gathered momentum in the last four to five years, driven by the humongous amounts of data that is available, the increasing power of cheaper computing that enables us to crunch and analyse this data in real-time, and advances in ML as well as DL that help us understand patterns in the data and build solutions accordingly.

ML is a subset of AI. It enables a computer to spot patterns and use data to make connections to accomplish specific tasks without the need for human programming, where the code is written manually using programming languages.

Search or recommendation engines are good examples since they do not need human developers to write code manually. Rather, they use algorithms to index pages and rank them. How else would you get answers to your questions when you type them in the search boxes provided by Google or Microsoft's Bing?

Further, have you noticed that when you are searching for an electronic gadget, for example, a mobile phone on a site such as Amazon, you immediately see related products such as chargers, wired and wireless earbuds, and even phone covers? Such tasks would require thousands of human developers to continuously track your buying patterns, making it virtually impossible. A recommendation engine algorithm, however, can track your past buying behaviour and even predict your next purchase since it is continuously noting your preferences.

DL, an advanced ML technique, uses layered (hence "deep") neural networks (neural nets) that are loosely modelled on the human brain. However, they are nothing like the human brain, which is estimated to have 80–100 billion neurons. For instance, birds have certainly inspired humans to design an aeroplane, but that does not make a plane a bird.

Neural nets enable image recognition, face recognition, speech recognition, self-driving cars and smart home automation devices,

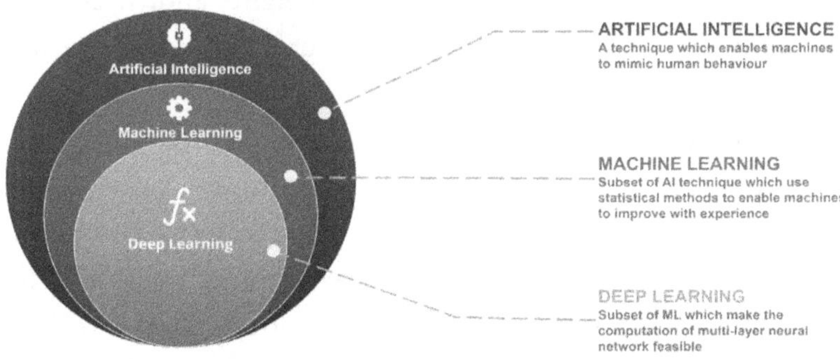

Image source: Tech-E

among other business applications. They were first proposed in 1944 by Warren McCullough and Walter Pitts, two University of Chicago researchers who later joined the Massachusetts Institute of Technology (MIT).

Neural nets are an ML technique that allows a computer to learn how to perform a specific task by analysing hundreds and thousands of examples. Their actions can be "supervised" by humans, "semi-supervised", or even totally "unsupervised" by humans.

For instance, if you feed thousands of labelled images of cats, dogs, and tigers to an object recognition system, it will learn from the images by detecting visual patterns that consistently correlate with the specific labels.

Neurons receive inputs layer by layer. The neurons in the first layer perform a calculation and send it (the output) to the neurons in the next layer. The process is repeated until there is overall output.

A node assigns a number known as a "weight" to each of its incoming connections. If that number is below a threshold value, the node passes no data to the next layer. Else, the node sends (or "fires") the number.

The weights and thresholds are continually adjusted until the training data with the same labels consistently yield similar outputs. There is also a process known as back-propagation, which tweaks the calculations of individual neurons to allow the network to learn to produce the desired output.

When the first trainable neural network, the perceptron, was demonstrated by Cornell University psychologist Frank Rosenblatt in 1957, it had only one layer with adjustable weights and thresholds between the input and output layers. Today's neural nets, of course, are very sophisticated.

Consider these cases. On December 7, 2017, AlphaZero—modelled on AlphaGo (the world's strongest player of the Chinese game Go)—took just four hours to learn all chess rules and master the game enough to defeat the world's strongest open-source chess engine, Stockfish. The AlphaZero algorithm is a more generic version of the AlphaGo Zero algorithm. It uses reinforcement learning—an unsupervised training method that uses rewards and punishments.

AlphaGo Zero does not need to train on human amateur and professional games to learn how to play the ancient Chinese game of Go. Further, the new version not only learnt from AlphaGo but also defeated it in October 2017.[3]

Ross Goodwin, an artist and creative technologist at Google, used the long short-term memory (LSTM) recurrent neural network (RNN) for his "Please Feed The Lions" project, which we have explained in detail in the following chapter.

RNNs are a class of neural networks that enable output from an earlier step to be used as input in the current step. RNN models are typically used for NLP and speech recognition since they feature hidden states that remember some information about a sequence. This is applicable when a model must predict the next word in a sentence, which requires it to remember some previous words to complete this task.

Godwin's LSTM RNN statistical model predicts the next text character repeatedly and is trained on thousands of poetry books. Hence, when someone submits a word, the algorithm figures out whether it's a noun or verb or any other part of speech. This is explained in the following chapter.

OpenAI's GPT-3 model, which we have also detailed in the next chapter with many examples, is much more complex. GPT-3, which is the third version of the nth series, uses neural nets with 175 billion parameters.

ML models need parameters to make predictions from new data. Examples of model parameters include the weights in a neural network. The parameters must be continually tuned to achieve the best results.

GPT-3, which is currently the world's largest language learning model, can potentially be used to write poems, articles, tweets, and books, or even to translate or write code as well as any human.

The GPT-3 model has already digested about 500 billion words from sources like the internet and books (499 billion tokens, or words, to be precise, from sources including Common Crawl and Wikipedia). Common Crawl is an open repository that can be accessed and analysed by anyone. It contains petabytes of data collected over eight years of web crawling. Moreover, GPT-3 can recall and instantly draw inferences from this data repository.[3]

AI is also assisting artists and working independently on portraits. When India held its first AI art exhibition at Nature Morte in New Delhi on August 17, 2018, the show titled "Gradient Descent" exhibited works of global artists who meld their skills with AI to create new artworks.

A month later, the London branch of Christie's, the world's largest auction house, put on sale the work of an algorithm developed by the French art collective, Obvious. The work was created using a model called a Generative Adversarial Network (GAN), which typically generates data from scratch, primarily images.

The artists first fed the GAN a data set of 15,000 portraits done between the fourteenth and twentieth centuries, following which the algorithm created new works based on the training set until it was able to fool a test designed to distinguish between human and machine-made images. The resulting work, titled Portrait of Edmond de Belamy, depicts a man in a dark coat and white collar with indecipherable facial features that resides somewhere in the uncanny valley. (Androids and avatars may look extremely realistic and lifelike, but when we examine them, they are not quite human. This makes people feel a sense of unease, strangeness, disgust, or even creepiness. This is referred to as the "uncanny valley".)

GANs are also being used by companies such as Data Grid and Neon to automatically generate high-resolution, full-body images of non-existent or fictitious people. These companies, of course, hope to use these whole-body model images as virtual models for advertising and apparel and for use in banks, retail shops, airports, and other outlets.

GANs, unfortunately, can be misused too. Given their potential to create fictitious people from scratch, GANs can also be used by lumpen elements and perverts to create fakes of celebrities too—better known as "deepfakes"—since GAN is a DL technique.

AI algorithms are also debating with humans. Project Debater, an AI tool from International Business Machines (IBM), engaged in the first-ever live public debates with humans in June 2018 when it argued on the topic of whether we should subsidise space exploration or not. The model is touted as IBM's next big milestone for AI and has been in the works for almost nine years.

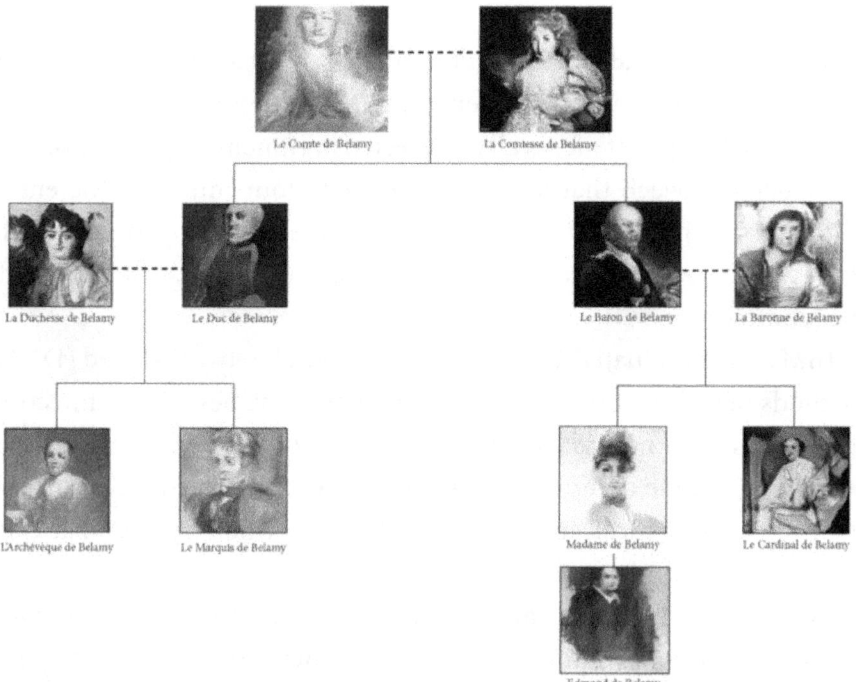

Image source: La famille de Belamy—all the portraits in GAN's fictitious Belamy family tree. Image © Obvious

A global IBM Research team led by IBM's Haifa, Israel lab endowed Project Debater with three capabilities. First, data-driven speech writing and delivery. Second, listening comprehension that can identify key claims hidden within long continuous spoken language. And third, modelling human dilemmas in a unique knowledge graph to enable principled arguments.

The system uses the Watson Speech-to-Text API (application programming interface). Project Debater's knowledge base comprises around 10 billion sentences from newspapers and journals. Using AI NLP technologies, it can recognise the same concept, even when stated differently.

Project Debater begins by searching for short pieces of text from its database to build its opening speech—to either defend or oppose a motion. Next, it constructs arguments to support its case by removing redundant argumentative texts. It then selects the strongest remaining claims and evidence and arranges these by theme, thus creating the base of its narrative.

Project Debater also uses a knowledge graph that allows it to search for arguments to support the general human dilemmas that are raised by the debate topic. It pieces all the selected arguments together to create a persuasive speech that lasts approximately four minutes. The entire process takes just a few minutes. After delivering its opening speech, Project Debater listens to the opponent's response, digests it and builds the rebuttal.

IBM says it evaluated 19 different deep neural network-based (DNN) methods of scoring arguments to help identify the best DL architecture for this task. To negate claims, for instance, the algorithm has a rule-based approach to determine what constitutes an effective negation and then uses a statistical approach to determine when an automatically generated negation can plausibly be used.

To combine argument units from different texts, IBM designed a joint inference method by jointly modelling argument–relation classification and stance classification.

IBM believes Project Debater can help humans avoid one-sided and doctored narratives such as fake news.

APPLICATIONS

Now that we have given you a fair idea of how AI algorithms work, let's take a look at how AI is being applied across sectors, both globally and in India. We have chosen five sectors—healthcare, banking, financial services and insurance (BFSI), and retail—to begin with. We will deal with some of these sectors in detail in the following chapter.

AI Doctor

Eric Horvitz, the chief scientist at Microsoft Research, nailed it when he termed AI the "sleeping giant for healthcare". It's the ability of doctors and technology companies to use AI to sift through humongous amounts of data, which is at the core of the healthcare revolution. In hospitals, for instance, radiologists use ML and DL to see visual patterns in X-rays and detect the risk of diseases like cancer with more accuracy and faster.

Microsoft India has a partnership with Apollo Hospitals for an AI-powered Cardiovascular Disease Risk Score API in India. Microsoft also uses AI for the early detection of diabetic retinopathy to prevent blindness, which we explained in the earlier chapter.

In July 2020, the Delhi-based Indraprastha Institute of Information Technology (IIIT), the Institute of Post-Graduate Medical Education and Research (IPGME&R), Kolkata, and the Inria Saclay-Île-de-France Research Centre, France, announced that they had jointly developed an AI algorithm to help quicken the search for a COVID-19 treatment. The AI algorithm uses a database of drugs called drugbank.ca, which lists more than 100 antivirals that have been approved.

Likewise, Bengaluru-based Niramai and the Indian Institute of Science (IISc) have developed an AI model that allows patients to WhatsApp their X-rays. The model then suggests whether it is likely to be COVID-19, pneumonia or viral pneumonia, following which a doctor can take suitable action.

Mumbai-based imaging AI provider, Qure.ai, received clearance from the US Food and Drug Administration (US FDA) in July for its head CT scan product "qER", which can be used for radiology scans with intracranial bleeds and cranial fractures, among other functions. The AI-powered solution can be used to prioritise (or "triage") nearly all critical abnormalities visible on routine head CT scans.

The real promise of AI appears to be in speeding up the process of designing, testing, and even making potential new drugs.

In January 2020, for instance, Google's DeepMind published an article about its ML system, AlphaFold, in the research journal *Nature*. AlphaFold can predict the 3D structure of a protein based on its genetic sequence far more quickly and accurately than pre-existing approaches. A protein's shape helps us guess its role within the cell, and this facilitates the development of the right drugs.

AI is also speeding up vaccine testing. Australia's Commonwealth Scientific and Industrial Research Organisation (CSIRO) announced it has been working on SARS-CoV-2 since January 2020. On April 2, it announced that it was testing potential COVID-19 vaccines at the Australian Centre for Disease Preparedness (ACDP) in Geelong, Victoria.

The genome of COVID-19 can be likened to the virus' blueprint. Since it's impossible to do it manually, ML is used to analyse the genome data sets in a bid to identify the most representative strain on which to test the vaccines.

Startups, too, are joining the AI-powered drug development chorus. In early February, companies like BenevolentAI—a UK-based startup, Deargen—a South Korean AI drug discovery specialist, and US-based Insilico Medicine pitched in with their respective AI-based solutions to tackle coronavirus.

Researchers from BenevolentAI and Imperial College, London, for instance, said they had used AI to find an already-approved drug that might limit the coronavirus's ability to infect people.

Similarly, Deargen said it used a pre-trained DL-based drug-target interaction model called Molecule Transformer-Drug Target Interaction (MT-DTI) to identify commercially available drugs that could act on the viral proteins of COVID-19. Their work is published on the bioRxiv preprint server.

Insilico Medicine, too, announced that its AI algorithms had designed six new molecules that could stop the virus from replicating in people's bodies. These molecules must be tested, so it remains to be seen whether these compounds ever become medicines.

AI Banker

More than two decades ago, Bill Gates said, "Banking is necessary, but banks are not." While physical banks may still be around, online banking, mobile banking, AI-powered chatbots and voicebots, banking on social media sites, cryptocurrencies, fintechs, blockchain, payment banks, and open banking initiatives (allows customers to share financial data with non-banking third parties like fintechs) have radically transformed not only the banking but the entire BFSI industry, vastly enriching customer experience.

Customer mindsets vary even in this digital age. Not everyone is comfortable with an interactive voice response (IVR) or chatting with bots. "Customers of Yesterday" continue to want a personal experience by walking into a branch or calling up the contact centre. "Customers of Today" are comfortable with mobile apps, online banking and ATMs.

And there are those who were born with the Uber and Airbnb type of services. We call them the "Customers of Tomorrow", who are always restless and looking at newer ways to interact and engage with a bank—be it through social media, conversational banking, or bots. A large part of the digital value comes from cutting across all three customer segments.

Banks are using automation, APIs, and technologies like AI to improve customer interactions and journeys, and predictive algorithms to predict what kind of products are more suitable for a customer—or for a relationship manager—when he or she meets a customer to recommend a product.

Predictive algorithms, or algos for short, are also being used to understand the risk profile portfolio. AI is being used in high-frequency algorithmic trading, where inputs are taken from multiple financial markets to make investment decisions in seconds.

Banks and insurance companies now leverage big data and ML when doing credit scoring and making loan decisions. By using robotic process automation (RPA), ML and other intelligent technologies, banks are adopting an "AI-first" perspective to create innovative services and improve internal efficiencies, notes a February 2019 report by Capgemini and the Indian Banks' Association (IBA).

As an example, ICICI Bank has automated hundreds of processes using an in-house RPA solution. In India, startup Signzy is helping banks with AI and RPA-assisted onboarding solutions. Voice Assistants (VAs) are being utilised in the front office to support questions on account balances, payments, and bills.

The report cites examples of how SBI Intelligent Voice Assistant (SIVA) helps customers with daily banking tasks, while HDFC Bank uses Amazon's Alexa to allow customers to check balances, find payment deadlines, and pay bills. HDFC Bank has a chatbot that works with Google's virtual assistant to answer customer questions. The Chennai branch of City Union Bank piloted a humanoid robot that would answer generic banking-related questions from customers. So did HDFC Bank.

Axis Bank, according to the Capgemini and IBA report, introduced an iris scan authentication feature for Aadhaar-based transactions through its micro-ATM tablets. ICICI Bank introduced voice recognition for customers dialling the bank's call centre. While HDFC Bank has Niki.ai, Kotak Mahindra Bank incorporated its chatbot Keya into its phone banking helpline to improve its IVR system.

AI is also being used to detect fraud. While the National Stock Exchange of India Ltd (NSE) uses ML to identify market patterns and automate low-complexity tasks in a bid to minimise trading-associated risk, BSE Ltd has been using AI-assisted solutions for rumour detection since 2016.

Last but not least, AI is helping regulatory bodies, such as the Reserve Bank of India (RBI) and the Insurance Regulatory Development Authority (IRDA), monitor compliance in a speedier and more efficient way.

AI Retail Manager

AI is being used by the retail sector in multiple ways. Reliance Retail, for instance, plans to leverage data analytics and AI to stock store-specific assortments. The retail giant also aims to use AI tools to enable its customers to buy online and even take a refund offline.

Tata Croma, on its part, has deployed CASA—a customer engagement platform powered by AI—into their Croma Privileges programme. This platform uses a mix of product, customer, sales, and other data to better understand their customers and design product and marketing strategies.

Flipkart plans to leverage AI, ML, and analytics capabilities to optimise its data for innovative merchandising, advertising, marketing, and customer service. The online retail giant is also expanding its presence in Silicon Valley in the US and focusing on AI-based products by making use of world-class research facilities in the Valley. This is being done through F7 Labs, Flipkart's US-based research arm in Palo Alto.

Flipkart's fashion unit, Myntra, also uses AI to enhance its products, logistics, and customer experience. Amazon India uses ML and AI, among other things, to correct addresses, improve catalogue quality, product size, and product search recommendations, and provide deals for events.

Much has also changed in the world of fashion. Twenty years ago, for instance, we all bought fabric, went to a local tailor to get our apparel stitched and paid the price the tailor demanded. Then came ready-to-wear products as brands started introducing better designs, and people began loving them. Some even said minor fitting issues could be ignored if they were fine with the design and price.

Now, in the new era of personalisation and standardisation, customers are demanding not only better design and a better fit but also want ease and convenience of shopping. Further, these concerns will hold a lot of relevance in the post-pandemic era too.

The reason is that even as the impact of the pandemic tapers, hygiene will assume a lot of importance when purchasing apparel—shirts, tops, jeans, trousers, etc. Shoppers may not be comfortable trying apparel in stores, and retail stores, too, may discourage trials for the same reason. Hence, brands will have to ensure that they provide a safe and convenient shopping environment for shoppers in their stores.

Retail giant Zara, for instance, uses augmented reality (AR) for in-store displays. Customers only need to hold their mobile phones in front of a select shop window to see models wearing pieces from the latest line. Gap uses the DressingRoom—an AR app that lets customers try on clothes anywhere using a Google Tango-enabled device.

Startups such as Stitch Fix, Wide Eyes and India-based Mirrorsize and Vue.ai, too, have similar technology options. Mirrorsize, for instance, has developed a 3D body measurement solution that uses AI, advanced computer vision, DL models, and mesh processing to instantly provide precise body measurements. All that the user needs to do is hold the phone in front of them and follow the instructions that the app provides in real-time. The app provides measurements for both tight- and regular-fit clothing and shows users their 3D avatars too.

Vue.ai uses image recognition and data science to extract data from catalogues, analyse it with user behaviour and help marketing, product, and cataloguing teams draw insights that can improve customer experiences, drive conversions, and reduce costs.

RED FLAGS

As we see, AI has tremendous potential. You can use it to develop smarter companies, smarter cities, smarter villages, and effect sharper governance too.

But before we get excited, let's understand that AI's current source of power—data—is also its Achilles' heel. Researchers continue to be perturbed by the fact that neural nets are "black boxes"—once they have been trained on the data sets, even their designers rarely have any idea how the results are generated.

This has also given rise to the name "Franken" (after Mary Shelley's *Frankenstein*) algorithms and the need for algorithms to be induced with a sense of ethics and fairness so that they can avoid biases. This is a major reason why AI has already received a lot of bad press, underscoring the danger of biased AI algorithms and increasing data privacy violations.

It was just last year that algorithm-based systems downgraded the results of thousands of students in Scotland and England. The governments of these countries had to revert to teacher assessments after students created a hue and cry, and the media highlighted the inherent biases in the algorithms that put poorer students at a disadvantage.

Facebook, for instance, was under fire in India in August 2020 for allegedly failing to selectively police hate speech posts. Similarly, a study conducted by the London-based Institute for Strategic Dialogue demonstrated that content recommendation algorithms of social network sites such as Facebook and Twitter can actively direct users to hate speech posts.[4]

The healthcare sector is another case in point. There's so much good that AI is doing. Doctors are using smart devices to remotely monitor the health of patients and are even performing remote surgeries with the help of robots. Radiologists are using ML and DL to seek patterns in X-rays and rapidly diagnose diseases. AI is quadrupling the speed of magnetic resonance imaging (MRI) scans.

Further, gene-editing tools such as CRISPR-Cas9 (and variants of it) are helping doctors find treatments for life-threatening diseases, and AI is helping them in this task.

But doctors could use the same data to create "designer" babies—genetically-modified children with customised traits like a music or math genius—for those parents who can afford this technology. Insurance companies could misuse the data to tweak health premiums that will not benefit patients with specific illnesses.

Cybercriminals, too, could steal our identities. Governments could, which they already do, use AI to police our social media habits and introduce policies to instil in us what they deem as "proper" behaviour.

AI's incredibly paced growth poses other challenges too.

Smart robots and automation will make, and are already making, routine jobs redundant even as they are creating new ones. Print journalists, for instance, use digital tools to tell their stories to cater to various online platforms like Google, Facebook, YouTube, Instagram, Snapshot, and TikTok. Those who can't be reskilled, however, bear the brunt and fall by the wayside.

Our society will also face vexing questions such as: Who will take responsibility if a fully autonomous Level 5 car kills a human—the owner, manufacturer, or software provider? And what if governments and terrorists begin using AI-powered weapons that leave no trace?

These are topics that we have dealt with in detail in a later chapter.

CAN INDIA BECOME AN AI SUPERPOWER?

These valid concerns of data misuse notwithstanding, the applications of AI across sectors reveal that India does have skilled manpower and the tech prowess to make it big on the AI global map. But can India challenge the supremacy of countries like the US and China in this field?

China has been consistently building an ecosystem to fuel its ambition to become a world leader in AI by 2030.

A report on China's AI development was released by Tsinghua University in September 2018, which said that from 2013 to the first quarter of 2018, the amount of investment and financing in AI technology in China accounted for 60 per cent of the world's, valued at

$27 billion in 2017. That figure would only have increased substantially.

However, while China is challenging the US for global AI supremacy, "… a lack of trust will hinder Chinese firms' ability to acquire significant global market share outside of nations that are taking part in China's subsidised Digital Silk Road initiatives," noted an August 19, 2019 report by the Centre for Data Innovation.

The report pointed out that several Chinese AI chip startups have received hundreds of millions of dollars in funding, and firms such as Huawei have developed impressive chip designs.

It qualified, though, that China's shortage of talent, the complexity of developing chips, and the lack of multiple Chinese semiconductor firms being in the top 15 globally for sales, indicate that China still needs to make significant progress to match the US in semiconductors.

The report also recommended that China should stop unfair trade practices such as forced technology transfers and intellectual property (IP) theft. Chinese apps, too, have always raised suspicions about cyber espionage attempts and security risks globally.

The pandemic has only increased the mistrust that the world had of China.

Chinese telecom hardware manufacturers Huawei and ZTE, who had been under the scanner for alleged security and privacy violations—not only in the US and some European countries but also in India—for many years, were among those who faced the flak.

While Huawei is the world's largest maker of telecom equipment and the second-largest maker of mobile phone parts, ZTE manufactures the patented equipment of many multinationals in China at very low costs.

On June 30, 2020, the US Federal Communications Commission (FCC) formally designated Chinese telecom vendors Huawei Technologies Company and ZTE Corporation, including their parent and subsidiaries and affiliate firms, as "national security threats".

A ban on these companies could cut both ways. It could impact the fortunes of these companies and, subsequently, that of China. On the other hand, it could substantially increase the cost of telecom equipment across the board at a time when countries across the world, including India, are gearing up to launch 5G services.

India must take advantage of this mistrust.

It did so in small measure when it imposed an interim ban on the popular Chinese video-creation platform TikTok and 58 other apps due to "security" reasons in June 2020. The decision to ban TikTok was taken at a time when Indian and Chinese security forces clashed in the Galwan Valley for a few weeks before calling it a truce.

TikTok was run by an American CEO but owned by a Chinese company, ByteDance. When the ban was imposed, ByteDance's TikTok had an estimated 30 per cent, around 120 million, of its global users coming from India.

Losing the Indian market would impact the company's valuation as the firm readies for an IPO listing. Even though the ban was interim, many TikTok users would have moved to other platforms like YouTube, Facebook, Hotstar and Jio.

However, India's regulators will have to devise policies that strike a balance between overreach and protecting the security and privacy of the data, especially since Chinese companies have made huge investments in many Indian companies.

About two dozen Chinese technology companies and venture funds, led by behemoths including Alibaba, ByteDance and Tencent, funded 92 Indian startups, including unicorns (those startups valued at $1 billion or more) such as Paytm, Byju's, Oyo and Ola, according to the foreign policy think tank, Gateway House.

In the Indian startup space, about 20 Indian unicorns have a Chinese investor. Paytm, one of India's most successful startups, is backed by Ant Financial, an affiliate of Alibaba. Ola Cabs, India's home-grown rival to Uber, raised funds from Didi. Delhivery, an Indian logistics startup, received money from Fosun International. Swiggy, a food-delivery startup, and Dream 11, a gaming startup, have raised money from Tencent.

Further, Apple phones are contract-manufactured by Taiwanese company Foxconn, which has plans to invest up to $1 billion to expand a factory in the Sriperumbudur plant in Tamil Nadu where it assembles Apple iPhones, according to a July 11, 2020 Reuters report.

India's regulators can learn valuable lessons from the European

Union (EU) and countries like Australia, Canada and the US. We will explore this theme in more detail in a later chapter.

SUMMING UP

First, we gave you a bit of AI's history to put the technology in today's context. We then gave you an overview of how AI works and the critical role that computing power and data currently play.

Second, we gave you examples of three AI applications—AI as a doctor, a banker and a retail manager. We showed you how businesses around the world and in India are using AI in these sectors.

Third, we highlighted some major concerns that are being raised as AI gets more and more powerful.

Fourth, we pointed out that while India does have skilled manpower and the tech prowess to make it big on the AI global map, it still has a long way to go before it can meaningfully challenge the supremacy of countries like the US and China in this field.

The takeaway is that India can gain from anti-China sentiments. However, this will happen only if it devises the right policies, strengthens its manufacturing industry, revamps its labour laws, strengthens its IP ecosystem, and invests substantially in R&D to become an AI-powered digital powerhouse.

The government has already taken some concrete steps in this direction. "Technology is evolving at such a fast pace that very soon artificial intelligence will dominate our way of life," Prime Minister Narendra Modi said during the launch of the National AI Mission in May 2020.

NITI Aayog has already decided to focus on five sectors that it believes will benefit the most from AI. These are healthcare, agriculture, education, smart cities and infrastructure, and smart mobility and transportation. We will examine some of the developments that have been made in these areas in the following chapters.

As we may have realised by now, India, which has prided itself as a mobile-first nation, is now pitching for the AI-first country tag. In this context, it's only fitting that India will now chair the Global Partnership on Artificial Intelligence (GPAI), a role it has taken over from council chair France. "India will work in cooperation with member states to put in place a framework around which power of AI can be exploited for the good of citizens across the globe-with guardrails to prevent misuse and user harm," minister of state for electronics and information technology, Rajeev Chandrasekhar, tweeted on November 21, 2022, when he represented India for the symbolic takeover.

Launched on June 15, 2020, GPAI facilitates international cooperation on AI by bringing together experts from science, industry, civil society, governments, international bodies, and academia to support cutting-edge research and applied activities. The consortium comprises 25 member countries, including the US, UK, EU, Australia, Canada, France, Germany, Italy, Japan, Mexico, New Zealand, South Korea, Singapore, and India. Montreal, Canada, hosted the inaugural edition on December 3 and 4, 2020, followed by Paris on November 11 and 12, 2021. Tokyo is the first Asian city to host this summit.

India may soon host this summit, given its keen interest in becoming an AI superpower in the region. At least on the AI applications side, India has millions of skilled engineers and software developers.

We believe that initiatives such as "Make in India", "Startup India", "Skill India" and "Atmanirbhar Bharat", among others, coupled with the AI thrust and sensible policies, will accelerate the pace at which India is becoming digitally intelligent and raise India's AI quotient.

Let's now explore how AI is being used around the world and in India.

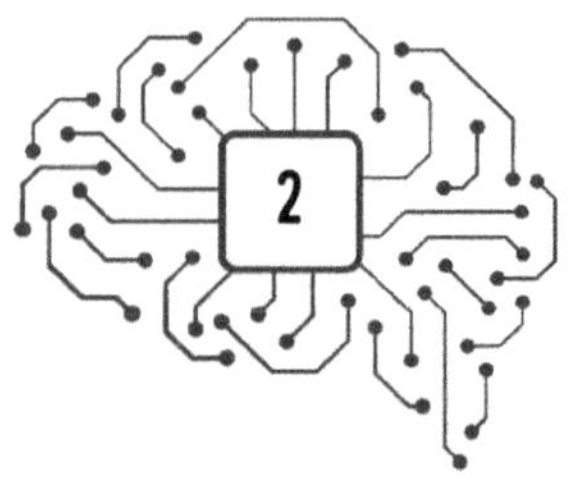

EXPLAINING DIGITAL INTELLIGENCE

"When patterns are broken, new worlds emerge."

—*Tuli Kupferberg*

"It was seven minutes to ten o'clock in the morning, and it was the only good thing that had happened." [09:53:46]

"A patch of green grass seemed to be seeking its face, but it was not much to see …" [10:36:11].

Do you feel there's something amiss in these sentences? You guessed right. These words were not penned by a human but written by an AI algorithm for a novel called *The Road* in 2017.

A year later, the human author of this algorithm, Ross Godwin, trained another algorithm to convert words into collective poetry. He worked with artist and designer Es Devlin on "Please Feed The Lions" in collaboration with Google Arts and Culture as part of the London Design Festival in 2018.

The project involved adding a lion to the four-strong pride at Trafalgar Square in London. Visitors were invited to "feed the lion" with words that would evolve into a collective poem. The AI-written poem was displayed on LEDs embedded in the lion's mouth by day and projected on to Nelson's Column in Trafalgar Square at night.

Godwin used a specific recurrent neural network (the LSTM–RNN) for this project. This model predicts the next text character repeatedly and is trained on thousands of poetry books. Hence, when someone submits a word, the AI algorithm figures out whether it's a noun or verb or any other part of speech. Simply put, an AI algorithm is a step-by-step procedure written in software code to help machines execute specific actions.

An AI, third-generation natural language processing (NLP) model called Generative Pre-Trained Transformer 3.0, or GPT-3, vastly enhances the capabilities of AI-written poems and novels. The GPT-3 model, in fact, can generate human-like text. Well, almost.

A college student, Liam Porr, used GPT-3 to produce a blog post called "Adolos". Thousands of people who read the post did not realise that it was written by OpenAI's third-generation language prediction model, which is better known as GPT-3. Ironically, Adolos means 'sincere' in Greek.

"In a strange way, an AI could help us all come together, but at what point does this relationship of human and machine start to undermine who we are as a species? Where do we draw the line between human and machine?"

You may find it hard to believe, but even these questions were generated by GPT-3 as part of an episode written in collaboration with a human for Tinkered Thinking. The paragraph was fed to a GPT-3 model, following which the AI language model generated more sequential text with a predefined word count. GPT-3, thus, wrote the

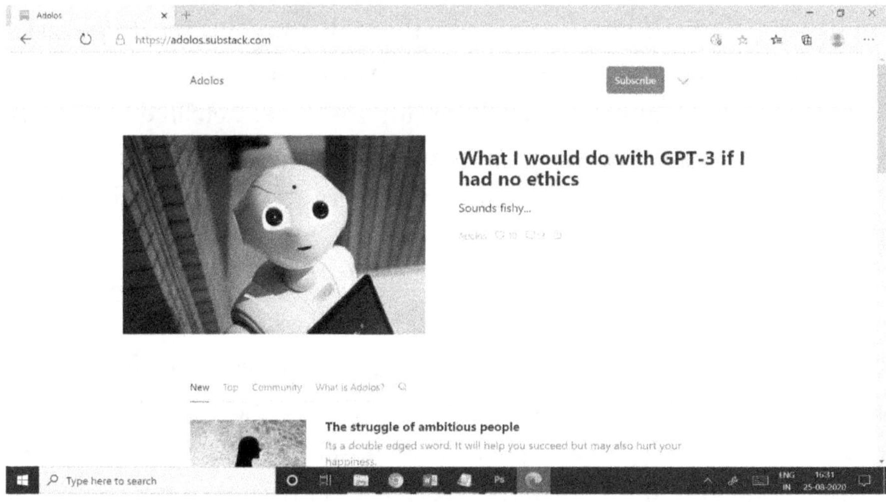

This is a screenshot of an AI-generated blog that made waves in 2020.

entire episode.

GPT-3 is currently the world's largest language learning model. In a July 2020 paper titled "Language Models Are Few-Shot Learners", the authors describe GPT-3 as an autoregressive language model with 175 parameters, implying it uses past values to predict future ones. Parameters help ML models make predictions on new data.

With computing power becoming increasingly cheaper, AI algorithms are becoming smarter by consistently training on data sets that are getting bigger and bigger.

An algorithm is a set of steps that enables a computer program to accomplish a specific task. Liken it to a recipe that shows you how to make dishes such as poha, daal, or butter chicken. ML comprises a series of algorithms that enables software to update and learn from previous outcomes without any need for human programming. To put it simply, while traditional algorithms specify precise steps to provide an answer, an AI algorithm (since ML is essentially a subset of AI) can learn from data and automate this task.

The fact is that intelligent algorithms today now not only power our smartphones and other mobile devices but also drive cars and write novels, poems, and even horror stories. They help machines compose music, make movies, and write sports and business stories to emulate reporters, paint, make portraits, and even cook and serve at restaurants.

AI algorithms are eventually expected to help machines outsmart humans in many activities, especially those that involve repetitive tasks and years of practice, such as quizzes, debates, and games.

IBM's supercomputer Deep Blue, for instance, defeated the then-world chess champion, Garry Kasparov, in May 1997. Fourteen years later, IBM Watson beat ace Jeopardy players Ken Jennings and Brad Rutter.

In March 2016, Alphabet-owned AI firm DeepMind's computer programme, AlphaGo, challenged Go champion Lee Sedol. The ancient Chinese board game Go is a complex game—the likely configurations are said to match the number of atoms in the universe. Sedol believed he could win since the game requires a remarkably high level of intuition that machines are not known to have. He was proved wrong.

Two years later, AI bots beat humans at another complex game—

Dota 2, a free-to-play multiplayer online battle arena video game.

AI will write a high-school essay by 2026, drive a truck by 2027, work in retail by 2031, write a bestselling book by 2049, and work as a surgeon by 2053, predicts a June 2017 survey done by a team from the University of Oxford and Yale University.

Researchers who took the survey also believe there is a 50 per cent chance of AI outperforming humans in all tasks within 45 years and automating all human jobs within 120 years.

These developments and predictions can amaze and alarm us simultaneously, raising questions such as: Will AI soon write children's books like Enid Blyton, churn out works like those from Shakespeare or Charles Dickens, write fiction like J.K. Rowling's Harry Potter series, or even a poem like William Wordsworth?

Will AI also be able to write stories and poems in Indian languages like Hindi, Marathi, Gujarati, Bengali, Telugu, Kannada or Malayalam, which will turn out to be as good as the best of human authors? More importantly, will AI algorithms take away our jobs and become powerful enough to subjugate us, as it's shown in sci-fi movies?

There are no easy answers, but here's how we perceive these concerns.

First, we remain optimistic that humans will be able to control the outcome by devising safeguards and effective policies, which we have discussed in detail in a later chapter.

Second, in his 2006 book *The Singularity is Near*, American author and futurist Ray Kurzweil goes a step further. He predicts that by 2099, machines will have attained equal legal status with humans. This harks back to movies like *Bicentennial Man*, in which the late Robin Williams was developed as a robot but evolved into a humanoid with tech advancements and was finally granted the status of a human by the courts when he was 200 years old.

However, current AI developments at least indicate that humans are unlikely to see a fully sentient AI-powered machine—one that can think, work, emote, create, and live like us—any time soon. Even the Hong Kong-based Hanson Robotics' AI-powered robot, Sophia, which is already a citizen of Saudi Arabia, is not even remotely close to being a human. Simply put, Sophia can be switched off; a human being cannot—we die from illnesses or simply old age.

Third, we believe it currently makes more sense to sharpen our focus on how AI has already changed the way we work, play, do business, and live, and try to leverage the advantages it is giving us in our daily lives and businesses, as we will demonstrate below.

THE COVID PUSH

The impact of AI-induced digital disruption is already being felt across every industry—smartphones, driverless cars and trucks, digital banking and payments, and healthcare, to name a few.

AI proved helpful even before the pandemic had gathered momentum. Consider this case. On December 30, 2019, a Toronto-based health surveillance company, BlueDot, issued a warning to its customers to avoid Wuhan—where the virus originated. An automated service called HealthMap at Boston Children's Hospital also detected those first signs. So did a model run by San Francisco-based Metabiota.

Companies like BlueDot and Metabiota and services like HealthMap use NLP algorithms to monitor news outlets and official healthcare reports. These are predictive algorithms that use air travel data to assess the risk at airports or other transit hubs where infected people may be arriving or departing.

The pandemic has only accelerated the pace of digital transformation. In 2020, it amply demonstrated how companies could effectively use AI-powered digital technologies, such as robots, 3D printers, IoT, mixed reality (a combination of virtual reality and augmented reality), and 5G to complement the traditional methods of increased hygiene, quarantines and enforced global travel bans by governments.

Robots, for instance, helped in many ways during the pandemic. They patrolled and cleaned infected areas, led patients in exercises, and even performed robo-dances to entertain bored quarantine patients at the Wuhan Wuchang Hospital in China.[1]

Robots from Belgium-based Zorabots were already being used in hospitals, care homes and hotels since 2013. When the pandemic broke out, the robots began assisting people at the Antwerp University Hospital by checking their body temperature and determining if they were wearing a mask correctly, among other things.[2]

Kochi-based startup Asimov Robotics developed a three-wheeled robot called "KARMI Bot" to serve food and medicines to COVID-19 patients, thus reducing the risk of infections for doctors and health workers.

5G-powered temperature measurement devices flagged patients with fever symptoms at the entrance of the smart hospital that was jointly built by telecom carrier China Mobile and communications company China Potevio Co. The robots were donated by CloudMinds Technology—a SoftBank-backed startup based in Beijing.

Drones, too, pitched in to deliver the goods during the pandemic. Civic officials in Mumbai used drones to track the spread of COVID-19 cases in the largest slum of Asia—Dharavi—in Mumbai, according to an April 17 report in the *Hindustan Times*. Brihanmumbai Municipal Corporation (BMC) officials also used drones to disperse a crowd thronging a market in the Dongri area, violating the countrywide lockdown that began on March 25, 2020.

The drone feed was beamed to a giant screen. These drones, along with traffic cameras and heat maps, helped the police in enforcing the lockdown in these densely populated areas.

Consider another example. When Northern India was attacked by locusts in June 2020, the Union Ministry of Agriculture claimed that India had become the first country to control locusts with the help of drones.

IoT devices also played an important role during the pandemic. Passengers at airports around the world are now routinely given wristbands along with a unique quick response (QR) code (the matrix barcode that you see on your mobile device) to track their movements. They can download the relevant apps on their smartphones and scan the QR.

When they reach their homes, they only need to walk around their apartment and calibrate the device. While the basic technology is known as Geofencing, wherein a virtual perimeter is created using GPS, radio frequency identification (RFID), Wi-Fi, Bluetooth, and the cellular network, the binding tech is the internet of things, or IoT—a concept

Drones fall under the broad umbrella of Unmanned Aerial Vehicles (UAVs).
Picture courtesy: *Hindustan Times*

that helps devices communicate with each other.

Further, many countries are using individual-level location-tracking of people via their smartphones to contain the spread of the pandemic. Aarogya Setu, launched by the Indian government on April 2, 2020, enables Bluetooth-based contact tracing, mapping of likely hotspots and dissemination of relevant information about COVID-19. The app had over 114 million users by May 2020.

But apps pose challenges too, such as invasion of privacy and security. Apps, for instance, collect sensitive information like location data, Bluetooth-enabled proximity information, and whether individuals are infected—all of which could lead to selective discrimination. Moreover, all this sensitive information can be hacked and sold to unscrupulous companies and scammers.

SOME EXAMPLES

Hence, it's important for governments to prevent misuse of the very tool that can help in saving countless lives. We will talk more about that in the chapter where we discuss AI, ethics, and privacy.

The pandemic also highlighted the use of mixed reality devices—those that used a combination of virtual reality (VR) and augmented reality (AR).

As an example, the Imperial College Healthcare NHS Trust—which includes Charing Cross Hospital, Hammersmith Hospital and St Mary's Hospital—said that using HoloLens had led to a fall in the amount of time staff are spending in high-risk areas of up to 83 per cent.[3]

HoloLens with Dynamics 365 Remote Assist uses Microsoft Teams to send a secure live video feed to a computer screen. This allows healthcare teams to remotely see how the doctor treats patients. HoloLens also allows the doctor to see information such as the patient's X-ray imaging and blood test results. The Trust, thus, could save on personal protective equipment (PPE) too.

Closer home, students who could not attend the 58th Convocation of IIT Bombay due to the pandemic viewed their own animated personalised avatars receiving medals, awards, and degrees from the chief guest and the director of the institute.

The entire ceremony, held on August 23, 2020, was broadcast live so that students, relatives, and friends, even in remote areas without internet access, could watch it on a large screen with their families.

3D printing, too, was extensively used to help save lives as governments battled to flatten the COVID-19 curve. The technology, which has been

Digital avatar of IIT Bombay director and a student receiving his degree. *Source:* IIT Bombay

around for almost three decades, belongs to a class of techniques known as additive manufacturing. The material, which is typically some form of plastic, ceramic or metal, is squirted from a 3D printer's nozzle to build an object layer by layer (hence the term "additive").

It started when companies like Isnnova and Lonati S.p.A. 3D printed valves for ventilators. Others, like RapidMade, produced lightweight plastic face masks with removable filters as well as face shields.

GE Additive designed a 3D-printed adapter that can convert a standard hard hat and visor into a face shield in less than a minute. HP Inc. partnered with researchers at Harvard University and Beth Israel Deaconess Medical Center to assist with gathering test data and refining 3D-printed test swab designs, materials, and printing capacity.

A Mumbai-based 3D printing firm, Boson Machines, pitched in by manufacturing 3D-printed face shields for doctors treating COVID-19 patients in India.

All these technologies, which are clubbed under terms like "digital transformation" and "Industry 4.0", would continue to play a key role as the rules of the post-COVID world are reimagined. More importantly, India offers an opportunity to use these technologies at a scale that is matched only by China.

This is already happening, as we see in the case of Jio Platforms, which is owned by Mukesh Ambani's Reliance Industries Ltd (RIL).

AI-POWERED 'SUPER APP'

On April 23, 2020, India's business magnate Mukesh Dhirubhai Ambani, RIL chairman and managing director, announced that the world's largest social networking site, Facebook, had taken a 9.99 per cent stake in Jio Platforms for $5.7 billion.

Silverlake Investments, General Atlantic Partners, Vista Equity Partners, L. Catterton, and KKR—all leading global private equity (PE) firms—took the cue and invested large sums of money in Jio Platforms. In July, Intel Capital also invested a little over $250 million. These transactions and others that followed valued Jio Platforms at a whopping $65 billion.

How did this digital platform, which also operates the Jio Infocomm telecom network, manage such a huge valuation amidst a pandemic that had almost crippled global economies and led to a massive capital crunch? The answer primarily lies in the question itself—the operative terms being "digital platform" in India and "for Indians".

Furthermore, since the pandemic forced people to stay indoors and maintain physical distance, digital tools and platforms were the only way to communicate with family, friends, and office colleagues, and do work and business.

The vision of Jio Platforms, according to RIL's 2019–20 annual report, is to enable a Digital India for the local population and businesses across the country, including small merchants, micro-businesses, and farmers, "so that all of them can enjoy the fruits of inclusive growth". The huge valuation, however, comes from the fact that the partnership with Facebook has created two huge pools—Indian consumers and their data.

Numbers buttress the story. At the time of signing the deal, Jio had approximately 388 million users who were subscribers of its telecom business and associated digital properties. On its part, Facebook had around 300 million users, while its unit WhatsApp had an estimated 400 million users.

Reliance has created a largely debt-free digital holding company for its telecom business, apps, and a few of its related acquisitions. A host of companies that RIL invested in are now part of Jio Platforms. These include music streaming service JioSaavn, online education platform Embibe, and AI-powered virtual assistant, Haptik.

Further, with Jio Mart—the merchant platform of Jio—RIL wants to target 60 million SME businesses, 30 million shopkeepers, and 120 million farmers.

Concurrent with the investment, Jio Platforms, Reliance Retail and WhatsApp also entered into a commercial partnership agreement to further accelerate Reliance Retail's digital commerce business on the JioMart platform using WhatsApp and to support small businesses on WhatsApp, according to RIL's latest annual report.[4]

This has effectively made Jio Platforms an ecosystem that offers everything from telecom to digital payments, media and entertainment content. The services include Network18, Viacom, Voot, Jio Studios,

JioGames, JioMoney and Jio Payments Bank, JioTV, JioCloud, JioHome and JioSmartLiving.

This is akin to having a Verizon Communications, a service like Google, a digital payments company like PayPal Holdings Inc. and a digital content provider such as Netflix Inc.—all combined on a single cohesive digital business platform.

RIL went a step further and announced the unthinkable on July 15, 2020. It got Google to take a 7.73 per cent equity stake for Rs 33,737 crore in Jio Platforms despite Facebook already having invested a substantial amount in the company. This partnership will help Google and Jio leverage each other's digital strengths to expand the number of internet users in the country.

Jio Platforms and Google simultaneously entered into a commercial agreement to jointly develop an affordable entry-level smartphone.

All these investments, acquisitions, and restructuring have helped RIL build a platform that is comparable with global ones ,such as Amazon, Tencent Holdings Ltd, and Alibaba.

We now can access thousands of apps on our mobiles for every conceivable task—be it to check our fitness level, buy clothes or books, listen to podcasts, do grocery shopping, buy food, or whatever. What if all these tasks can be bundled into one app? You're on the right track if you're thinking of a web portal for smartphones. We call it a "Super App"—the smartphone mobile app version of the all-in-one platform that caters to an average user's daily needs.

As my colleague Kolla has explained in a detailed chapter on super apps, the super app started as a phenomenon in East Asia, with Chinese company Tencent's popular mobile instant messaging app—WeChat— evolving into a "platform of apps".

Jio will eventually resemble an AI-powered super app in the post-COVID-19 world, enabling users to access media and entertainment content, buy stuff online, and communicate with other users.

TRILLION-DOLLAR DIGITAL INDIA

Jio Platforms is simply a case in point, albeit a stellar one, of how India can become a digital superpower.

Salt-to-software conglomerate Tata Group, too, is working on its own super app through Tata Digital to expand its presence in consumer-facing businesses. The idea is to aggregate all Tata Group services—groceries, lifestyle, electronics, healthcare, finance, etc.—under a single 'omnichannel' platform. "It will be a super app, a lot of apps in apps and so on … We have a very big opportunity," Tata Sons Chairman Natarajan Chandrasekaran told *Financial Times* in August 2021.[5]

India needs more such ecosystems if it wants to achieve a digital revenue of over $1 trillion in the next five years.

The economic value of India's digital economy, which was pegged at around $200 billion in 2019, is forecast to rise to over $1 trillion in 2025, according to a report by the Ministry of Electronics and Information Technology (MeitY) and consultancy firm McKinsey & Co.

"The trillion-dollar economy report is the symbol of opportunity that India offers. Digital India is also an opportunity for people in the digital space to do business in India. The size and scale that India offers is a big business opportunity for global companies," said Ravi Shankar Prasad, Minister of Information Technology, when releasing the report on February 20, 2019.

Information technology and business process management (IT-BPM) companies, digital communication services (including telecom), e-commerce, domestic electronics manufacturing, digital payments, and direct subsidy transfers accounted for a substantial portion of the $200 billion figure in 2019. They are forecast to contribute around $500 billion to the digital economy by 2025.

The remaining 50 per cent of the potential economic value of $1 trillion, according to the MeitY–McKinsey report, could come from new digital ecosystems, including financial services, agriculture, healthcare, logistics, jobs and skills market, e-governance, and other areas.

This potential, the authors of the report argue, would create a rapidly growing market for a host of digital services, platforms, applications, content, and solutions.

To be sure, this rising market opportunity will also result in more jobs, but the skill sets will not remain the same. A report released by

McKinsey Global Institute in March 2019 noted that the productivity unlocked by the digital economy could create 60–65 million jobs that will require digital skills by 2025. The report, however, cautioned that retraining and redeployment will be essential to help some 40–45 million workers whose jobs could be displaced or transformed by the digital revolution by 2025.

What works in India's favour is that the country has around 1.2 billion phones and over 500 million active internet users who were five years old and above as of November 2019, according to a report by the Internet and Mobile Association of India (IAMAI) and Nielsen Holdings plc that was released on May 5, 2020.[6]

It's encouraging to see many young people accessing the internet—433 million were over 12 years old, and 71 million were 5–11 years old, who accessed the internet on the devices of family members.

Further, even though internet penetration in urban areas is higher than in rural areas, penetration in villages is growing at a faster clip and can improve if villages get better quality connectivity and more affordable mobile internet plans.

Gender equality is increasing too. The report revealed that 26 million new female internet users were added in November 2019—a 21 per cent increase compared to a 9 per cent rise in male users.

Mobile remains the device of choice for accessing the internet in both urban and rural areas, the report noted. Given the affordability of mobile devices along with the availability of cheaper data plans, accessing the internet on mobile devices, mostly smartphones, has clearly become the first choice. As of November 2022, India had over 1.2 billion mobile phone users and 600 million smartphone users, according to data provided by the government.

Digital payments, too, have gained a lot of traction as the pandemic encouraged people and merchants to maintain a safe physical distance. Banks are coming to terms with the fact that young customers, primarily those living in urban areas, prefer net banking and mobile banking, and would seldom, or never, want to visit a bank branch if offered that choice.

The pandemic has only boosted the adoption of digital payments due to the self- and enforced-quarantine periods.

Fintechs, meanwhile, have made the payments ecosystem more inclusive, disruptive, and challenging with their innovative technology solutions, such as AI-powered bots and contactless payments, to name a few.

In India especially, the government's Aadhaar-enabled payments system and the Unified Payments Interface (UPI) have revolutionised the payments ecosystem. Currently, about 135 banks offer UPI. Further, QR codes will continue to be used for payments, and IoT is set to dominate micropayments by transforming connected devices into payment channels.

All these developments spell good news for the making of a true Digital India.

SUMMING UP

We first demonstrated that AI-powered robots, drones, automated guided vehicles, 3D printing and wearable devices, among other digital technologies, have the potential to radically transform the Indian manufacturing and services sectors. As per a NASSCOM prediction, data and AI could add $450–500 billion in terms of GDP by 2025 and drive India's vision of inclusive development.

Second, we showed why India needs super apps—such as the ones being created by RIL and the Tata Group—to up its digital game. We concluded with an overview of the ecosystem that India is developing as it targets a $1 trillion revenue from its digital economy.

We believe India can achieve this goal. What may also work in its favour is the strong likelihood of a global realignment of trade as companies seek to move manufacturing out of China, which has invested heavily in AI.

Third, we believe that with government support and sensible policies, this is India's chance to take AI to the next level, as envisioned by the National AI mission launched in May 2020.

NITI Aayog, a policy think tank of the Indian government, has already acknowledged that AI is poised to disrupt our world and that

India—being the fastest-growing economy with the second-largest population in the world—has a "significant stake in the AI revolution".

NITI Aayog's claim is amply supported by the fact that numerous companies across sectors are using AI in India. We will explore how some of these companies are using AI to enhance the efficiency of their businesses in the following chapter.

PART–2

ARTIFICIAL INTELLIGENCE IN INDIA

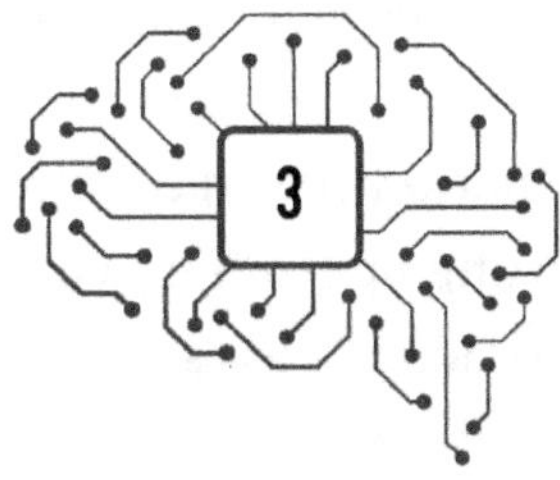

HOW AI IS HELPING INDIAN COMPANIES

"Software is eating the world, but AI is going to eat software."
—*Jensen Huang*

Around the time that AI hit the inflexion point in 2017 and was ready to go mainstream, I was advising some companies on how to formulate their digital transformation strategies and implementation plans. These companies had begun allocating technology budgets and prepping their executives to effect change management and a digital mindset across the company.

They were simultaneously readying themselves to adopt and integrate digital technologies such as Web 2.0, mobile apps, cloud computing, social media and customer engagement tools, and data analytics with their legacy software and infrastructure in a bid to improve their business process efficiency.

During our discussions, it struck us that many AI solutions, which were ready for adoption around that time, also fit the bill. In fact, many of these AI solutions were promising to solve our business problems with more efficiency and, more importantly, at a faster pace. Hence, we included AI tools as a part of the digital transformation exercise of these companies.

More than four years have passed since we began the journey of digital transformation with those companies. The efforts have paid off manifold, reconfirming the fact that it pays to invest in AI. But then, I was merely stating the obvious since the world has seen the disruptive power of digital transformation. We have already witnessed examples of how digital startups sprung up from nowhere to take on the might of incumbents and win customers across sectors.

Uber, Ola, Lyft, Airbnb and Oyo, for instance, used digital technologies to challenge traditional cab-hailing and hospitality industries without owning a single taxi or hotel. Similarly, online groceries such as Amazon successfully tackled the likes of Walmart and Costco in e-commerce. Other behemoths like Reliance Fresh and Reliance Digital, which are part of the Mukesh Ambani-owned Reliance Industries, also successfully challenged established retail shops such as DMart and Future Group besides online biggies such as Amazon and Walmart in India with the help of digital technologies.

Companies such as Uber, Ola and Oyo are categorised as digital natives. Users only need to access their mobile apps to call a taxi or book a hotel. Others, such as Amazon, Walmart, and Reliance, are digital hybrids and are recognised as phygital companies. The reason is that they combine their digital presence with a physical or offline one by building warehouses and retail shops in the real world.

It's important, however, not to miss the fact that all those companies that adopted digital transformation have one thing in common— regardless of whether they are digital natives or digital hybrids (phygitals), they are continually using AI tools as part of their digital transformation strategy to give them a consistent edge.

For example, most of us log on to e-commerce sites such as Flipkart or Amazon India for our shopping needs. This is the digital part of the experience. But these companies also have physical warehouses where they store the inventory so that they can deliver the goods to you on time. This is why digital transformation has to be effective both online and in physical warehouses. But these e-commerce companies were born as digital natives. Tata's Croma and Reliance Digital, on the other hand, have both physical stores and online shopping. We call these companies phygitals or digital hybrids.

In this context, it may come as a pleasant surprise that many companies adopting AI are non-core technology companies. Core technology companies refer primarily to digital technologies-led industries and companies, such as IT products and services, telecom services providers, consumer internet companies, and enterprise software companies. Non-core technology companies, on the other hand, comprise industries that use machines and digital technologies as enablers for their core offerings. Examples include companies in the oil and gas, healthcare, automotive, banking and financial services, education, and insurance sectors.

For instance, how many of us would typically associate oil and gas companies with cutting-edge technology terms like AI, ML and IoT? The fact, however, is that all major upstream and downstream oil and gas companies around the world, including India, use these technologies for the exploration of oil, predictive maintenance (where ML is used to alert workers and managers of a faulty leak or potential danger and urge them to repair it before it becomes a serious problem), and improving customer experience.

Let's take the example of India's second-largest oil and gas company, Bharat Petroleum Corporation Ltd (BPCL), which announced a partnership with consulting firm Accenture to digitally transform its extensive sales and distribution network in April 2021. Accenture plans to use its capabilities in data, AI, and cloud technologies to build, design, and implement a digital platform christened IRIS.

This platform will help BPCL integrate real-time data from across its countrywide network, which includes more than 18,000 fuel retail outlets, 25,000 tank trucks, 75 oil installations and depots, 52 liquefied petroleum gas (LPG) bottling plants, and 250 additional industrial and commercial locations, to provide a consolidated view of its extensive operations, according to an April 13, 2021 press statement.

The IRIS platform will use analytics based on AI and ML technologies to trigger automated alerts and actions. This will also empower the more than 1,00,000 BPCL workforce across the country to react swiftly and make faster and more accurate decisions, including preventative maintenance. This can help increase sales at retail fuel outlets by minimising infrastructure downtime and ensuring consistent fuel quality, as well as improving the experience for customers.

IRIS can accept more than three million inputs per second from automated sensors, cameras, and IoT devices deployed at all key locations. It can track performance based on key parameters such as fuel stock, safety, compliance, equipment health and boosting asset uptime. BPCL's field workforce and partner network will have a seamless experience thanks to support from a portal, mobile app, and call centres in Noida and Chennai. The digital sales and distribution platform will use BPCL's cloud infrastructure, only making it more agile and scalable.

BPCL is simply a case in point of a non-core technology company adopting AI-powered digital tools. Let's now look at another sector and consider the case of consumer electronics brand Samsung's AI-enabled bilingual washing machine that has a Hindi and English user interface. This washing machine line-up, with 21 new models, learns and remembers laundry habits and suggests the most frequently used wash cycle.

Since this washing machine is also IoT-enabled, it can connect with Samsung smart devices, such as Galaxy smartphones, Samsung Smart TVs and Family Hub refrigerators, as well as voice devices, such as Alexa and Google Home, to allow you to operate it remotely. According to a press statement, this washing machine "has been customised for India with over 2000 wash combinations and 2.8 million big data analysis points for different types of fabrics and can be controlled with a smartphone or a Samsung connected device".

As these examples suggest, many AI solutions are being implemented across a wide range of industries and companies. Just like mobile telecommunication, cloud computing, GPS, and even electricity, AI has application and adoption potential in every industry. AI, according to a NASSCOM report, has the potential to add $450–500 billion to the gross domestic product (GDP) of India by 2025.

The target is achievable since AI does improve the capabilities of companies to increase their revenue. There are two reasons for this, according to the Boston Consulting Group (BCG). The first reason is that "AI's ability to detect very weak signals helps companies develop,

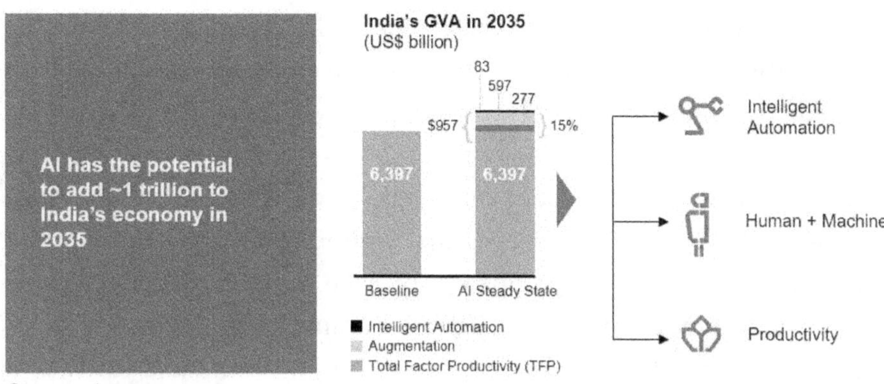

Source: Accenture

refine, and generate numerous forecasts (such as those for demand, supply, inventory, prices, and logistics)".

The second is that AI works at a pace that provides companies with the ability to analyse large amounts of data to make decisions in real-time. "By improving the accuracy of forecasts and by enabling real-time decisions, AI helps companies generate more revenue," BCG notes.[1]

Given this context, let's explore how AI helps companies earn more money with some examples. As it is well said, the proof of the pudding lies in the eating.

TAKING THE HELP OF MONEY-MINDED SMART BOTS

Let's start with the banking, financial services, and insurance (BFSI) sector. As we pointed out in brief in Chapter 1, AI in the BFSI sector is typically used to onboard new customers, including those that are under-banked or have never opened a bank account (the unbanked). This helps the cause of financial inclusion by giving more and more underprivileged people access to the banking system. It also helps them keep away from the clutches of moneylenders who charge exorbitant amounts by way of interest, burdening such people with debt for life.

Poorer sections of society also have poor or no credit scores, which prevents them from getting loans at lower rates. It is estimated that 50 per cent of first-time loan applicants face rejection from financial institutions. While traditional lending systems have relied solely on credit scores, legacy processes and tedious paperwork, AI is being used by banks and non-banking financial companies (NBFCs) to determine the creditworthiness of a borrower without a credit score with the help of predictive analytics, digital footprints, and other complex algorithms and data points.

Financial service providers can, thus, rely on the digital presence of a loan applicant by assessing their online shopping habits, utility and telephone bill payment history, or even social media profiles for determining creditworthiness. As most online transactions are done through a smartphone today, lenders are now easily able to track a prospective customer's online activity. Rather than using credit scores and credit history, fintech companies are now using something called a "social loan quotient" to assess a loan applicant and determine their creditworthiness.

AI is also used to enhance customer experience and service delivery optimisation, and internal efficiency optimisation. This leads to the improvement of internal efficiency and turnaround time for processing claims and cuts down financial losses. The BFSI sector can introduce "radical personalisation" with the help of AI. This implies personalising product offerings to target individual consumers based on multi-modal data (mobile, social media, location, etc.).

AI can help companies discover new trends and anomalies by identifying fraudulent activity using customer transactions and other relevant data. AI helps in predictive analytics, which implies evaluating customer credit risk using applications and other relevant data so that bankers and insurers can disburse loans in real-time without allowing their personal biases to creep in.

AI's predictive maintenance ability helps companies predict the risk of churn for individual customers and clients, and recommends renegotiation strategies. The use of predictive analytics is 90 per cent accurate in detecting the repayment behaviour of a prospective customer; thus it helps in bringing down delinquencies. Further, AI-powered chatbots can be used by insurance companies to review claims, verify policy details, and inspect them with fraud detection algorithms before the final settlement.

ICICI Bank, for instance, is leveraging NLP, ML, cognitive tools, optical character recognition, data analytics, and bots, among others. The bank's operations team is using AI to review documents submitted by customers to increase speed and efficiency. It also uses chatbots for customer services to respond to customer queries and aid/inform employees on the actions required to address customer needs. The bank's iPal chatbot is available on desktops, laptops, and smartphones too. All answers given by iPal are automated, but iPal is trained to understand queries and improve the responses.

Further, ICICI Bank's software bots perform more than one million banking transactions per working day. These software bots are configured to capture and interpret information from systems, recognise patterns, and run business processes across multiple applications to execute activities, including data entry and validation, automated formatting, multi-format message creation, text mining, workflow acceleration, reconciliations, and currency exchange rate processing, among others.

Similarly, HDFC Bank's EVA (Electronic Virtual Assistant) uses NLP to locate branch addresses and answer common queries such as interest rates, remittances, and IFSC codes in real-time. Since its launch in March 2020, EVA has addressed millions of customer questions and conversations. The AI bot can assimilate knowledge from thousands of sources and provide simple answers in less than 0.4 seconds, according to HDFC Bank.

DBS, a leading financial services group in Asia, offers DBS Wealth Chat. It's a service that allows its high-net-worth clients to interact, share ideas, and transact with their relationship managers (RMs) via the instant messaging platform WhatsApp. Even the state-owned State Bank of India's (SBI) AI-powered chat assistant, christened SIA, is capable of handling nearly 10,000 enquiries per second or 864 million in a day.

Financial institutions use AI chatbots to access stock market data too. Axis Direct, the stockbroking and financial services subsidiary of Axis Bank, uses a WhatsApp-based virtual assistant to offer its customers services, including research ideas, personalised alerts, and market updates. The bot can also offer information on stock quotes and live portfolio values and answer all sorts of investor queries on WhatsApp chat. Likewise, IDFC Neo Equity Portfolio is a unique portfolio management system (PMS) that is powered by AI.

The AI bot can analyse data from multiple traditional and non-traditional sources available in the public domain to identify stock opportunities to build a portfolio with steady outperformance and low volatility. Non-traditional sources leveraged by AI include goods and shipping movements and traffic patterns to better estimate demand, footfalls at malls to track customer behaviour, social media sentiments, credit card spending patterns, etc. Of course, there is a fund manager who has the final say on the investment at all stages.

HELPING DOCTORS DO A BETTER JOB

Developing countries like India face an incredibly challenging healthcare problem. As Srinivas Prasad, founder and CEO of Neusights, puts it: "... the imbalance between the already inadequate healthcare workforce and patients is widening. There is a need for 2.3 million doctors by 2030, but only 50,000 doctors graduate every year. A significant portion of the increasing (15 per cent inflation) hospital costs is financed by loans and the sale of assets. This is pushing thousands of people below the poverty line every year".[2]

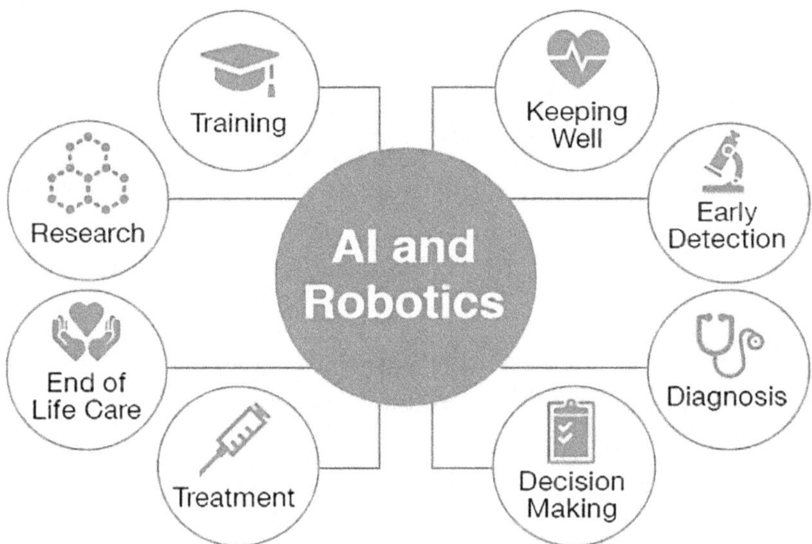

Source:: PWC, "No longer science fiction, AI and robotics are transforming healthcare.

AI, he insists, can play a pivotal role in addressing these challenges. And he is right. As we emphasised in Chapter 1, the ability of doctors and technology companies to use AI to sift through humongous amounts of data is at the core of the healthcare revolution. The real promise of AI, as we see it, appears to be in speeding up the process of designing, testing, and even making potential new drugs.

In Chapter 1, for instance, we explained in some detail how AI algorithms helped quicken the search for COVID-19 vaccines. Consider this example. When UK startup Exscientia partnered with Sumitomo Dainippon Pharma to develop a new drug to treat obsessive-compulsive disorders, AI helped them speed up the process. As a result, the new drug was ready for clinical trials in 12 months as compared to the industry average of 36–48 months.

Further, AI is already being used in the healthcare and pharma sectors for predictive analytics in a bid to diagnose known diseases from scans, biopsies, audio, and other data. Doctors, for instance, routinely use ML to help them detect diseases such as breast cancer, diabetic retinopathy, malaria, and tuberculosis. Patients benefit tremendously if these diseases are detected in their early stages. It's here that doctors can increase the speed of detection with the help of AI. In other words, AI is complementary and does not make a doctor redundant.

Hospitals are using AI to predict personalised health outcomes to optimise recommended treatments. They are optimising labour staffing and resource allocation with the help of AI. They are identifying fraud, waste, and abuse patterns in diverse clinical and operations data. Hospitals are even forecasting individual hospital admission rates using historical and real-time data. Remote health monitoring systems use ML algorithms for real-time data analysis.

Let's consider some examples now. Apollo Hospitals launched ProHealth—an AI-supported preventive healthcare programme in 2019—through its 370 centres across the country, including its hospitals and clinics. It partnered with UK-based DXC Technology to create this AI tool. ProHealth has been developed based on the experience of over 20 million health checks conducted at the Apollo network of hospitals. The database is huge and has not been done by any other institution across the globe.

The system uses AI analytics to predict health concerns, and a health mentor is assigned to guide and provide care before and after the health check-ups. This includes but is not limited to appointments, home sample collections, telemedicine consultations, personalised health tips, etc. Apollo Hospitals also uses Amazon Alexa Skill, a bot to help users find the nearest Apollo Hospitals, clinics, and pharmacies, and book appointments with doctors of their choice using simple voice commands.

Similarly, Fortis partnered with Bengaluru based Phable to provide an AI powered guidance and prediction system that helps patients and doctors by alerting them of early warning indicators. Their app-based virtual assistant improves the quality of life of patients by helping them manage medication, tests, diet, exercise, etc.

The AI solution integrates several home-care health devices and can detect anomalies in health conditions, thereby becoming a potential life-saver. The platform supports over 18 major chronic ailments and uses AI to deliver personalised guidance to patients. Phable was founded by Sumit Sinha, Mukesh Bansal and Prasanth Reddy in 2017 and received its seed funding from Omphalos Ventures.

Doctors are also using AI-powered robots to assist them during procedures. The Apex Heart Institute (Ahmedabad) and Amrita Institute of Medical Sciences (Kochi), for instance, use AI-powered robotics to guide surgeons during operations. Fortis Hospital on Bannerghatta Road in Bengaluru is the only hospital in the state of Karnataka that uses the da Vinci AI-assisted surgical system. This robot assists doctors with minimally-invasive general surgeries and the treatment of prostate cancer and uterine conditions (da Vinci Hysterectomy and Myomectomy), among other things.

The use of AI-powered robotic systems can reduce complications in surgeries and augment traditional modes of learning. Further, as pointed out in Chapter 1, ML tools could also shorten the innovation time for drug discovery and information retrieval.

This is not to undermine the fact that AI systems can deliver inaccurate decisions, introduce biases, be hacked and compromise sensitive health information of individuals. We have dealt with this fact in some detail in Chapter 1 and have focused a chapter later in the book on how this lacuna can be addressed. For now, let's focus solely on the benefits of AI.

ENTERTAINMENT ROULETTE: MAKING MONEY FROM YOUR STRESS, BOREDOM

How many of us would ever admit to binge-watching on Netflix, Amazon, HBO, or YouTube? Binge-watching occurs when you continue watching episode after episode of the same show in a single sitting. Regardless, the fact is that entertainment is almost an addiction for most of us, especially given that most of us have been working from home due to the ongoing COVID-19 pandemic.

Gone are the days when we relied only on cinema theatres and the idiot box—the television or TV—for our dose of online entertainment. Even the idiot box today has become smart since you can simply plug into the internet with USB sticks and devices like Amazon Fire Stick and Roku.

So much so that Netflix CEO Reed Hastings has explicitly stated that his company's biggest rivals aren't Amazon, YouTube or even traditional broadcasters. Rather, it's "our need for sleep". Hastings hit the nail on the head when he made that statement. In May 2020, SleepStandards surveyed 1,032 respondents across the US on how Netflix affects their sleep.

First, as most of us would have guessed, millennials are the most likely to watch Netflix compared to other generations. Hence, it was not surprising that a little over 82 per cent of millennials admitted to binge-watching Netflix for more than five hours on occasion. While streaming sites may revel in these findings, the survey's results are disturbing too. The reason is that we know today that lack of sleep can exhaust your brain. Sleep-deprived people become irritable. They cannot focus on work, and it can even lead to accidents when driving a vehicle.

Regardless of whether you lose sleep over this or not, streaming sites need more and more subscribers. For instance, Netflix makes billions of dollars from its nearly 120 million global subscriptions—the more subscribers, the more revenue it generates. It, therefore, uses AI algorithms to continuously engage its viewers and reduce cancellations.

Netflix, for instance, uses ML to power its recommendation algorithms. In other words, when you are watching a movie or a serial, Netflix uses AI to automatically recommend similar shows that you might be interested in. Netflix also uses AI to optimise the production of original movies and TV shows in its studio. The giant streaming site uses AI to power " ... our advertising spend, channel mix, and advertising creative so that we can find new members who will enjoy Netflix."[3]

Netflix is only a case in point of how media and entertainment companies use AI. Hotstar, for instance, also uses ML to provide personalised content feeds and ad experiences to users based on their watch history. They also use ML models to deal with the diversity of users across regions.

Media houses, in fact, routinely use AI to analyse various parameters from their customer data like demographics, current trends, market scenarios, etc. This helps them gain unique insights to engage better with their customers with more targeted content that results in more revenue. Advanced analytics capabilities also allow companies to modify their content, marketing plans, and even distribution channels.

Media houses are also using AI to help develop AR/VR interactive content based on the storyline and themes for content, gaming, and events. Live events and reality shows that use AI-powered AR/VR content garner more eyeballs and more revenue. Further, companies are using AI-based video intelligence tools to analyse the content of videos frame by frame and identify objects to add appropriate tags.

Leading media and broadcasting companies use AI tools to generate channel performance reports from raw analytics data shared by the Broadcast Audience Research Council of India (BARC). This weekly data is typically in the form of cumbersome Excel sheets. By using AI-enabled data analysis and natural language generation (NLG)-based reporting automation tools, media companies create performance reports in a language that's easy to understand, making the whole process efficient and speedier.

AI is also being used to automatically generate multilingual subtitles for video content since human translators would need hundreds of hours to write subtitles for multiple shows and movies in dozens of languages. Besides, doing it in real-time would be an incredibly challenging task and prone to error. As an example, YouTube's AI allows its publishers to automatically generate closed captions for videos uploaded on the platform. AI is also helping media companies be secure. Network18, for instance, has deployed Darktrace's AI technology to safeguard its IP from sophisticated cyber-attacks.

Simply put, as customer experience personalisation becomes critical for the media and entertainment industry, they will have to increasingly use AI tools to engage and retain their users.

SUMMING UP

We must realise, though, that AI is still an evolutionary technology. In terms of deployable solutions, the current state of AI development can be broadly put into four buckets: products, early-stage products, very-early-stage products, and research. Advanced analytics-based AI solutions, such as search engine results, social media alerts, e-commerce and streaming services' recommendation engines, dynamic pricing engines of airlines and hotels, and profiling engines, can be categorised as AI products. Even chatbots, considering the recent advancements in text-based NLP, maturity, and the wide-scale adoption they have witnessed, can be categorised as AI products.

However, although voice-based NLP products such as Amazon's Alexa, Apple's Siri, Microsoft's Cortana, and Google Now have been launched and are being used by millions of consumers, they still have significant headroom. For instance, identifying the subtle differences in tone and voice modulation for accurate sentiment and intent analysis still has a lot of room for improvement in voice-based AI solutions.

Further, although these solutions have covered a significant distance in terms of accents, there is a lot more to be done. Because of this state of voice-based NLP solutions development, they can be segmented as early-stage products. Computer vision-based AI solutions for image recognition and video analytics are "very-early-stage products" and "research".

Given this context, the ROI for companies adopting AI will depend primarily on achieving the business objective they set out to meet when implementing the project. In other words, companies seeking ROI from AI should ask: Has AI helped us in making our business process speedier, more efficient, and less expensive?

For instance, many Indian companies have deployed AI chatbots to provide better customer care and customer experience. Now the ROI of implementing an AI-enabled chatbot is essentially the cost saving that one will make since you will not need to hire a call centre or telemarketing executive. Companies in India that have implemented AI-based solutions in the form of text chatbots, which provide canned responses, have succeeded in reducing the number of customer care employees. The cost saved, thus, can be viewed as ROI from AI for the company.

Some companies that implement AI see a direct increase in revenue, making the ROI factor evident. The e-commerce industry has many such examples. Amazon, for instance, garners around 35 per cent of its revenue from its recommended product algorithms, which are essentially ML-based or AI solutions. In the brick-and-mortar retail sector, AI solutions typically provide direct ROI in terms of increased sales and increased revenue. In such cases, too, executives clearly see the ROI.

Going forward, AI systems will only become more autonomous. Consider the case of Rio Tinto and Caterpillar teaming up to develop the world's first intelligent mine in Australia. Called "Mine of the Future", AI will be used for scheduling and enabling real-time operating decisions.[4] The mine will boast of automated trucks, drills, and trains. AI-driven systems will connect all these elements for scheduling—from ore planning to delivery. The AI-driven system will boost revenue by increasing output, ensuring quicker deliveries, and providing more-accurate forecasts of customer demand. Here, too, there's a clear case for the ROI from AI implementation.

That said, estimating ROI from AI solutions will become increasingly complex as the adoption of AI solutions increases. Simply put, since AI will be present in many solutions and become as ubiquitous as electricity, it is going to be much more difficult to estimate its value since AI will touch and power almost every aspect of companies and

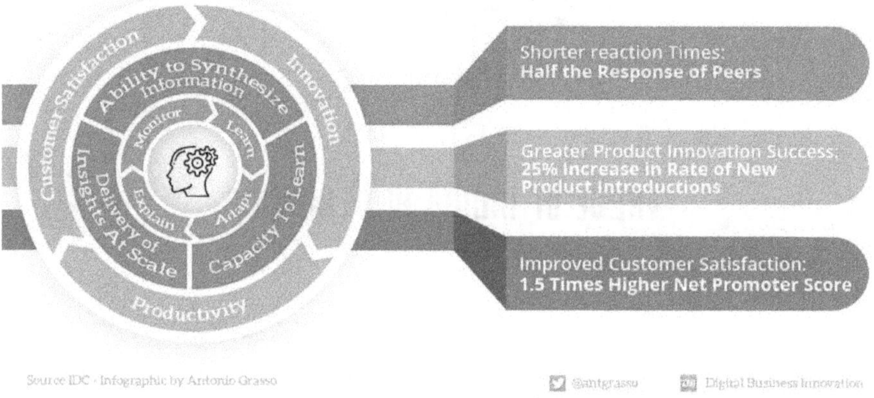

industries. A good example of this is the recommendation engines of media streaming companies such as Netflix, YouTube, and Spotify. The discovery and recommendation engines of almost all these companies are ML algorithms.

They are so deeply embedded and integrated with the companies' products that it's exceedingly difficult to distinguish them from the companies' core products. For instance, Netflix's value lies in adding more subscribers. But it's the power of algorithms that help Netflix engage and retain these subscribers. Simultaneously, it's also true that Netflix's success relies on providing good original movies with brilliant actors, and pushy, creative marketing and sales, among other things. In other words, the ROI here is in realising that AI is a critical driver for such an industry. In these cases, companies need to acknowledge that if they do not invest in AI, they will be caught napping and will eventually be ousted from business.

India's AI spending is predicted to grow from $300.7 million in 2019 to $880.5 million in 2023, according to IDC's Worldwide Artificial Intelligence Spending Guide Forecast released in September 2020. While Indian companies do have a long way to go in making good use of AI applications, this forecast augurs well for the industry. In the following chapter, we will see how AI startups are boosting the overall digital ecosystem by both disrupting and complementing the business models of big companies across sectors.

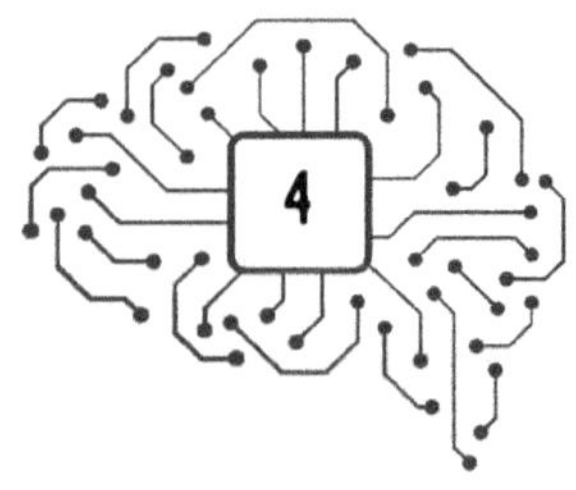

VALUE OF INDIAN AI STARTUPS

"The very best startup ideas have three things in common: They're something the founders themselves want, that they themselves can build, and that few others realise are worth doing. Microsoft, Apple, Yahoo Google, and Facebook all began this way."
—Paul Graham, co-founder of Y-Combinator

Four years is a very long time in the world of AI. Here's one example. When we at Convergence Catalyst published our AI market industry report in June 2017, an unsupervised computer vision-based ML algorithm had to be trained on anywhere between 19 million and 40 million images of cats to identify a cat.

Computer vision is an AI tool that uses ML and DL to identify and process objects in images and videos, just like humans do. The technology is commonly used to power AR glasses, build self-driving cars, in surveillance cameras to monitor suspicious activities at airports, etc., or for facial recognition.

In technical terms, computer vision involves the use of technologies such as image classification, object recognition, object detection, and image segmentation algorithms for tracking and face recognition. Hence, when we feed a computer with millions of images of cats, the algorithms analyse features like colours, shapes, and distances to identify a cat from a random mixture of unlabelled images without any human aid.

Six months later, I was advising a two-member New York-based AI startup that was building "Shazam-for-food"—a mobile app that would identify any food item that its camera was focused on. To build this solution, the two co-founders spent three weeks collating, structuring, and vectoring the data (making the software code execute faster). This time around, though, only one million images were required to train their computer vision algorithm. What required 19–40 million images to identify a single entity could now be achieved with just a million images. Moreover, the team took only a few weeks to complete the project as compared to the few months that a similar project would have taken five years ago. This was possible because of the tremendous advancement and innovation in designing ML algorithms, which could do the same work with fewer amounts of data and in a shorter time.

AI has only improved exponentially since then. By June 2018, a three-member Bengaluru-based computer vision AI startup, Cerebrum Edge, cracked something known as "one-shot imitation learning". The company's facial recognition algorithm is now used to identify a person's face based on a single image (or a photograph). The founder-CEO of Cerebrum Edge, Hrishikesh Kumar (he likes to be called "Hrishi"), used to present to potential clients on a graphics processing unit (GPU) based laptop that would help him run his facial recognition algorithm in real-time. The algorithm used the web camera of the laptop, and the solution would identify the people from their images and display their name, gender, age, company, and other demographic data that was fed.

Hrishi or his colleague use their own photographs to pre-feed and train the algorithm. Hence, when the laptop's webcam faced the potential customer's executive, the algorithm was unable to identify the person since it was not trained to recognise their image. Hrishi would then perform a simple Google search on the customer's name. This, of course, was done with the customer's permission. Hrishi would typically find the customer's LinkedIn profile, download the picture from there and feed it into the training data set of the facial recognition algorithm along with some basic demographic data of the executive, such as name, gender, designation and company. He would then compile and run the computer vision software and turn the laptop around so that its webcam could capture the customer's face once again. This time, the algorithm would rightly identify the person and display all the demographic data instantly on the screen. This entire process was done in minutes, leaving the customer amazed and delighted.

Cerebrum is just a case in point. Thousands of such AI startups are making India proud. In fact, India is the third-largest ecosystem of startups in the world, with 24 unicorns valued at a little over $100 billion, according to NASSCOM. Startups valued at over $1 billion are called unicorns. A company valued at more than $10 billion gets the title of a Decacorn. Hectocorn is reserved for a startup valued at over $100 billion. India also moved up three places—from the 23rd position out of 100 countries in 2020 to 20th in 2021—out of 100 countries. The US, UK and Israel were ranked the top three countries in StartupBlink's Global Startup Ecosystem Index 2021. They are known as the "Big 3 Club".[1]

StartupBlink measures ecosystems based on the number of startups, their quality, and the business environment. But it also ranks cities independently, and it's here that India has three cities in the top 20—Bengaluru rose four spots to reach the 10th position while New Delhi jumped six spots, and Mumbai climbed a spot to rank 14th and 16th, respectively. With nine new Indian cities entering the ranking this year, India currently has 43 cities in the top 1,000, three in the top 100, eight in the top 200, and 20 in the top 500. The report notes that India increased its ranking by three spots in 2021 to re-enter the global top 20 after dropping six spots in 2020. India is the fifth-highest-ranked ecosystem in the Asia-Pacific region, ranking eighth globally in education and tenth in transportation technology.

One such unicorn that made waves in July 2021 was the AI-powered food delivery app, Zomato. It was subscribed 38 times when it was listed in India on the BSE. On July 23, 2021, Zomato's stock price jumped to Rs 138 in intra-day trading to close at 127, recording a market capitalisation of over Rs one lakh crore in intra-day trading and Rs 98,731.59 crore at close. Interestingly, Zomato's listing took place around 30 years after India's second-largest IT services provider, Infosys, was listed on the BSE. The market cap of Infosys stood at Rs 6,77,343.70 crore on

Indian startup system continues to be the 3rd largest in the world

NASSCOM Zinnov

	China[2]	USA[2]	India	UK[1]	Germany[1]	Israel[2]
Numbers of Unicorns[3]	206	203	24	21	11	7
Avg. Time to Unicorn (Years)	4–6	6–8	7–9	6–8	5–7	
Avg. Valuation per Unicorn ($ Bn)	~3.8	~3.5	~3.2	~2.4	~2.0	~1.3
Innovation Clusters with min. 1 Unicorn[4]	18	24	5	4	4	4

Notes (1) CEInsights - the complete list of unicorns (2) Hurun Global Unicorn List 2019 (3) Data as on Oct 2019 (4) Cities have been bundled into clusters. For example, Silicon Valley includes Palo Alto, San Jose, Mountain View, Santa Clara, Cupertino, Campbell, Los Altos, Los Gatos, Milpitas, San Matso, Sara Toga, Sunnyvale. Similarly, Delhi-NCR includes Delhi, Noida and Gurgaon.

July 23, 2021. But when it listed on the bourses on June 14, 1993, Infosys was valued at just Rs 54 crore, paling in comparison to the China-headquartered Ant Group-backed Zomato's valuation at over $14 billion. You may call this the lure of an AI-powered startup.

BUT WHAT EXACTLY IS AN AI STARTUP?

How do we know that a startup is an AI startup, especially given that every tech startup claims to be using AI? To answer this question, let's first understand the broad definition of a startup. NASSCOM defines a startup as an "entity working towards innovation, development, deployment, and commercialization of new products, processes, or services driven by technology or intellectual property". Global innovation mapping and research company Startup Blink defines a startup as "any business that applies an innovative solution which validates a scalable economical model". For instance, Alphabet (Google's parent company) that was founded in 1998 and Facebook, which was launched in 2004, were startups to begin with but now figure among the world's largest companies in terms of market capitalisation.

Now that we have a broad idea of what a startup means, let's understand what an AI startup does. An AI startup falls under the category of deep tech startups, which NASSCOM defines as those tech startups "which create, deploy or use advanced technology in their product or service". These advanced technologies include AI-ML, IoT, blockchain, AR/VR, and others like robotics and 3D printing. Hence, not every tech or deep-tech startup is an AI startup. But all AI startups do fall under the category of deep-tech and tech startups.

Broadly speaking, AI startups are effectively those companies that use AI tools such as ML, DL, NLP, NLU, computer vision, intelligent automation, and robotics to develop products and services and scale up their own businesses. As we have seen in the earlier chapters too, these startups can be spotted across sectors including healthcare, finance (fintech), education (edtech), retail, food delivery, transportation (taxi-hailing apps), agriculture (precision agriculture), and hospitality. There were an estimated 12,000 tech startups in 2020, according to NASSCOM, of which 2,100 were leveraging deep tech or advanced technologies. AI and IoT accounted for two-thirds of all deep tech startups in this period. The number would have only increased.[2]

HOW AI STARTUPS WORK

As we have pointed out with numerous examples in earlier chapters, AI is being used in the healthcare sector since ML algorithms reduce drug discovery times, provide virtual assistance to patients, and improve the accuracy of medical imaging and diagnostic procedures, among other things. In retail, companies leverage AI algorithms for visual search, NLP, shopper behavioural analytics, in-store analytics, etc. Companies use AI algorithms for cross-platform advertising, intelligent email marketing, content-aware video advertising, etc. In the manufacturing sector, companies use AI algorithms for predictive maintenance using industrial IoT data, wearable computing, and voice platforms for connected devices, among other things.

Food delivery startups like Zomato and Swiggy, for instance, use AI and data analytics to provide a curated list of restaurants on the customer's landing page based on their location and preferences. They also use an image classifier to group images under food categories as well as NLP and NLU to allow users to search for food items using colloquial language vocabulary too.

Rezo.ai, for instance, uses ML, NLP and other proprietary algorithms to help companies across sectors automate interactions in their contact

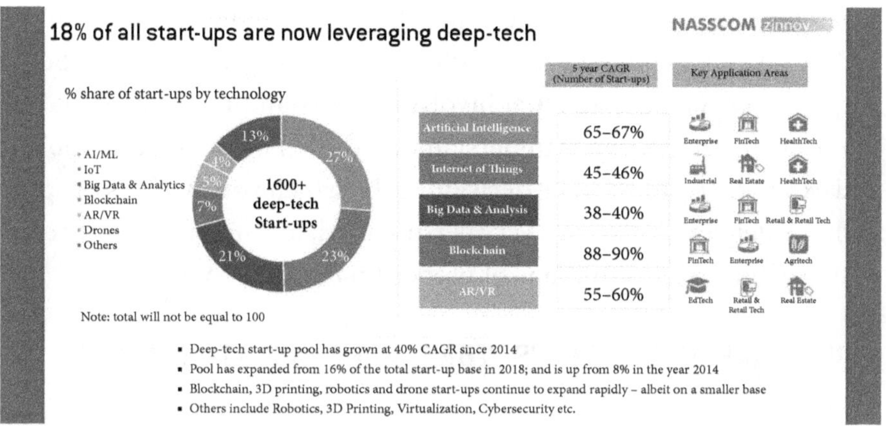

- Deep-tech start-up pool has grown at 40% CAGR since 2014
- Pool has expanded from 16% of the total start-up base in 2018; and is up from 8% in the year 2014
- Blockchain, 3D printing, robotics and drone start-ups continue to expand rapidly – albeit on a smaller base
- Others include Robotics, 3D Printing, Virtualization, Cybersecurity etc.

centres across multiple channels such as email, chat, voice, and social media. By doing so, Rezo.ai claims it has helped its partners reduce their operational costs by 20–30 per cent. Rezo.ai analyses customer–agent interactions, coaches and trains agents, and enhances the customer experience (CX) with in-built RPA. Unlike AI, which is driven by data, RPA is process-driven. RPA, or software robotics, only follows the processes defined by an end user. AI-powered bots, on the other hand, use ML to detect patterns in data, particularly unstructured data, and learn over time. You can program RPA robots to follow specific workflows and rules, thus minimising human error. Rezo.ai also uses proprietary AI, NLP and NLU algorithms to train models from unstructured voice and text data. These models, once trained for an enterprise, get deployed as virtual agents with the ability to talk and revert to customer queries just like an enterprise "best agent".

Let's take another example. Versa Innovation, a local language technology platform that runs Dailyhunt and Josh, currently runs a data set on AI, which is over 6–7 petabytes and is growing by over 8–10 terabytes every day. Its learning models are being trained on over 250 million pieces of content across audio, video, imagery, and text across 14 local languages. All the content resides on its platform. Versa Innovation has more than 80 proprietary AI/ML tech models that run to understand the content and the context. For instance, if they make a comparison of three mobile phone players, they look at the social media embeds in those posts. If there is a video, they dissect the video and break it up by frames to understand the content. They also isolate the audio and look for pattern recognition in terms of what it's saying. So AI plays a threefold role. The first involves understanding the content and the context. The second is understanding the behaviour—both implicit and explicit. The third is the decisioning by which you marry the supply with the demand to create a very personalised, meaningful feed for each of those hundreds of millions of users who use the product.[3]

FIVE CHARACTERISTICS THAT MAKE AN AI STARTUP VALUABLE

Focus on niche areas: AI startups focusing on niche areas and not generalised AI are witnessing significant growth and VC interest. The latter point is critical if the startup is seeking funding to grow in scale. Startups that avoid working on generalised AI algorithms and not competing with large companies are also more likely to be successful. Big companies such as Google, Facebook, Baidu, and Amazon are not only investing heavily in AI and ML but have adopted the strategy of open-sourcing their tools and platforms. These companies are hard to compete with, given their access to funding and unique proprietary data sets. AI startups, as seen above, would be better off choosing an industry vertical and specific real-world problem to focus on.

Bengaluru-based Gnani.ai, for instance, is working in the niche space of automatic speech recognition and NLP in Indic languages to build smart voice assistants. Simply put, it enables users to interact with voice applications in their native language. Gnani.ai has a proprietary all-neural speech recognition engine. Its conversational bots are trained to have a human-like naturalised conversation, while its in-house voice biometrics module is capable of scanning over 140 features of the human voice. Voice biometrics is a part of AI-based speech recognition technology that uses a voice imprint to authenticate an individual's identity. It analyses vocal features and attributes such as pronunciation, pitch, tone, dialect, and style of speech before completing the authentication process for users.

Applications include automated lead qualification using

conversational AI voicebots, which allows more leads to be processed in the same amount of time. Without intelligent automation, a sales team would have to manually qualify each lead, wasting time that could be spent on refining the sales pipeline from lead nurturing to conversion. Gnani's AI-powered conversational assistant uses ML and NLU to automate the entire inbound and outbound customer service workflow—from conversational IVR to handling complex queries.

Relevant, proprietary, and scalable data source: Large technology companies typically have huge, proprietary data sets that span across many industries. And open-source community efforts are quickly democratising access to the most sophisticated ML algorithms. This makes it impossible for an AI startup to develop a competitive advantage solely around algorithm development. If a company is planning to compete with others using AI and ML, it better have the best data to solve a specific problem, failing which it should adopt a strategy that is different from its competitors. In addition to the data sources being unique and defensible, they must also be relevant to the challenge being solved. Next-generation AI depends on the complexity of the data that the company is mining. Unstructured images, video, and audio data are far more difficult to mine than text. What is of significance is whether the company is working with fast-moving data or static data. Algorithms for fast-moving data, such as the real-time images processed by a self-driving car, are often much more complex and valuable.

Consider this example. Kappa, a product from Hyperstate Tech, uses AI to transform media such as videos, pictures, and gifs into interactive content pieces to increase user attention and engagement. The idea is to help brands and marketing executives create interactive content on the go and distribute it through any channel. Kappa's proprietary AI-powered algorithms allow brands to publish smart videos that are intuitive, interactive, and sensitive to a user's behaviour. Kappa has an intuitive drag-and-drop, no-code editor built for non-tech teams. Kappa technology, for instance, was used to convert consumer attention into effective brand actions for the Mercedes GLE campaign by transforming an existing brand asset into an interactive video, thus saving costs while increasing user engagement. It is a software-as-a-service (SaaS) that helps companies add app-kind of functionalities to their videos in real-time. Hyperstate likens Kappa to putting "your videos on steroids" with the help of AI.

Focus on domain expertise over AI expertise: Technology should always be treated as a means to an end, especially when it concerns businesses. Hence, AI and ML should never be the end goals—they should help you achieve your specific business goals. Hence, it's also important for AI startups to have diverse members in their teams—not just data scientists and AI specialists.

Let's take the example of Niramai, which stands for Non-Invasive Risk Assessment with Machine Intelligence. Niramai also means 'being free from illness' in Sanskrit. The startup has developed a low-cost, software-based, automated, portable cancer screening tool that can be used in any clinic. The core technology has been developed using patented ML algorithms. Niramai's AI-based, radiation-free breast cancer screening test has received CE mark approval, ISO 13485 and MDSAP (Medical Device Single Audit Programme) international certifications. The CE mark approval indicates that the product may be sold freely in any part of the European Economic Area. The ISO 13485 and MDSAP certifications endorse medical device manufacturers for their compliance with international medical device quality standards and regulatory requirements. The test is already being used in renowned hospitals and clinics across various Indian cities, including HCG Hospital, Apollo Clinics, and HealthSpring Diagnostics.

At the core of the Niramai solution lies Thermalytix—an AI-powered computer-aided diagnostic engine that uses a high-resolution thermal sensing device and a cloud-hosted analytics solution to analyse thermal images. Niramai's cancer screening tool, SMILE, has been tested on more than 4,000 women in 12 hospitals/diagnostic centres as well as screening camps. According to the Niramai website, clinical trials indicate that the Thermalytix solution is "highly accurate" and is "comparable and sometimes better than Mammography". Niramai has also developed a cloud-hosted AI-based service that analyses chest X-rays using ML algorithms. The solution, called XraySetu, generates a patient report showing suspicious abnormal regions in the lungs and detects if the person is likely positive for COVID, pneumonia, or other lung abnormalities. Niramai developed this solution in partnership with ARTPARK—a not-for-profit company promoted by the IISc.

Companies such as Niramai include domain experts, business leaders, and salespeople, not just engineering teams. It has been observed that homogenous startup teams, especially when comprised solely of AI researchers with no industry-specific experience, tend to fail more often.

Sellers of picks and shovels: There is significant business value in providing tools for other companies to develop and use AI technologies, essentially becoming the picks and shovels sellers in the AI gold rush. Algorithmia, for instance, is an AI startup that has built a kind of app store for algorithms. The service aims to make it easier for any company to use ML. VCs love this company. Algorithmia has raised $10.5 million from the recent Google AI fund. Numerai is a crowdsourced hedge fund platform that allows AI engineers and data scientists to create algorithms for stock trading. It had 7,500 data scientists creating algorithms on its platform and raised $6 million in 2016. Similarly, Element AI is a platform for companies—that lack specific AI talent and other resources—to build AI solutions and go about their core business. Element AI raised $102 million in its first round (Series A) of funding.

Patents lend a greater edge: More than 70 per cent of the technology patents filed in India relates to one or more emerging technology domains. At an international level, patent filing grew at 4 per cent in the year 2020. Interestingly, AI accounts for 6 per cent of all emerging tech patents in India, according to a recent report published by NASSCOM and INDIAai—an online hub run jointly by MeitY, National e-Governance Division (NeGD), and NASSCOM.[4]

The report also notes that over 5,000 AI patents were filed over the last decade in India, of which 94 per cent were filed in the last five years. Of these, more than 60 per cent originated in India. The technology sector led the race for AI patents with a share of 47 per cent. ML was the most popular AI technique for patents, while computer vision was the leading functional area. Most of the patents were filed by companies in the consumer electronics, personal computing devices, and healthcare sectors.

BIG AI FIRMS FISH FOR SMALLER ONES

While companies are trying to integrate ML and DL into their products, AI talent does not come easy. This is one of the primary reasons why big companies keep a hawk's eye on top AI startups, many of which are still in the early stages of research and funding. Not surprisingly, tech giants like Facebook, Amazon, Microsoft, Google, and Apple (FAMGA) have been "aggressively acquiring AI startups for the last decade", according to CB Insights.[5] Apple leads the pack with 29 AI acquisitions since 2010, followed by Google with 15 acquisitions. Microsoft comes third with 13 acquisitions, followed by Facebook with 12, and Amazon with 7. Other top acquirers include major tech players like Intel, Salesforce, Twitter, and IBM.

Apple has used these AI acquisitions to develop new iPhone features. For instance, Apple bought the Israeli AI company RealFace in February 2017. This was a three-year-old ML startup at that time and was known for its facial recognition technology. Apple now has FaceID—the technology that allows users to unlock their iPhones by looking at them. CB Insights points out that Apple's Siri or Google's contributions to healthcare through DeepMind have also emerged from acquisitions of AI companies.

We are seeing a similar trend in India, with RIL acquiring stakes in technology firms that use AI tools, blockchain, cloud, AR, and gaming and banking software, and even buying out AI startups in some cases. For instance, RIL bought one of the world's largest conversational AI platforms for Rs 700 crore with the aim of providing users conversational AI-enabled devices with multilingual capabilities. It also acquired local language technology service startup Reverie Technologies—a cloud-based, language-as-a-service (LaaS) platform that helps apps and content go multilingual. RIL has also invested about $25 million in US-based AI startup Netradyne—an AI-powered startup that focuses on driver and fleet safety.

Similarly, consultancy firm EY India acquired AI-backed human resource (HR) technology startup Spotmentor Technologies in 2020. The company uses insights from unstructured data on jobs, people performance, and capabilities to identify skill gaps for each employee. It then searches for the best possible learning content on the web to create suitable learning plans and calculates the effectiveness of learning programs and their business impact. Spotmentor has three patent-pending algorithms.[6] VerSe Innovation acquired Cognirel Technologies—a Bengaluru-based AI solutions provider. VerSe will bring on board Cognirel founder Ram Prakash to head its newly instituted AI lab, which will focus on developing models through computer vision and DL to enhance video content.

WHY AI STARTUPS HAVE A BRIGHT FUTURE

The Indian startup ecosystem may be less developed than those in other geographies, yet there are many reasons why we can bet on deep tech and AI startups in the country. I have listed seven reasons. You can surely think of many more.

First, given the relatively-lower valuations, Indian startups are becoming an attractive proposition for global investors to expand into new sectors and newer geographies. Second, India will be able to produce the talent that AI and deep tech startups require with the help of programmes like NASSCOM Future Skills, the Government of India's Skill India, and multiple corporate initiatives in this space. Intel, Google and Microsoft, for instance, have committed to skilling more than 2,00,000 engineers. In addition, companies such as Google, Ericsson, and Microsoft have set up their global AI research centres in India.

Third, with whitepapers and policies such as the National Strategy for Artificial Intelligence, National Drones Policy, and National Digital Communications Policy 2018, among others, policymakers are creating a conducive environment for startups to build solutions with a clear understanding of rules and regulations. Fourth, there is funding pouring in for deep tech and AI startups, which attracted a total funding of \$836.3 million in 2020, according to a report by AIMResearch titled "Indian AI Startup Funding in 2020".[7] What's also heartening and encouraging, according to a NASSCOM–Zinnov report, is that successful entrepreneurs are turning into angel investors to support the startup ecosystem. Besides, India has more than 335 active accelerators and incubators with the capacity to support over 5,000 startups annually. The numbers are set to expand to over 450 by 2025 with policy support from central and state government agencies.

Fifth, as the NASSCOM–Zinnov report points out, access to large data sets and improved lab facilities with sector-specific capabilities allows entrepreneurs to reduce time-to-market. A good example would be innovation facilities being set up by the Indian Space Research Organization (ISRO) across the country. Sixth, sector-specific policies and initiatives are steadily opening up market opportunities for startups. An example is the policy focus of the central and state governments on electric vehicles, which opens market opportunities for startups in this space.

Seventh, experienced founders with global exposure are entering the startup ecosystem. This helps them lean on their domain expertise when focusing on problems that need to be solved. Of course, there are many more reasons why we can, or rather should, bet on AI startups.

Simply put, the ecosystem of a steady and good supply of talent, along with adequate funding from investors and policy support from governments, will go a long way in helping entrepreneurs use AI tools to solve business and societal problems. I haven't spoken about the latter since we have dedicated a whole chapter to that topic. In the next chapter, we will explore the relationship between data and AI.

McKinsey Global Institute research suggests that by 2030, AI could deliver an additional global economic output of \$13 trillion per year. The firm, however, acknowledges that there are risks associated with AI adoption. It lists five such risks: The first three, which it terms as enablers of AI, are data difficulties, technology troubles, and security snags. The other two "are linked with the algorithms and human-machine

Outlook 2025 for the Indian startups ecosystem

NASSCOM

	2014[1]	2019[6]	2025[2]
# of Unicorns[5]	05	24	95–105
Cumulative Valuation[3]	$10–20Bn	$95–101Bn	$350–390Bn
# of Direct Jobs[3]	80–85k	390–430k	1100–1250k
# of Indirect Jobs[4]	240–300k	1400–1600k	3900–4400k

Note: (1) Analysis of companies founded between 2009-14. Estimated numbers as on Dec 2014. Includes Flipkart in Unicorns. (2) Analysis of companies founded between 2005-25 (3) Calculated based on analysis of all funded and 500 unfunded start-ups. Valuation Est. is based on data model (4) Calculated based on DPIIT model with adjustment for outliers witnessing strong growth (5) For Unicorns, start-ups founded in or after 2000 are considered. (6) Analysis of companies founded between 2009-19.

interactions that are central to the operation of the AI itself".[8] These are risks that are not restricted to startups. They are applicable to every company that seeks to adopt AI. But from the numerous examples cited in this chapter, the earlier chapters, and the ones that will follow, it will become evident that the benefits of AI outweigh the risks if balanced with proper policies. In the next chapter, we will explore one of these risks in detail—data difficulties and the relationship of good data with AI.

Speaking at the NASSCOM Technology and Leadership Forum (NTLF) 2021, Indian Prime Minister Narendra Modi said, "I have a message for startup founders. Don't limit yourself to valuation and exit strategies. Think how you can create institutions that will outlast this century. Think how you can create world-class products that will set the global benchmark on excellence. There can be no compromise on these goals. Without these, we will be a follower and not a global leader."[9] Startups, AI or otherwise, will do well to pay heed to his words.

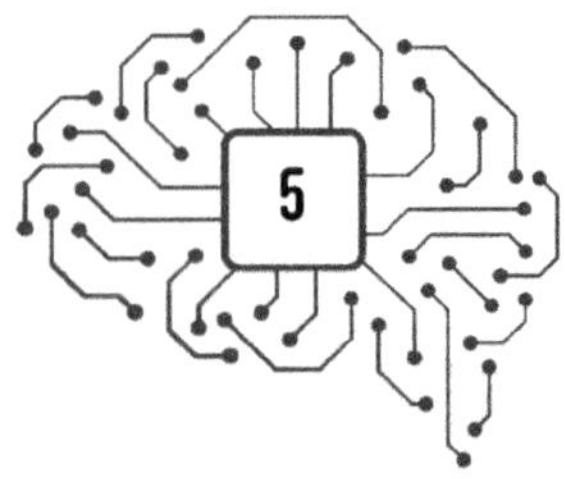

WHY GOOD DATA IS OIL FOR AI

"The goal is to turn data into information, and information into insight."
—*Carly Fiorina*

Do you recall how we shopped till even a decade ago? It was simple. We would walk into a shop, identify a product, pay for it at the counter by cash or card, and exit the shop with the product. You can still do so if you buy goods from your neighbourhood grocer or any mom-and-pop store. But if you are among those who prefer to shop in big retail outlets, your experience will be quite different. Not only will you be inundated with a choice of products, but once you've made a choice, you will have to queue up at the counter to pay for the product. And just when you think you're done, the story gets interesting.

The staff at the counter will begin by asking for your phone number, email ID or membership card. They will then swipe the membership card or enter all that information into a database if you're new to the shop. Only then will they ask you how you wish to pay—cash, card, or with the help of a digital payment app. Once you tick all these boxes, you will be allowed to exit the mall with your goodies.

Why do these retail malls insist on you parting with all this data? First, they use it to provide you with an online receipt since they can save money by avoiding physical receipts. Second, they can use all this information to know your preferences and recommend similar products by email if you opt to do so. Last but not least, they need all this information, especially if you have asked them to deliver the goods to your place. If you are shopping for goods online, then you would have provided all this information and so much more, which includes your credit card and the sensitive (card verification value) CVV number. For instance, as pointed out in the earlier chapters too, if you ordered food, apparel, or even asked for a taxi or hotel room using an app, you would have shared all this personal information with the respective services provider, without which you will not be able to get the service.

Companies need to collect all this data to train their AI models that will, when deployed, decipher patterns to help these companies predict consumer behaviour. The AI team also helps companies to analyse this data, draw insights, and suggest specific lines of action to grow sales, revenue, etc.—an exercise that is better known as data science. However, collecting data, training the AI models, and deploying them in companies is easier said than done. It involves multiple iterations to train the AI model till the developers believe the model will serve its intended purpose successfully. Further, even after you have deployed the AI model, you will have to consistently update it to keep it relevant with the changing data inputs.

If companies diligently perform this entire exercise, they will get the desired results. For instance, if you have shopped for a laptop, you are likely to buy a laptop bag, laptop stand, charger and/or computer table with the help of the ML-powered recommendation engines that these retail outlets use. Retail outlets, thus, can offer you a lot of discounts and customised offers since they now have a good insight into your shopping habits. As an example, a food delivery app like Zomato or Swiggy can offer you a complimentary coke with a pizza or some cash discount if you're a regular app user.

It's not just companies that thrive on data. Even governments need your data if you want to avail of public services. For instance, a majority of those who want to get vaccinated would have accessed the cowin. gov.in website at least once to either book a slot, download a vaccine certificate, or check the status of COVID-19 vaccinations in our state or the country at large. We have, thus, already sampled the power of how data can be collected and intelligently analysed with the help of technology tools. Using the COVID Vaccine Intelligence Network (CoWIN), you can see all COVID-related data on the dashboard that the site provides. The portal's success even caught the world's attention, following which the Indian government offered the CoWIN platform as a free "digital public good" to various countries.

Like many other countries, India too has a contact-tracing Aarogya Setu app, which collects personal information such as name, phone number, age, sex, Aadhaar card number, and countries visited in the last 30 days. This data is stored on a central server, following which a unique digital ID (DiD) is pushed to your app. Every time you complete a self-assessment test, the app collects your location data with the help of Bluetooth technology and uploads the results of your self-assessment along with your DiD on the server. The app is currently available in 12 languages. The idea of collecting all this data is to analyse it and let you know if you are at risk from other COVID-infected patients in your vicinity so that you can keep a safe distance.

The government made another smart move. It opened up CoWIN's application programming interface (API) to the public, giving developers free access to the app's framework. This prompted many developers to integrate the CoWIN app into their own platform, similar to how food delivery services sync their apps with Google Maps. The government is simultaneously integrating the CoWIN app with technologies like AI and IoT to monitor vaccine movement during transit, get updates on data storage, and manage the supply chain and inventory in real-time.

The reason for using AI is that it can connect the data dots better than human beings, as we have seen in the earlier chapters, and help us solve problems in real-time. Data gets a booster with AI, and, in turn, AI gets better with increasingly large amounts of training data, which is why we call it "big data". It enables smarter analysis of data since AI can access not only structured data (found in Excel sheets, databases, etc.) with ML tools but also unstructured data (social media chats, tweets, etc.) with DL techniques. Consider this. If you visit a doctor for the first time, they will ask you about the history of illnesses in your family. This will give the doctor a better idea of how to treat you. The next time you visit the same doctor, you may not have to repeat the same details, as they would have kept your records for reference. The doctor already knows your history, so they will ask you incremental questions to treat you better.

AI takes this exercise many steps further since AI models are trained on data from millions of patients, as we have pointed out in earlier chapters too. This is how an AI-powered chatbot, Introbot AI, for instance, can use WhatsApp to provide verified updates on the availability of hospital beds and oxygen cylinders. Similarly, sites such as under45.in, getjab. in, findslot, Insurtech WIMWIsure, and VaccinateMe.in allow for real-time tracking of vaccine slots with the help of data and AI.

YOUR DATA TELLS THE GOVERNMENT WHO YOU ARE

The government of India, as with most governments around the world, has access to mountains of data—your income-tax records, PAN, Aadhaar number, bank transactions, land records, medical records, etc. In its August 2020 report titled "Unlock Value from Data and AI: the India Opportunity", NASSCOM rightly pointed out that India is becoming a digital leader on the back of the Jan Dhan-Aadhaar-Mobile (JAM) trinity. The JAM trinity was aimed at increasing financial inclusion for the poorer sections of society and providing them subsidies and other benefits that could be directly deposited in their bank accounts.

The initiative has met with success to a great extent. Now, consider the amount of data that is being generated, with around 80 per cent of India's adult population holding a bank account, over 450 million citizens having mobile internet access, and 1.25 billion Indians being biometrically registered with Aadhaar. "All of this translates into an enormous amount of data, considering it is estimated that 1.7 MB of data is being created every second for every human being on earth," the NASSCOM report notes.[1]

Aadhaar alone generates humongous amounts of data. In 2019, the Unique Identification Authority of India (UIDAI) announced that the Aadhaar project had crossed the 125 crore mark, implying that over 1.25 billion residents of India have a 12-digit unique identity. It works thus. When you share your Aadhaar number to open a bank account, avail of a subsidy, or any other public service, your Aadhaar number and demographic information are matched instantly with the information available in the Central Identities Data Repository (CIDR), following which you receive a one-time password (OTP) with limited time validity on your mobile number and/or e-mail address. Then, your Aadhaar number and biometric information are matched with the biometric information—fingerprints or iris-based authentication—stored in the CIDR.

When you share your Aadhaar number with your banks, mutual fund companies, or mobile phone companies for authentication, they only send the Aadhaar number and biometrics (which you provided at the time of authentication) to verify your identity. They do not send your bank account details to the body. UIDAI insists on its website that "Aadhaar is an identifier, not a profiling tool." That said, Aadhaar-based services like the Aadhaar-enabled Payment System (AePS) have helped bring bank services to remote villages and towns besides helping people prove their identity for jobs, travel, and services such as bank accounts, gas connections, mobile SIMs, etc.

Aadhaar-based authentication services have been used close to 37,000 crore times since inception, according to UIDAI. Moreover, UIDAI receives about three crore authentication requests every day. It has so far recorded close to 331 crore successful Aadhaar updates (biometric and demographic) to date and receives about three to four lakh Aadhaar update requests daily.[2]

Of course, personal data can always be hacked or misused. UIDAI, however, claims that the Aadhaar database in CIDR "has never been breached in all these years of its existence" despite many reports that periodically allege that Aadhaar data has been hacked.[3] In this chapter, though, we will be only focusing on the power of data analytics since we have covered the potential misuse of data and AI extensively in a separate chapter.

WHAT YOU FEED IS WHAT YOU GET

AI and data have an intimate relationship. AI's success, as we have pointed out in the earlier chapters, is primarily driven by three factors.

First is the humongous amounts of data that is available for training AI models, which we have explained at length in Chapter 1. Second is the increasing power of cheaper computing that enables these models to crunch and analyse the data in real-time. The third factor comprises the advances in ML and DL that help us understand patterns in the data and build solutions accordingly.

ML, as we pointed out in Chapter 2, does not involve the manual coding that human programmers do when writing traditional algorithms. ML algorithms use sample or "training" data to build mathematical models that are used to make predictions or decisions without being explicitly programmed to do so.

ML algorithms are used in applications such as search engines, movie recommendations from streaming services, and product recommendations on e-commerce platforms. ML algorithms are also used to teach computers to drive cars. In this case, a self-driving car from Tesla, or Google's Waymo, would have trained on data from thousands of driving hours by various drivers. In other words, the more data it trains on, the better the results.

Speaking about data in this digital age, you may have invariably come across the much-repeated quote that is credited to Clive Humby, a British mathematician and entrepreneur in the field of data science—"Data is the new oil."[4] Indeed! India's digital push could transform it into a data-rich economy. AI, as NASSCOM insists, will play a crucial role in realising the government's vision to use this data to make India a $5 trillion economy by 2024–25.

New research from the Capgemini Research Institute complements this line of thinking. It reveals that organisations across the world involved in sharing, exchanging, and collaborating with data can rake in financial benefits of up to $940 million or 9 per cent of the annual revenue of a typical organisation with an annual turnover of $10 billion. Yet only 61 per cent of organisations primarily engage in data ecosystems involving simple data sharing and low levels of collaboration, and just 39 per cent are turning data-driven insights into a sustained competitive advantage, the firm noted in a July 14, 2021, press statement. Sharing anonymised data, the report adds, allows organisations to act in a less intrusive manner.

The reason AI is successful is that it helps companies analyse very large amounts of data in a much shorter time than when they would do it in Excel spreadsheets. This, in turn, improves the accuracy of forecasts and enables real-time decisions to help companies generate more revenue. In fact, data and AI could add $450–500 billion to India's GDP by 2025, representing about 10 per cent of the $5 trillion target.[5] Moreover, data and AI could create over 20 million technical-related jobs and more in peripheral roles.

According to NASSCOM, three sectors—consumer goods and retail, agriculture, and banking and insurance—could likely deliver nearly 45 per cent of this value. The rest will come from sectors such as telecom, media, and IT; transport and logistics; public sector; and healthcare, notes the above-cited NASSCOM report.

Potential contribution of Data and AI to India's GDP by 2025

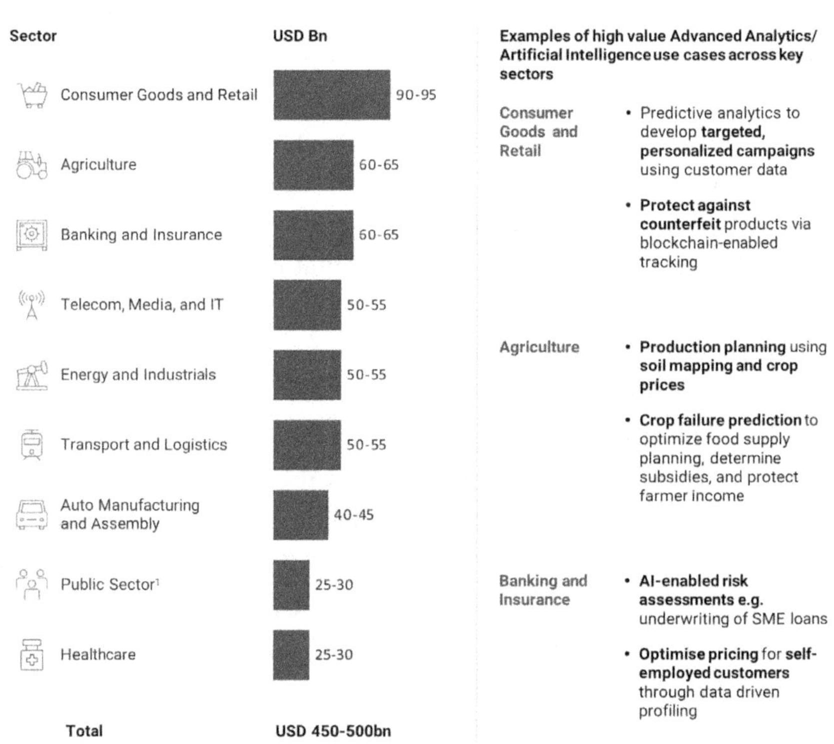

HOW AI USES DATA

NASSCOM has identified three focus areas where data and AI can be used effectively to realise India's 2025 vision of inclusive development. First, data and AI can support governments and businesses to provide an effective COVID-19 response and catalyse economic recovery. Second, it can support social initiatives and equitable growth. Third, it can enhance talent and capabilities to position India as the global hub for data and AI services.

Let's begin with how the combination of data and AI can help the medical fraternity. AI models can help doctors since these models are trained on data from millions of patients.

Virus containment can be supported, for instance, by AI models and digital platforms for health systems to plan supply and demand for testing, infrastructure (isolation to intensive care), health workers (nurses, intensivists, and others), medical devices (e.g., ventilators), medicines, and PPE, according to NASSCOM. AI models can also be used to support businesses by predicting employee sickness due to COVID-19 or monitoring social distancing using computer vision.

In this context, there are hundreds of healthcare tech startups in India. These startups, typically founded by engineers who were prompted by a healthcare emergency and/or an episode in their personal lives, are finding solutions to such problems with the help of technologies like IoT, AI, ML, data analytics, and, of course, leading doctors as advisers on their boards. Many such solutions have failed to make sufficient mainstream inroads and died along the way. But those healthcare startups that survive end up enriching the medical ecosystem with a host of innovative and life-saving solutions that are also reasonably priced.

MediBuddy, for instance, is a digital healthcare platform for inpatient hospitalisation, outpatient services, and corporate wellness benefits. CureFit provides a combination of fitness engagement, coaching and delivery through online and offline channels. Qure.ai builds DL solutions that aid physicians with routine diagnosis and treatment. Wysa is an AI conversational agent that has been shown to help improve mental health. Dozee offers contactless remote patient monitoring and AI-based triaging systems to automatically group patients based on the severity of their injuries and the likelihood of their survival. Niramai uses ML and AI to fight against the inaccessibility of breast examinations.

These, of course, are just a few examples of how hundreds of healthcare startups in India are using data and AI to help the medical community speedily diagnose diseases and save more lives in the bargain. Other than the numerous innovative healthcare startups in the country, India's healthcare ecosystem comprises hospitals and insurance companies owned by government institutions and private companies. Hence, in terms of beneficiaries of data collection, analysis, analytics and prediction, the primary beneficiaries are insurance companies and hospitals that have access to the medical data that patients provide. Doctors can analyse all this data with the help of AI tools to make critical, life-saving decisions.

Similarly, predictive logistics planning processes can help improve supply chain resilience and reduce the impact on costs due to shortages. Likewise, AI can be leveraged to use real-time cash flow data to forecast payment delays or defaults, which can help improve financial planning. AI can also be used to develop a digital sales interface with automated features (e.g., alerts to signal possible delays) for effective remote operations.

On the social front, AI models can support projects like the Jal Shakti Abhiyan (National Water Mission) with the help of an Early Warning System (EWS) to manage flood and coastal erosion, and integrated water management systems to monitor water levels and quality in groundwater and basins. Similarly, AI can be used to devise location-based policies for pollution control (e.g., minimise emissions from crop burning by identifying target areas for clean equipment subsidies).

The NASSCOM report also highlights that AI can be used to reduce road fatalities and aid in traffic management. AI can help increase farmer lending using credit risk assessment models based on farm characteristics and output data, which, in turn, can improve farmer income and provide money at lower costs. Moreover, given that nearly 4.5 million people are employed by the Indian IT services industry, including over 5,00,000 in AI/ML, data and AI could create over 20 million jobs in technical roles alone and have the potential to create more jobs in peripheral roles.[6]

DATA IS HELPING BUILD AN AI ECOSYSTEM

India, as we can surmise from the above data, already has a robust public digital infrastructure comprising Aadhaar, UPI, and millions of internet connections and mobile internet phones. This Jan Dhan-Aadhaar-Mobile or JAM trinity, which we also referred to in the early part of this chapter, provided the government of India a platform to establish the building blocks of a National Digital Health Mission (NDHM) in August 2020.

The National Health Authority (NHA)—which is the nodal government agency responsible for implementing India's public health insurance scheme, Ayushman Bharat—has been entrusted with the

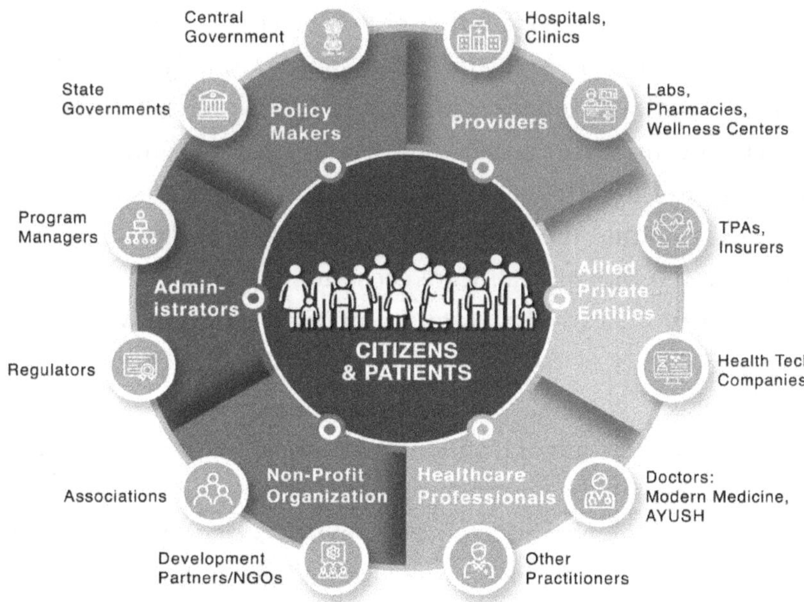

Source: Ministry of Health website

role of designing the strategy, building the technical infrastructure, and implementing NDHM.

NDHM was launched with four key features in the first phase—Health ID, Personal Health Records (PHR), Digi Doctor and Health Facility Registry. Of these, only the Health ID has been developed and implemented currently in the six union territories of India. As of December 2020, over 3,00,000 users have obtained their Health IDs on NDHM. A Consent Manager and Gateway and Health Information User (HIU) application are slated to be developed. Together, these six features form the building blocks of NDHM.

The National Health Stack (NHS) is another credible healthcare platform that can benefit India's healthcare ecosystem. It is being built by the same volunteer-led technology think tank, the Indian Software Product Industry Round Table (iSPIRT), which built the India Stack and UPI. The base layer of NHS comprises a set of generic building blocks. These include bank accounts, digital identities, and mobile numbers, and they form the basic ingredients needed to identify, transact with, and communicate with individuals and businesses. Many components of the India Stack, such as the eSign and DigiLocker, leverage and augment these building blocks.

The next layer of the NHS is the "plumbing layer". This layer contains fundamental pillars needed to enable simple, intelligent, and secure healthcare solutions. The three main pillars of the NHS plumbing layer are electronic registries, a personal health record framework, and a claims engine. The third layer of the NHS is an augmentation layer that is intended to utilise the three pillars of the NHS to introduce greater efficiency to the Indian healthcare ecosystem. The doctor-patient ratio in this country is relatively low and cannot be changed overnight. The augmentation layer of the NHS is designed to drive up doctor efficiency with technology.

Examples of this kind of technology could include a matching engine to pair patients with the most relevant doctor or a system to help doctors securely and remotely monitor the bio-markers (measurable biological functions like heart rate, blood pressure, and even blood tests) of their patients. Unlike the plumbing layer, the augmentation layer of the NHS is not yet close to completion. The fourth and final layer of the NHS is the application layer. It comprises all government and private sector applications that aim to serve the diverse needs of Indian patients.

The NDHM and NHS are credible platforms and steps in the right direction. Yet, they have limitations. For instance, their data collation is voluntary and individual-based, and the success of their platforms and frameworks depends a lot on interoperability or a seamless exchange of data between the numerous systems and software that belong to countless departments and entities. Instead, India needs a healthcare model similar to what the Tamil Nadu government has achieved.

For a little over 15 years, the Tamil Nadu government has been bringing all the national health programmes at the state and district level under one umbrella to make them function through individual subcommittees. This will not only help in pooling all resources available in the implementation of the programme but also provide for a seamless exchange of data so that the AI models can be trained on large amounts of good-quality data.

As NITI Aayog points out in its discussion paper, "the application of AI in healthcare can help address issues of high barriers to access to healthcare facilities, particularly in rural areas that suffer from poor connectivity and limited supply of healthcare professionals. This can be achieved through the implementation of use cases such as AI-driven diagnostics, personalised treatment, early identification of potential pandemics, and imaging diagnostics, among others".[7]

A 2017 FICCI-KPMG study predicted that the healthcare sector in India would grow to $280 billion by 2020. In this context, the adoption of AI for healthcare applications is expected to touch $6.6 billion by 2021.[8] The above-cited NITI Aayog study insists that AI combined with robotics and the Internet of Medical Things (IoMT) "could potentially be the new nervous system for healthcare, presenting solutions to address healthcare problems and helping the government in meeting the above objectives". However, we reiterate that much of the success of AI in healthcare, or any other sector for that matter, will depend on the input data quality.

DATA QUALITY SCORES OVER QUANTITY

We all insist on the potential of data but seldom do we underscore the fact that the quality of data is far more important than the data itself. In other words, the training data can be messy, insufficient or wrongly labelled. The training of AI models, thus, will be good only if they have learned from quality data. Liken this to a student learning from a good textbook or a good teacher. But if the book or the teacher is bad, the student will not gain much knowledge. Worse, the student may simply lose interest in a particular subject.

Hence, it was not surprising when Michael Palmer qualified Humby's quote of data being the new oil by remarking, "Data is just like crude. It's valuable, but if unrefined it cannot really be used. It has to be changed into gas, plastic, chemicals, etc., to create a valuable entity that drives profitable activity; so must data be broken down, analysed for it to have value."[9]

NASSCOM has made a similar critique. It acknowledges that despite the potential that all this data holds to transform the delivery of government services, create inclusive policies, and make Indian enterprises globally competitive, the quality of the data is suspect in many cases, which could limit monetisation. In its report, NASSCOM noted that data sets (essentially, data in spreadsheets like Excel, etc.) in India exist in silos across public-sector platforms, which makes them hard to discover and results "in creation of duplicate datasets and incompatible data models".[10]

ML solutions, for instance, can help a pathologist make a quality diagnosis. However, the AI model will be efficient only if it has access to quality annotated pathology data sets. To address this problem, NITI Aayog is working to develop a national repository of annotated and curated pathology images. This "Digital Pathology" repository will require all glass slides generated to be scanned at high resolution and magnification. It will further require accurate, precise, and comprehensive annotation of the scanned images using various data sources and levels of clinical and pathological information available from day-to-day patient care.

Increase accessibility and utilization of data in India using a data marketplace

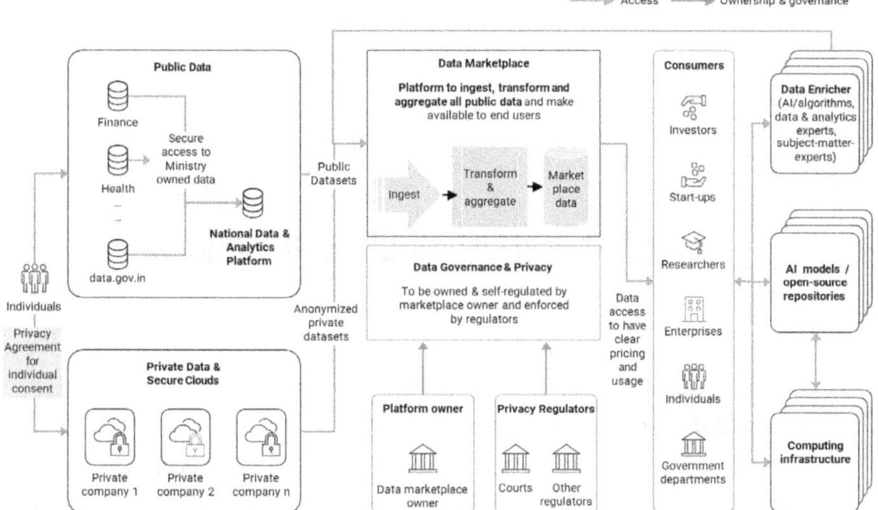

Source: NASSCOM

NASSCOM, meanwhile, has identified a list of the top 10 data sets that are of national importance. These are finance (banking, credit history and digital transaction history), healthcare, farm (actual yields of crop varieties and data on soil health), grain value chain (which includes data from mandis and ration shops), land records, data from road traffic, weather, satellite imagery, power and grids, and education.

NASSCOM recommends that these data sets should be made available on a data marketplace that aggregates data from the public and private sectors for effective data utilisation. It insists, though, that all this data should be collected only with user consent and be anonymised before being made available on the data marketplace and to AI models for training.

In the next chapter, we will explore how AI is being used to enhance the ecosystem of digital payments. Before we conclude, though, let me reiterate that it is unreasonable to expect AI models to work at 100 per cent efficiency, given the current limitations of ML software. That said, AI tools can definitely enhance business value manifold with the help of good data.

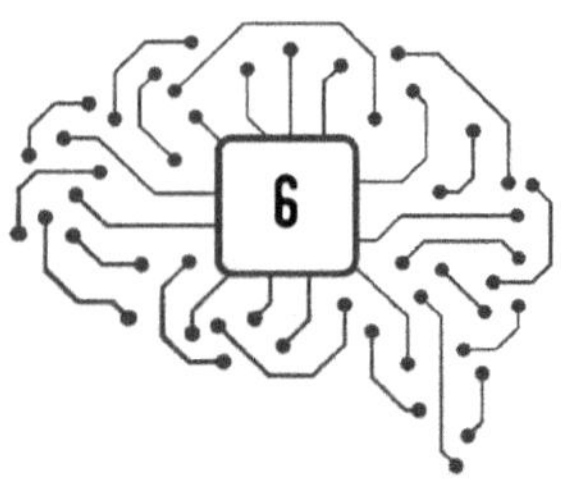

DIGITAL PAYMENTS WITH AI BRAIN

The pandemic, ironically, was one of the primary reasons for fintech firms to leverage access to data, technology, and advanced analytics in 2021, almost making it a watershed moment for digital adoption in India.

I love going on long drives. On one such occasion, I was driving from Bengaluru to Pune. It's an almost 14-hour drive, which forces one to take breaks. The idea is to have lunch or simply sip a cup of tea and nibble on some unhealthy but tasty oily snacks. I stopped at one such stall a few kilometres from Belgaum. And I wasn't disappointed. The tea was invigorating, and the snacks were tasty. Satiated, I was eager to get back on the road. I went up to the counter to pay for my meal. But when I opened my wallet, I realised, to my embarrassment, that I had forgotten to withdraw cash from the ATM before leaving. I looked sheepishly at the owner and asked if he accepted credit cards. He said nothing, but his look said it all: "Man! Are you dumb? You think I would keep a swipe machine and accept credit cards in such a small stall that is so far away from the city?"

I was wondering what to do when he seemed to divine my thoughts and asked, "*Tumhare paas phone nahin hai kya?*" (Don't you have a phone?) I sensed the sarcasm and was embarrassed again. "Why did it not strike me despite seeing the small white plastic stand with a QR code on it?" I whipped out my smartphone, scanned the code, paid the money, thanked him and left the shop with part of my dignity intact.

The fact is that cash is still king, having been in existence for over 3,000 years in different forms, and it is not going to disappear in a hurry since trust and security will continue to remain the operative words in digital payments with the increase in the number of cybercrimes. Yet, it is an inescapable fact that the Indian government's UPI platform, which was developed in 2016, has revolutionised the payments ecosystem.

It was this ecosystem that helped me pay the owner at that stall. The owner benefited too, since he did not have to pay any fee to Visa or Mastercard for using the point-of-sale (POS) machine, which he would have had to shell out if I had used a credit or debit card at his stall. This charge is known as the merchant discount rate or MDR and is defined as the rate charged to a merchant for processing payment services. The fee is charged by banks on credit and debit card payments accepted from consumers for any services availed or goods bought.

The MDR levied on debit cards is capped at 0.90 per cent. There is no such charge for RuPay debit cards, though. However, credit card transactions could be charged anywhere between 1.5 and 3.5 per cent, while MDR charges on wallet transactions could be 2–2.5 per cent. Of course, the government is mulling a cap on these charges. If effected, this could hurt the revenue of the companies involved but benefit small stall owners especially.

Regardless of the government's decision, digital or mobile wallets will remain the payment method of choice among global e-commerce consumers. They accounted for 44.5 per cent of e-commerce transaction volume in 2020, up 6.5 per cent from 2019, according to the 2021 Global Payments Report by Worldpay from FIS.[1] According to the report, Chinese consumers lead the way, accounting for 72.1 per cent of e-commerce purchases. Even in the US, where digital/mobile wallet adoption lagged global averages, digital wallets grew to represent 29.8 per cent of e-commerce transactions, up 23.7 per cent over 2019 levels.

The pandemic started to change the shopping habits of Indians, and while cash still tops the preference list at 34 per cent, many consumers continue to shift to mobile or digital wallets, and debit cards, the report

Source: Shot by self

notes. "It's more gratifying for Indian consumers to shop physically, but online retail also continues to increase as infrastructure and technology advancements are made," says the report.

A joint report by Boku and Juniper Research titled the "2021 Mobile Wallets Report", rightly points out that in developed markets, the debit and credit card penetration "dramatically exceeds the rest of the world".[2] Hence, mobile wallets are far more likely to utilise payment card and contactless mobile device hardware, like near-field communication (NFC) chips that allow us to simply tap on a POS machine and make the payment.

In many other parts of the world, stored-value wallets, such as Paytm, Google Pay, PhonePe, Bhim, and Amazon Pay, use QR codes at the POS, which saved my day during my above-cited road trip to Pune. Moreover, while the Indian government's much-debated move to demonetise banknotes in 2016 inconvenienced thousands of citizens, they also became a catalyst for mobile wallet adoption, with Paytm nearly doubling from 140 million to 270 million users in about a year.

According to the Boku report, 55 stored-value mobile wallets processed over $1 billion in annual transactions in 2020. The figure is forecast to rise to 69 stored-value mobile wallets that will process more than $1 billion in transactions.

The report underscores that China is undoubtedly the most mature mobile payment market in the world. But the scene is a bit different in China, with WeChat Pay and AliPay forming a duopoly for mobile wallets, with 1 billion and 1.2 billion users, respectively (the figures when the report was published). China clearly had a head start on the rest of the world when it came to mobile payment acceptance. The volume and value of transactions reflect that fact. That said, while user growth in China is set to stagnate over the next five years, the report expects to see continued growth in transaction volume and value.

India is another high-growth market for mobile wallets and one of the more well-established mobile payment markets in the world. With over 200 million wallet users in 2020, which is expected to grow to over 434 million by 2025, mobile payments have taken hold. In 2016, India's demonetisation policies led to the rapid adoption of Paytm, with the wallet first reaching 10 million users in 2017. In India, though, the UPI scheme is supported by all major banks and used almost exclusively by mobile apps. UPI has quickly become the top mobile payment method within India and saw over 2.7 billion transactions in March 2021. The use of UPI creates a level playing field, which is stimulating India's

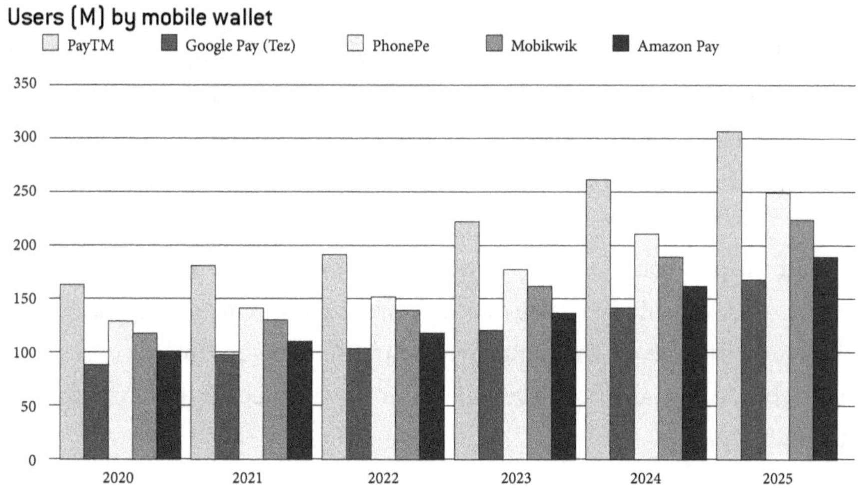

wallets growth, according to the Boku report.

According to India's MeitY, the value of digital transactions increased from Rs 1,085 crore in FY 2016–17 to Rs 5,554 crore in 2020–21, at a CAGR of 50.42 per cent.

The report concludes that the high response rate for a need for a digital payment method should be seen as an indicator to merchants that mobile wallet users in India are signalling high intent for online commerce. It also rightly points out that promotions such as cashback offers, both from wallet providers and retailers, have not only been effective in attracting new consumers to mobile wallets but are also likely to have contributed to the competition and fragmentation that exists in the market.

AI AND DIGITAL PAYMENTS

By now, you may be wondering why we have included a chapter on digital payments in a book on artificial intelligence. If you think so, consider these five reasons, which are in no way exhaustive.

First and foremost, how would you have used smart AI-powered apps like Google Pay, Amazon Pay, BHIM, or WhatsApp without AI-powered smartphones? Further, these apps and smartphones are only getting smarter as AI keeps evolving by training the models on increasingly better-quality data.

Amazon Pay, for instance, is a service that Amazon offers its customers other than the use of debit and credit cards. For instance, you can click on the Amazon Pay button when checking out from online stores, manage your payment methods in your account on Amazon. com, or use Amazon Pay on Alexa—its AI-powered voice assistant. Further, the integration of payment methods through Amazon's Echo smart speaker allows customers to buy products online through voice recognition. Amazon points out that 44 per cent of global consumers report they are likely to use voice services in at least some part of their shopping journey in the next three years. AI-powered voice experiences have the potential to change the retail experience in the coming years, it says.[3]

Google, in late 2021, launched a new app, Google Pay, which allows businesses to capitalise on the increasing adoption of digital payments in India. The app is aimed at enabling small- and medium-sized businesses (SMBs) to facilitate digital payments without onboarding and verification processes, a statement from Google said. The company also announced the rollout of tokenised cards for debit and credit cardholders. This feature will allow users to process digital payments by using a digital token generated on the smartphone rather than an actual credit card number, as desired by the RBI. The tokenised modes of payment that are operational on debit and credit cards for banks are expected to strengthen security measures that will prevent hackers from tampering with the cards and swindling gullible users.

Similarly, fintech startup PayU uses AI, ML, data intelligence and predictive analytics to mitigate fraud and risk and improve the security of transactions with the help of the company's proprietary risk engine, developed globally for the PayU platform.[4]

Second, the banking, financial services, and insurance (BFSI) sector uses advanced analytics based on ML models to draw meaningful insights from the data they collect and make predictions. Technologies such as AI, ML, and the IoT will be increasingly used to provide fast, safe, customised digital payment solutions. AI and ML are also expected to play a critical role in cybersecurity to help identify threats, enable fraud preventive measures, and mitigate risk in the digital payment space.

AI, for instance, can help prevent and detect fraud by flagging suspicious transactions. These could include instances where the amount involved is very large, a transaction is initiated by some unknown entity, or where the organisation has never transacted with the destination company or country that is sending or receiving the payment. AI tools can also detect and monitor unusual staff behaviour, such as logging on to banking systems outside of working hours.

AI-powered chatbots already respond to simple queries from clients and carry out basic tasks, such as creating or cancelling a standing order or direct debit or giving more information on a payment that the client doesn't recognise. Some financial organisations use chatbots to carry out FX trades.

Third, talking specifically about payments, AI can be used to improve the speed and efficiency of the payment process by reducing the extent to which humans need to be involved. It can do so by automating workflows, providing decision support, and applying image recognition to documents. Further, developments in speech recognition technology imply that banks can increasingly process payments initiated via voice, where the initiator has used a smartphone or smart speaker. This can be done in different languages, too, which we will elaborate in the following chapter on AI and languages.

Fourth, AI can also be used to help banks onboard new customers by automating the documentation process required for Know Your Customer (KYC) purposes. Machines will be able to use NLP to read through the documents, make sense of them and disclose their findings to humans, who will be the final decision-makers. They will also be able to cross-reference the documents with external sources to detect any anomalies.

Fifth, regulatory compliance is another area where AI is likely to have an impact on transaction banking. The technology could be used to validate client transactions against money laundering and sanctions rules, and detect patterns that indicate illegal activity. While there is no evidence of widespread usage of AI for this purpose yet, it is likely to come in future.

THE CRYPTO WORLD IS BECOMING SMARTER TOO

Whenever we talk about digital payments, we must remember that we are mostly referring to payments that are regulated by the country's central bank or the RBI. Yet, there is a whole world of digital currencies—in fact, thousands of them—that are unregulated or outside the purview of central banks around the world. We call them cryptocurrencies.

This, again, is an area that many of us are trying to wrap our heads around. For one, the ecosystem itself is evolving. Second, there is a lot of uncertainty in this sector given that governments are not comfortable with the idea of cryptocurrencies that can be bought, sold, or traded without any regulation—which also explains the volatility in prices.

Third, blockchain, which is the technology on which cryptocurrencies are built, is ironically finding favour with the much-regulated banking sector, which is using this technology for smart contracts and the like.

First, however, let us understand what the word cryptocurrency means. Next, we will try to understand words like non-fungible tokens (NFTs). We will then conclude with the relationship of AI and cryptocurrencies, blockchain and NFTs, and cover a bit of Web 3.0, which is the world of decentralised finance that is being spun with all these technologies.

The financial world's excitement over adopting the cryptocurrency Bitcoin has undoubtedly see-sawed ever since the code was first released on January 9, 2009 by a person who assumed the name Satoshi Nakamoto.[5]

Let's, however, get one thing straight—there's nothing like a physical bitcoin. It's a digital asset. Users can buy and sell bitcoins or any of the thousands of other cryptocurrencies for that matter, such as Ether, Tether, Cardano, Shiba Inu, Dogecoin, Uniswap, Tron, Polygon, and WRX (WazirX), without any kind of intermediation from banks or other financial institutions, which is why we call it a decentralised system.

A public ledger called the blockchain contains every transaction ever processed, allowing a user's computer to verify the validity of each transaction, according to Bitcoin.com, a website promoted by the Bitcoin Foundation. The authenticity of each transaction is protected by a digital signature corresponding to the sender's address, allowing users to have full control over sending bitcoins from their own bitcoin addresses. So, digital money is also known as a "cryptocurrency". Anyone can process transactions using the computing power of specialised hardware and earn a reward in bitcoins for this service—a process known as mining.

To make things a bit more complex, there are AI-powered cryptos too. So, here's a question—what do names like SingularityNET, Ocean Protocol, Numeraire, DeepBrain Chain or Prometheus Network have in common? The simple answer—these are all AI-powered cryptocurrencies.

SingularityNET, for instance, is a decentralised marketplace that allows anyone to adopt AI algorithms, allowing organisations, companies, and developers to purchase and sell AI at scale. The Numeraire cryptocurrency from hedge fund company Numerai is aimed at helping researchers anticipate financial models utilising encrypted data. Fetch.ai is a platform that means to associate IoT devices and algorithms to empower their collective learning.

DeepBrain Chain (DBC) is a blockchain-based computing platform for AI aimed at reducing user costs for processing power. Developed by Prometheus Labs, Prometheus Network is a decentralised ecosystem intended to take care of real issues in data brokerage, made for the influencer marketing, medical, and insurance data market industries.

RISE OF NFTS

Today, it's hard to have a conversation about cryptocurrencies without talking about non-fungible tokens or NFTs that have been around since 2014. However, the recent exponential growth has been fuelled by our increasingly digital lives and excess market liquidity during COVID-19. The most popular NFT types are collectables, which represent rare assets that give owners a form of social status. The collectables segment had a 76 per cent market share in sales in the July–September quarter, said the NFT database Nonfungible.com. Digital art was next, with a 9 per cent share.

In March 2021, an Indian crypto trader known as Metakovan paid $69 million for a digital collage created by an artist called Beeple. But many in the art world are divided. Some claim this is a new way to make good money, while others argue NFTs are not a good long-term investment because these are not physical copies.

NFTs are digital tokens built on an existing blockchain network, similar to other cryptocurrencies. The difference, though, is that they are not "fungible". This implies that while one bitcoin can replace another on the blockchain, you can't replace one NFT with the next. You may liken NFTs to trading cards, where you can trade one for another, but both cards will retain their unique identities. Once created, an NFT will forever reflect your ownership of the digital item and can't be changed.

Indian celebrities, including Bollywood stars and cricketers, have joined the bandwagon. In July 2021, TV host and actor Vishaal Malhotra released his NFT in collaboration with artist Ishita Banerjee on the global platform Foundation. A month later, Amitabh Bachchan showcased some NFTs that included an autographed poster of the film *Sholay* and poems narrated by him, all of which were later hosted on a platform called BeyondLife.Club.

Cricketers, too, have shown interest. Homegrown digital collectables platform Rario announced that it had partnered with cricketers Zaheer Khan and South African Faf du Plessis for the platform. Singapore-based blockchain platform Cricket Foundation, too, announced an NFT platform dedicated to cricket earlier this month. It is backed by cricketers V.V.S. Laxman, Parthiv Patel, Wasim Akram, R.P. Singh, Piyush Chawla, Deep Dasgupta, Pragyan Ojha, Lance Klusener and others. The platform uses homegrown blockchain firm Zebi's platform to run its marketplace.

Not to be left behind, companies and brands like Nike, Gucci, MG Motors, McDonald's, and even the famed National Basketball Association (NBA) have made their foray into the crypto collectables space. NFT sales even made about 8 per cent of British auction house Christie's contemporary art in 2021.

Bored Ape NFTs, too, are part of a bigger NFT buying trend. The 10,000 digital images are basically avatars that you can use online. All 10,000 are different images, with each ape being dressed differently, having different expressions and so on. They come from a website called Bored Ape Yacht Club (BAYC) and are developed by a company called Yuga Labs. Buying one of these NFTs gives the buyer access to this club, including access to "The Bathroom"—a digital graffiti board akin to a dive bar bathroom. It launched on April 30 and has amassed over $600 million in sales to date, according to Dappradar, a decentralised apps tracker.

And, of course, just like AI-powered cryptos, we have AI-powered NFTs too. Digital artists such as Refik Anadol, for example, are experimenting with techniques such as generative adversarial networks (GANs), and even a bit of quantum computing, to train models in

Source: Bored Ape Yacht Club

hundreds of millions of images and audio clips to create breathtaking visuals.

Platforms such as Alethea AI or Fetch.ai are trying to incorporate language and speech capabilities to establish a dialogue with users. Alethea Tech Pte Ltd, for instance, talks about developing an iNFT (Intelligent NFT) with an AI personality. The concept of an iNFT was developed by Arif Khan, the CEO of Alethea. The company partnered with auction house Sotheby and artist Rober Alice to create and auction an intelligent virtual character called Alice. We will see many more such developments in the coming years.

DARK SHADES OF THE CRYPTO WORLD

It's no wonder that there's so much interest in cryptos around the globe despite regulatory hassles. In India, entrepreneurs have shown enthusiasm towards the bitcoin system even as all eyes remain on the Indian government, which is yet to decide the fate of cryptocurrency. That said, there was no escaping the word 'cryptocurrency' in 2021. The cryptocurrency capitalisation globally now exceeds $2.2 trillion, according to coinmarketcap.com. In comparison, India's GDP as of 2021 was estimated to be $3 trillion. Globally, there are currently about 300 million crypto users, with 160 million of them in Asia alone.

That said, one must acknowledge that cryptocurrencies do have a dark side, which does warrant reasonable regulation. For instance, data shared by blockchain-based research platform, Chainalysis, reveals the total amount of cryptocurrency deposited to illicit wallet addresses almost doubled in 2021 as compared to 2020. The company said that illicit wallets received $14 billion in 2021, as compared to $7.8 billion in 2020. However, the report added that while crypto crimes grew by 79 per cent over the year, the total transaction volume across crypto assets grew by 550 per cent in 2021, touching $15.8 trillion in 2021.

Crypto crimes constitute hacks of crypto exchanges, decentralised finance (DeFi) protocols, crypto scams, and more. The Chainalysis report noted that "roughly $3.2 billion" worth of crypto was stolen in 2021, a 508 per cent increase from 2020. About $2.2 billion of these funds were stolen from DeFi protocols. DeFi refers to financial products built on blockchain platforms, which use algorithmic smart contracts to facilitate banking products without involving traditional banks or other financial intermediaries in between.

Other reports corroborated this trend. October 2021 data from The Block Research, another blockchain-based research firm, said the total amount of funds stolen from DeFi networks in 2021 stood at $681.14 million at the time, increasing from $30.72 million exactly a year ago. It noted that hacks of such systems grew by 22.5x year-on-year. In December 2021, blockchain security and analytics firm PeckShield reported that $120 million worth of Ether and Bitcoin were stolen from a DeFi protocol called BadgerDAO. A September 2021 report from virtual private network (VPN) provider Atlas VPN said that DeFi hacks accounted for 76 per cent of all major hacks in the year so far.

It's no wonder that governments remain suspicious of cryptocurrencies, other than the fact that central banks cannot regulate digital currency, allowing unscrupulous people to swindle gullible investors.

As for now, cryptocurrency backers can take some comfort from the fact that India's Union Finance Minister Nirmala Sitharaman has called for collective, global action to regulate an evolving technology such as cryptocurrencies. Even Gita Gopinath, chief economist of the International Monetary Fund (IMF), believes that emerging economies should not outright ban cryptocurrencies but instead regulate them. Addressing an event at the National Council of Applied Economic Research (NCAER) in November 2021, Gopinath acknowledged the challenges involved in banning cryptos, given that many exchanges are offshore and not subject to the regulations of a particular country. She, too, believes in a collective, global policy on regulating the use and application of cryptocurrencies. "No individual country can solve this problem on their own, and there is a need for global policy on it urgently," she said.

Cryptocurrencies may eventually make way for a Central Bank Digital Currency (CBDC). Many countries are launching their own CBDC, and the Indian government, too, appears to be leaning in this direction but is yet to list the Cryptocurrency and Regulation of Official Digital Currency Bill. It's unclear for now how this will exactly work, but it's safe to assume that the CBDC in India will essentially be a legal tender that is governed by the RBI but issued in a digital form and managed on a digital ledger—a blockchain. That said, going into the merits and demerits of a CBDC is outside the scope of this book.

SUMMING IT UP

Ironically, while cryptocurrencies remain a thorn in the side of governments, they appear to be comfortable with the underlying technology that powers bitcoin—blockchain. On December 6, for instance, India's MeitY released a national strategy for adopting blockchain technology for government systems, especially e-governance services. The 52-page document sought to "create trusted digital platforms through shared blockchain infrastructure" and promote "research and development, innovation, technology and application development" around the technology.

The ministry has identified 44 key areas where blockchains can be applied, including the transfer of land and property, managing digital certificates, pharmaceutical supply chain, e-notary services, e-voting, smart grid management, and electronic health record management. The document has also taken into consideration blockchain-based platforms operated by governments in China, Brazil, the UAE, and Europe and highlights various government-led initiatives on blockchain that are underway.

Blockchain is a distributed ledger shared via a peer-to-peer network that maintains an expanding list of data records. Each participant has a copy of the ledger's data, giving everyone a ledger that reflects the most recent transactions or changes. Thus, blockchain reduces the need for establishing trust using traditional methods. Blockchain acts as an open ledger and reduces the duplication of access to data or checking of data. The other benefits are scalability and lower cost.

Blockchain holds the potential for all participants in a business network to share a system of record. This replicated, shared ledger provides consensus, provenance, immutability, and finality around the transfer of assets within business networks—reducing costs, complexity and time, underpinning shared, trusted processes, enabling trusted record-keeping, and improving discoverability, according to a Finextra white paper by IBM.

Many companies are trying to build applications on top of blockchain to offer solutions across industries. For instance, making an intelligent application over blockchain to store and handle patient data can find use in the healthcare space and would do away with the need for a central authority to manage all the details of a patient. Banks are another case in point. Blockchain works on a model of code-breaking and crowdsourcing, and the technology decentralises the way a traditional bank works—blockchain itself verifies a person's identity or credit risk.

For instance, 15 banks in India have partnered to establish a new company named Indian Banks' Blockchain Infrastructure Co. Pvt. Ltd

(IBBIC). The idea is to use blockchain technology to process inland letters of credit (LCs). The banks include ICICI Bank, HDFC Bank, Kotak Mahindra Bank, Axis Bank, and SBI. Meanwhile, the Institute for Development and Research in Banking Technology (IDRBT), the technology and research arm of RBI, is also in the process of developing a model blockchain platform for banking needs.

To be sure, these are private (governed by a central authority) or permissioned (limited to specific participants) blockchains, unlike the Bitcoin or Ethereum blockchains that are public, allowing anyone to participate. IBBIC can be likened to the private blockchains owned by Chinese banks that have clocked large transaction volumes. For instance, an Ethereum-based private blockchain platform developed by China Construction Bank called BC Trade clocked transactions worth $50 billion, thereby making it the largest trade finance platform in the world.[6]

The fact remains that ever since the day Nakamoto developed the bitcoin, thousands of cryptocurrencies of all shades and colours have been adopted for everything from international money transfers, online narco-trafficking, NFTs, and now also for use in the AI-powered metaverse—a concept we will cover extensively in the final chapter of this book.

For now, you may understand the metaverse as a place where technologies like AI, AR, and VR merge to allow for a very immersive experience that combines the virtual and real worlds. Examples of metaverses include 3D walk-throughs of real-world locations like oil and gas rigs, automotive factories, or retail outlets.

Going forward, the metaverse will also be accessible via next-generation TVs and smartphones, for which companies are in the process of designing interfaces, according to Emergen Research.[7] It adds that metaverse platforms powered by blockchain technology will enable users to create, own, and trade decentralised digital assets and virtual land assets with cryptocurrencies and NFTs.

Till then, we can only sit back and watch this exciting space evolve. Meanwhile, let's dwell a bit on how AI can help society, which we will do in the following chapter.

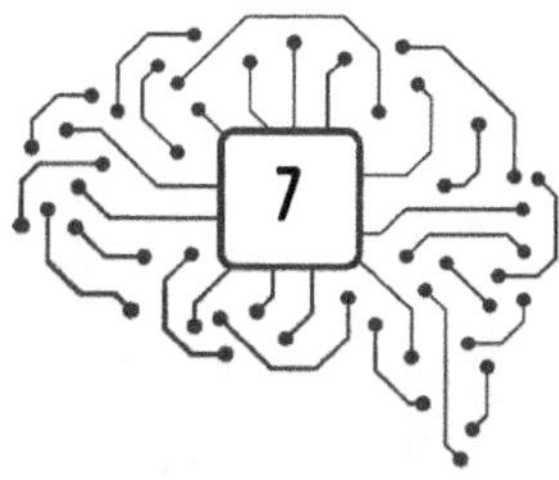

AN AI BLUEPRINT FOR SOCIAL CHANGE

"We're making this analogy that AI is the new electricity. Electricity transformed industries: agriculture, transportation, communication, manufacturing."

—Andrew Ng

About 60 years ago, an estimated 20,000 people in India lost their lives to severe cyclonic storms, according to a paper published by the Ministry of Earth Sciences. Just one single Cyclone, Chirala, which hit the coast of Odisha (then Orissa), claimed around 10,000 lives.

There has been a dramatic shift since then. In the 2010–20 decade, there were as many as 20 cyclones that hit both coasts of India—many of them as severe as Chirala and a few of them even more ferocious. But the net human toll from all 20 cyclones was only 658.[1]

While we will all agree that even a single life lost due to these natural calamities is one too many, the fact remains that India has been able to "mitigate" the human cost of these events. How has India managed to reduce the death toll? The major factor is the predictive analysis of data.

It is now possible to predict the movement of cyclones precisely—not in real-time but ahead of time. An early warning system allows the administration to evacuate people that lie in the route of the cyclone and take all preventive measures to ensure there is minimal loss of life. Data collected by the Met department over the last few decades is used to not only predict the path of the cyclone but also calculate related factors

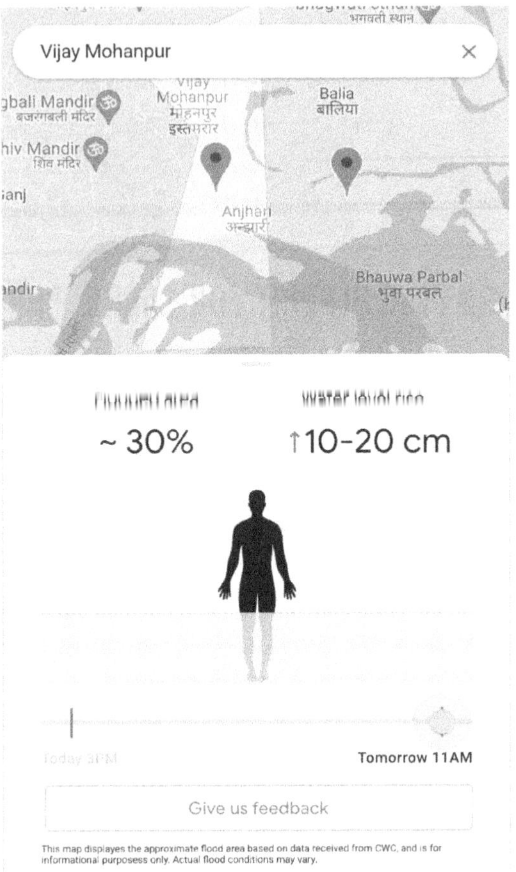

Source: Google blog (https://blog.google/technology/ai/expanding-our-ml-based-flood-forecasting/)

such as wind speed and epicentre of landfall accurately enough to ensure that the administration can take action to prevent large-scale death and destruction. These models are possible today due to the availability of data and tools to create the models for simulation. Most global flood alerts, for instance, provide information on how much a river will rise. This may not always help people understand the implication for them and their villages. Google's flood alerts display inundation maps that reveal the extent and depth of flooding right atop Google Maps. This helps people visualise this critical information more easily.

In another case, India's Central Water Commission has partnered with Google to predict the occurrence of floods and forecast them ahead of their happening.

Farmpal is a relatively unknown agritech company based in Pune. They decided to address the post-harvest supply chain for the producers and help them identify newer sales channels for more efficient distribution of the farmers' produce. The result—the wastage factor due to logistics has reduced from around 35 per cent to 5 per cent.[2]

These are just a few examples. Across dispersed sectors ranging from education to pharma to governance, AI is delivering massive results leading to severe disruption of age-old practices and threatening to usher in a brand new way of doing things.

DATA IS THE NEW OIL

The brand new way has data at its heart. Massive amounts of data harvested over the last several decades are providing decision-makers with a new set of solutions that were simply not available before. Whether it is natural calamities (cyclones, floods, earthquakes) or managing healthcare exigencies (such as COVID-19) or even business decisions in the areas of retail, banking, providing credit facilities or preventing loan frauds, data is providing early warning systems that allow the decision-maker to take decisions before they happen, and not, as was traditionally done—AFTER the event.

If oil was the driver of the global economy in the twentieth century, data and its mining, and extracting insights thereof, will be the driver of this century.

And the results are already showing on the ground. A Bengaluru-based medical technology company, Forus Health, decided to focus on preventive blindness as compared to treating existing blindness. Partnering with Microsoft, they developed an AI-based solution that detects retinal diseases such as blindness caused by diabetes, which is one of the most popular causes of blindness in India.[3]

In September 2015, the General Assembly of the UN adopted the 2030 Agenda for Sustainable Development, which includes 17 Sustainable Development Goals (SDGs). Building on the principle of "leaving no one behind", the new agenda emphasises a holistic approach to achieving sustainable development for all.[4]

A casual analysis of the SDGs will leave us wondering. For instance, how does one drive the balance between "Industry, Innovation and Infrastructure" and "Sustainability"? Also, how does one balance "Life Below Water" and "Life on Land" as they may, in many instances, be counterproductive to each other? While there could be many practical difficulties, the main objective for AI practitioners must be to ensure that most of the SDGs are achieved to the maximum possible extent without one having a deleterious effect on the other.

AI FOR SOCIAL GOOD

AI for Social Good (AI4SG) is a theme that has emerged over the years to apply AI to address societal issues and improve the overall well-being of society. Given the complexity of Indian society and the legacy of a shortage economy (the high level of demand in a shortage economy will enable sellers to charge more for the goods in question, resulting in higher prices), one needs disruptive thinking and practice to make breakthroughs in every single social aspect. To that extent, AI4SG has very high applicability in the Indian context. Against the backdrop of the UN SDGs, AI4SG has a much more universal application across Indian society, where every aspect of an individual's life can be impacted using AI technologies and solutions.

In India, NITI Aayog has decided to focus on five sectors that are envisioned to benefit the most from AI in solving societal needs. These include healthcare: increased access and affordability of quality healthcare; agriculture: enhanced farmers' income, increased farm productivity and reduction of wastage; education: improved access and quality of education; smart cities and infrastructure: efficiency and connectivity for the burgeoning urban population, and smart mobility and transportation: smarter and safer modes of transportation and better ways to address traffic and congestion problems.[5]

Some seminal approaches to implementing AI in some of these sectors are given below.

Education: In 2020, the Indian government introduced the New Education Policy (NEP), wherein the existing K12 and the university education system, which has been functioning for the last 75 years, was sought to be drastically revamped. The main objective of NEP was to universalise the education system from Early Child Care Education (ECCE) to secondary education by 2030, in alignment with SDG 4. NEP is also mandated to dismantle the current affiliation system and provide a high degree of autonomy to the providers. At the same time, NEP also dictates common standards of learning between public and private schools—a chasm that is currently seen as one too wide to bridge.

One of the key mandates of AI in implementing NEP is to analyse the reams of data and come up with patterns of how a particular child will holistically progress throughout her educational journey. Since we are focusing on holistic learning as against stream-based learning, every child's journey will be different from the other. Therefore, there has to be an objective assessment of the learnings that the child has had and the options available for the child, given the proclivities and aspirations of the subject. While algorithmic solutions will need to be developed using data, solutions will need to be individual-driven. Such a solution will depend on the teaching methods available and those that can be developed, content consumption patterns, individual students' learning ability, retention ability, and application ability.

The second aspect will be that of measurement. Once the student has undergone the programme, AI solutions will need to be deployed to objectively evaluate the parameters that have been put in place for gauging the metrics. This is easier said than done. Clearly, no amount of human effort will be able to put all of this and measure the outcomes realistically in a reasonable time frame.

Finally, the very pedagogy will be impacted by AI intervention. Creating multiple versions of the subject and introducing elements of related topics in the pedagogy that are of interest and relevance to the student will mean a level of customisation that will be enormous, given the size of our student population.

Healthcare: Is one area that has a huge immediate, direct impact on society. Google recently started six AI-based research projects in India that focus on addressing the social, humanitarian, and environmental challenges in sectors such as healthcare, education, disaster prevention and conservation. The initiatives[6] include a project where AI is used to improve health information for high HIV/AIDS-risk communities; to predict the risk of expectant mothers to increase positive healthcare outcomes for mothers and their babies; to improve consistency of healthcare information inputs; to predict human-wildlife conflict in the state of Maharashtra in a bid to help inform data-driven policymaking; to inform dam and barrage water releases and build early warning systems to give alerts of the risk of disasters; and a project where researchers are building open-source input tools for underserved Indian languages to accelerate the publishing of openly licensed content.

In healthcare, AI could be beneficial in mining medical records, designing treatment plans, forecasting health events, assisting repetitive jobs, doing online consultations, assisting in clinical decision-making, medication management, drug creation, making healthier choices and decisions, and solving public health problems. AI could be very helpful in areas where human resources are scarce, such as rural and remote areas.

AI technology has been helpful in dealing with COVID-19 in India. It has helped in the preliminary screening of COVID-19 cases, containment of coronavirus, contact tracing, enforcing quarantine and social distancing, tracking suspects, tracking the pandemic, treatment and remote monitoring of COVID-19 patients, vaccine and drug development, etc. The path to the adoption of AI-driven healthcare in India is filled with a lot of challenges. The unstructured data sets, interoperability issues, lack of open sets of medical data, inadequate analytics solutions that could work with big data, limited funds, inadequate infrastructure, lack of manpower skilled in AI, regulatory weaknesses, inadequate framework, and issues related to data protection are some of the key challenges for AI-driven healthcare.

The key issue related to applying AI in healthcare is to provide universal healthcare to all Indian citizens. During the early days of COVID-19, Wadhwani Centre developed a "cough analyser" that had data from millions of cough samples and could hence detect if a person's cough was symptomatic of COVID-19.

Another major issue is one of patients' records and mining the same across the entire value chain of healthcare in India. So, if a person in a remote village in Bihar travels to New Delhi's government hospital to seek an advanced medicare solution that is not available in his village or state, the patient record must be accessible by the Delhi-based doctor effortlessly.

Thirdly, the patient data needs to be analysed to create a model that can predict the onset or the existence of the disease by either geo-based or work-based parameters. This will help the administration take preventive steps to manage the disease in its very early stages and not wait till it reaches alarming levels.

Agriculture: contributes around 16 per cent of India's GDP and consumes close to 49 per cent of the adult workforce, and yet it is in the midst of an existential crisis. While food production has shot up consistently year after year, the net farm income per hectare of land has not shown a proportional increase. The agricultural sector is facing challenges across all facets—production, distribution, and monetisation.

And this is one area where AI can play a massive role. From soil analysis to pesticide sprays, AI solutions have been developed to ensure that the farmer has accurate, real-time information as to the nature of his soil and hence can take the right decision on what crops to sow.

Sunnyvale-based Blue River Technologies, a subsidiary of John Deere, has developed an AI-based solution that integrates computer vision and ML technology, which enables the farmer to calibrate the spread of herbicides and spray only in places where there are weeds and not resort to carpet-bombing of herbicide that can potentially increase the toxicity of the soil. This leads to an optimal use of inputs that not only reduces the cost but also has the potential to reduce toxicity and improve yields.[7]

International Crop Research Institute for Semi-Arid Tropics (ICRISAT), a Hyderabad-based organisation, has developed a smart solution that advises farmers on the sowing date by collating information related to soil test-based fertiliser application, farmyard manure application, seed treatment, optimum sowing depth, etc. And given the local mobile usage patterns, ICRISAT has ensured that the solution can work on a feature phone! The results were immediate. Across Karnataka and Andhra Pradesh, where the pilot was conducted, the yields increased by as much as 30 per cent.

Similarly, Imago is an India-based agritech startup that aims to use AI to increase crop yields and reduce food waste. The company combines ML and computer vision to automate tedious tasks, such as measuring crop quality and weighing yields. This won't just speed up the process, but it will also help farmers identify plants that have diseases.[8]

In distribution, AI can help in identifying spare warehouse capacity by using past data and can advise the farmer and the local mandi in identifying the nearest warehouse to reduce transportation costs. AI models that identify geography-based offtake, which can further reduce storage time, thus reducing the wastage incurred during the storage phase, have also been developed.

However, monetisation of the produce is where AI can have a dramatic and grassroots impact. With the passing of the three major farm laws in 2020—the Farmers' Produce Trade and Commerce (Promotion and Facilitation) Act, 2020; the Farmers (Empowerment and Protection) Agreement on Price Assurance and Farm Services Act, 2020; and the Essential Commodities (Amendment) Act, 2020—the Indian farmer today has the freedom to sell his produce to any agency and is not restricted to selling only to the local Agricultural Produce Market Committee (APMC). As a result, the farmer will need pricing information that can be predicted using AI tools and can get alerts to indicate different pricing patterns across the country. As a result, he can sell directly to any wholesaler in any part of the country and also slash his middlemen commissions which, traditionally, have been substantial.

Smart cities: Application of AI for smart cities and creating infrastructure is a no-brainer in the sense that AI will form the backbone of the smart cities. From smart traffic management using past traffic patterns and real-time data to smart homes that optimise energy consumption to smart infrastructure that enables the administration to accurately forecast citizen density to reduce energy usage and increase public space utilities, AI solutions will play a central role in the creation of smart cities. With the Indian government announcing the creation of 99 smart cities at a total cost of Rs 2 lakh crore, many of these urban agglomerations will start reaping the benefits of AI solutions for better living.

In Bengaluru, for instance, the traffic police has over 700 cameras spread across the city that provide real-time feeds to a central control facility, which then uses the data not just for optimal traffic management but even shares the data with other branches of the police for citizen safety. In a recent incident, the traffic police spotted a vehicle violating traffic rules. On a routine check, it was found that the said vehicle had been notified as having committed an offence already. Thus alerted by the traffic police, the city's crime branch used the data to apprehend the offender as now they had exact movement data of the offending vehicle.

The Pune streetlight project, on its part, uses SCADA (Supervisory Control And Data Acquisition) systems to remotely control the lights and ensure a higher degree of citizen safety.

Crowd management: Another innovative application of AI could be in the area of crowd management. After the experience of the second wave of COVID-19 in May 2021, there was a discussion as to whether it was possible in the future to actually manage the crowds in events such as the Kumbh Mela, which has millions of people from across the world congregating in one particular place.

Since the data about the travellers can be made available by linking the transport systems to the administration, the authorities can accurately predict the flow of people on a day-to-day basis. This will help them plan amenities, health checks and crowd management at specific places and even create a workflow for the pilgrims to ensure that there are no adverse events such as stampedes, etc.

CHALLENGES

While the opportunities and the resultant benefits of AI in creating social welfare and a better life for all the constituencies in society may seem obvious there are many challenges too. We can broadly divide the challenges into two parts: institutional challenges and intent-based challenges.

Institutional Challenges

It will be altruistic to say that the successful implementation of AI is predicated on the availability of vast amounts of data. Without data, there can be no AI. There will be nothing to analyse and parse. And herein lies the first problem. Given the size of the country and the quasi-federal structure of the polity, the sheer availability of data is a near-impossibility. Added to that is the issue of accurate data. In India, as in any other large developed country, there is a vast amount of data lying in silos across different departments in every state. Even within the state, there has been no consistent process by which the data was being aggregated in a central repository. If we now multiply the situation by the number of states in India, the problem becomes even more exacerbated.

The recent experience with COVID-19 is an eye-opener in that context. While the Central Government was collating data from every state on an end-of-day basis, some states were more forthcoming than others as far as sharing of the data was concerned. This led to a situation where any analysis of data had to be done on what was available at the Centre and not what was available in every state. Consequently, the forecast related to the second wave, which could have been predicted earlier, was late, leading to another round of massive shutdowns, which led to massive economic repercussions.

It is often said that data is only as accurate as it is recorded at the original entry. Once the data is recorded, it is well-nigh impossible to do a veracity check, especially if the size of the database is large. Consequently, any error in recording the data at the first instance will have a compounding effect on the analysis and could lead to errors in the creation of any models.

Add to the above the amount of unstructured data that is available in different formats across the country. Unstructured data includes data lying in various public offices across the country in different formats and is therefore unreported, data in social media platforms, in chats, in email conversations, and other discussion forums. The sheer volume of such data is so high that it needs a technological intervention to aggregate even a fraction of it.

Also, while much of the unstructured data may not be very useful, there will still be a large amount of data that can be mined, leveraged, and analysed to gain valuable insights. Finally, even if some of the unstructured data can be merged with the structured database, it will provide an enormous amount of value to the intelligence of the resultant information.

There have been recent efforts in harnessing NLP using AI tools and techniques to leverage unstructured data, particularly in the area of citizen safety, provision of public services, and identifying criminal patterns.

Even if the data were available, there would be a problem with the interoperability of data sets. Since the data comes from diverse sources, there will be a need to create a data "sandbox" wherein the data can be parsed and then collated to be merged and analysed. This will therefore force us to define fixed templates and, more importantly, enforce strict adherence to the templates by the data collection agencies.

Data collection and social inequities: More often than not, one sees that structured data is better available from larger urban agglomerations, while there is very little structured data that comes from rural and poor India. Any analysis of such data will be inherently skewed towards the more affluent parts of the country, leaving large swathes of the country living with solutions that are far removed from their reality. Any implementation of a social solution will only then lead to an increase in the disparity and increase the divide.

To solve this issue, the data collection must be ground up, and gaps thereof must be highlighted early and regularly. An excellent example of this was seen during the COVID management measures, where every state government was mandated to collect data at the village panchayat level, which was then aggregated on a pyramidical model to reflect the block, the district and, finally, the state. This resulted in the state government's ability to create "red zones" even at the village level, leading to much better management of the pandemic.

Lack of regulatory frameworks: Notwithstanding the IT Act, data protection norms in India are followed more in their absence. Despite the government's intention to address data violations in a strong manner, the attitude of much of civil society towards data—whether it is their own or others—is marked by a remarkable degree of sanguinity. More often than not, it is the feeling that "it won't happen to me" or sometimes, "the data is not important" and even "what will anyone do with my data?" This has led to a situation where even institutions like banks don't think twice before letting a third party access their customers' data.

Intent-based Challenges

These reflect our attitude and intent towards implementing AI-based solutions to solving social problems.

The obvious question that arises is: why would anyone oppose creating a solution to a larger problem if it can alleviate a social issue? The answers could be many, but what will be a common thread is the intent of the person that will be the underlying motive.

For instance, in the aftermath of the second wave of COVID, an analysis was done on the RT-PCR tests conducted on visitors to the Kumbh Mela. Investigations revealed that nearly 1 lakh fake tests were conducted during the event in April 2021. What is inescapable is the fact that such large-scale data manipulation will lead to a completely incorrect conclusion. Any data modelling that is based on such data will, therefore, be incorrect. Consequently, any AI solution that is developed using the model will be, at best, ineffective and, at worst, inimical to public welfare.

Many of the AI solutions—such as better monetisation of the farmers' produce by direct dealing with the end wholesaler—will have their echo in changing social equations. For a farmer, who has been forced to sell his produce to the middleman for over a century, it could be a boon to improve his financial and social standing. On the other hand, for the middleman and the layers that lie between the farmer and the ultimate wholesaler, it could lead to loss of income, however justified or unjustified the argument may be. This will lead to resistance among the middlemen to implement the solution—a resistance that could be passive or sometimes even active and violent.

There are other intent-based challenges. For long there has been a debate about "how much AI is good?" While it may be too early to seek answers to that question, the essential nature of AI needs to be understood. There have also been attempts to demonise AI and to project a society that is run by automatons—robots that are AI-driven, who lord over humans. Some research has also emerged of an "AI bias", which is inherently created by the human bias that is fed into the system and the self-sustaining data sets that seek to perpetuate the bias.

Max Tegmark, president of Future of Life Institute, says, "The concerns about AI are not about malevolence but competence." He points out that the best example of AI is the human species itself. While humans may not be the strongest animals on the face of the earth, they control it because they are the smartest. So, will it be possible someday to create an AI solution that could be smarter than the human who created the basic algorithms that eventually created the AI solution?[9]

Tegmark's "competence" can be read as intent in our context. So, when society is sought to be fundamentally changed by introducing disruptions that are powered by an intelligent solution that can see the problem holistically and then solve it one piece at a time, there are bound to be winners and losers. The winners will be those who will benefit from these disruptions, and the losers will be those who will lose their existing hegemony, rightfully or wrongfully. In these situations, there will be a tendency to disrupt the disruptions and restore the status quo.

Intent cannot be eliminated by technology as all solutions—technological and otherwise—emanate from an intent. However, AI can only thwart some of the obvious actions that are intended to impede social change.

FINAL WORD

A study by PwC suggested that the economic impact of implementing AI could lead to an increase of 14 per cent in global GDP by 2035—in absolute terms, an increase of $15.7 trillion.[10]

A NITI Aayog report suggests that, according to Accenture, AI has the potential to add roughly $1 trillion to the Indian economy by 2035.[11]

Whatever number one goes by, the implications are simply astounding. However, over and beyond the economic impact of AI, there will be a massive tectonic shift that is likely to take place once this journey begins.

Implementation of AI in rural or semi-urban agglomerations will have multiple social implications. On the one hand, it will dramatically improve the productivity of the labour force and will lead to higher income per household—either directly, by the implementation of the solutions, and indirectly, by freeing up manpower resources that can then indulge in other accretive economic activities.

On the other hand, it will also lead to bridging the economic gap between the erstwhile poor farmer and the more affluent sections of society. Given the rigid social structures within the societal fabric, the emergence of the rich local farmer and his release from economic bondage will lead to a redrawing of the social equations. Consequently, any implementation of AI will need to take into account the social factors and a realisation of the current inequalities and inequities in Indian society.

In the following chapter, we will explore one more aspect of AI for social good in the context of making the digital riches of the online world accessible to one and all in their respective languages. In other words, taking a step closer to bridging the digital divide.

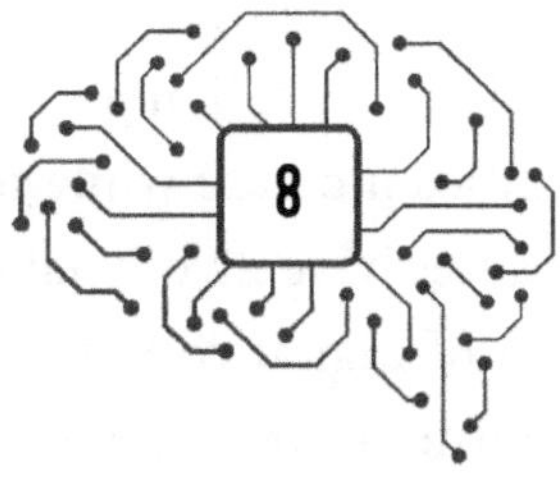

WHEN AI SPEAKS IN INDIAN TONGUES

As humans, we love to chat. But we do not have to run any software program to do so. We simply start talking since conversation comes naturally to us. We learn multiple languages as kids from our parents and peers, hone our speaking and writing skills, and build our vocabularies as we learn from others. Moreover, in many countries, people speak different languages and varied dialects too. Once again, they do all this without the help of any technology or software skills since the human brain is incredibly powerful, with billions of neurons performing this task.

In some cases, humans also use the help of other human translators to understand another language. Translation from one language to another, however, requires much effort and time. Besides, what would you do if a translator is not readily available during an important conference or for some business deal?

It's here that automation of the task comes in handy. Researchers have been trying to impart a human kind of intelligence to machines, which has made conversational AI a key area of AI research. In simple words, they want to provide machines with the ability to speak and understand languages like humans. This is easier said than done since what comes naturally to humans is not the same for machines. Besides, Indian languages, comprising Dravidian and Aryan subdivisions, are complicated. The complexities increase while translating languages for India, where 29 different states have 22 official languages.

Further, there's a dearth of digital content in Indian languages that can be pulled from the internet to train neural networks. Even though digital content is available, a lot of it cannot be used as it doesn't follow standard encoding like Unicode.

A computer understands binary language. In other words, it only understands 0 and 1, but can it directly understand alphabets, numbers, pictures, and symbols? Hence, we use alphanumeric codes to accomplish this task. ASCII, which stands for the American Standard Code for Information Interchange, has 256 characters but uses a 7-bit encoding (extended ASCII uses 8-bit). Unicode covers more than 1,28,000 characters, allowing for characters from many other languages other than just English. Unicode also accommodates glyphs and emojis and is used as a global standard.

And even with all the advancements that AI companies have made, conversational AI is still not very interactive. It's mostly transactional. The two major conversational AI solutions—text-based (chatbots) and voice-based (personal assistants)—are yet to deliver effective and efficient human-machine conversations that make them credible options for human speech.

Human-machine conversations comprise natural language understanding (NLU), which implies that the user can comprehend the language of a machine. Natural language generation (NLG) is all about formulating a reasonable and relevant response to the user. However, response generation is not simply a product of collecting and analysing lots of data. NLP, of which NLU is a subset, is difficult because the tasks regarding linguistics need to include variations in human psychology, cultures, and linguistic diversities. Further, most conversational experiences today are either very broad but shallow (e.g., "What's the time?" = "The time is 10.00 a.m.") or very narrow but deep (e.g., a multi-turn conversation in a quiz game).

To advance beyond these limited experiences, we will need to get to a world of both wide and deep conversations. This will require the machine's ability to scale beyond the current technical limitations of recognising between only a few hundred intents (the purpose or what we hope to achieve) at a time. Another limitation of machine conversations is personalisation. In a natural conversation between two people, each will normally draw on previous experiences with the other person and tailor the responses accordingly. Computer conversations that don't do this tend to feel unnatural and even annoying. Addressing this in the long term will require solving challenges such as speaker identification, so that the computer knows who you are and can respond differently to you versus someone else.

BEYOND JUST ENGLISH

Around the world, barring the US and China, there are practically no markets where large multi-billion-dollar tech digital media businesses have been created. The top Chinese search, e-commerce and social media networking tech giants—Baidu, Alibaba and Tencent (collectively known as BAT)—rival US digital media companies such as Facebook, Apple, Amazon, Netflix, and Google (FAANG).

Because in most or all of those markets, the duopoly of the global tech giants dominates, they dominate the time spent, and they dominate the monetisation. In India, however, there are over a billion people who consume television media. But almost 90 per cent of that consumption is not in English. While Hindi accounts for around 40–50 per cent of that consumption, the rest is by regional languages.

India, we should well remember, has 22 official languages and over a hundred widely-used languages with different scripts. Hence, when we refer to regional languages, it's Hindi and those languages combined—the only exception being English. The internet has around 550 million active users today. About 250 million of these users consume content in English, and a little more than 350 million in local languages. Nine of the 10 new users that come online every day are local language audiences. By the time the internet has a billion users, it is estimated that about 750 million will be local language users.

The early efforts to develop digitised Indic languages products and solutions were made by the mobile devices industry way back in 2004–05. The then leading device players in India, such as Nokia, Motorola, LG, and Sony Ericsson, tried to launch SMS in vernacular languages. While the underlying software and languages package was built either in-house or sourced from Nuance Communications (acquired by Microsoft), the hardware—local language keys on feature phones—was built by the mobile manufacturers themselves. And, due to the lack of standardisation and logistics issues (lack of predictability of demand for different regions, with different language keypads on the phones) coupled with indifference and lacklustre demand from the users, the mobile device brands could not sustain this effort.

As the internet subscriber base hit the inflexion point at 200 million users sometime in 2013–14, the need for vernacular languages-based online content started growing. Especially considering that only 10 per cent of the Indian population could read or write in English, for the internet to grow beyond that segment of the population required content to be developed in various Indian languages. And the initial fonts, designs, and standardisation of these digital fonts were led by the Centre for Development of Advanced Computing (C-DAC) and Google.

C-DAC, in fact, was the first company that worked on Indian languages digitisation at scale. Over the past three decades, the institution has developed several true-type fonts (TTFs) and open font formats for various Indian languages. Moreover, the Applied Artificial Intelligence (AAI) Group at C-DAC has been working on some of the fundamental applications in the field of NLP, machine translation, intelligent language teaching, and decision support systems. The MAchiNe assisted TRAnslation tool, or MANTRA, was one of C-DAC's major achievements.

The institution also developed an 'Expert English to Indian Languages Machine Translation System' (EILMT) that allows translating text from English to Indian languages, namely Hindi, Bengali, Marathi, Urdu, Tamil, Oriya, Gujarati and Bodo. The idea is to use this solution in the areas of tourism, healthcare, and agriculture.

Further, the Technology Development for Indian Languages (TDIL) programme of MeitY has developed many such solutions, including the Hindi WordNet, which is a system to bring together different lexical and semantic relations between Hindi words. According to the MeitY website, it organises lexical information in terms of word meanings and can be termed a lexicon based on psycholinguistic principles. The design of the Hindi WordNet is inspired by the English WordNet.

WordNet, incidentally, is freely and publicly available for download at https://wordnet.princeton.edu/download. It groups words together based on their meanings, akin to a thesaurus. But WordNet is much more complex. It interlinks not just word forms—strings of letters—but specific senses of words. Also, unlike the grouping of words in a thesaurus, WordNet labels the semantic relations among words.

According to the Princeton website, the main relation among words in WordNet is synonymy, "as between the words shut and close or car and automobile". "Synonyms—words that denote the same concept and are interchangeable in many contexts—are grouped into unordered sets (synsets). Each of WordNet's 1,17,000 synsets is linked to other synsets by means of a small number of 'conceptual relations'. Additionally, a synset contains a brief definition ('gloss') and, in most cases, one or more short sentences illustrating the use of the synset members. Word forms with several distinct meanings are represented in as many distinct synsets. Thus, each form-meaning pair in WordNet is unique."[1]

In the Hindi WordNet, the words are grouped together according to their similarity of meanings. Two words that can be interchanged in a context are synonymous in that context. For each word, there is a synonym set, or synset, in the Hindi WordNet, representing one lexical concept. This is done to remove ambiguity in cases where a single word has multiple meanings.

MeitY also has another solution, christened AnglaMT, a machine-aided translation methodology specifically designed to translate English to Indian languages. AnglaMT is a pattern-directed, rule-based system with a structure for English. It generates a "pseudo-target" applicable to a group of Indian languages such as the Indo–Aryan family comprising languages such as Hindi, Bangla, Asamiya, Punjabi, Marathi, Oriya, and Gujarati; and languages such as Tamil, Telugu, Kannada, and Malayalam from the Dravidian family. Some of the major design considerations of AnglaMT have been aimed at providing practical aid for translation wherein an attempt is made to get 90 per cent of the task done by the machine, and 10 per cent is left to the human post-editing, according to the MeitY website.

Other efforts include that of AI4Bharat—a non-profit, open-source community of engineers, domain experts, policymakers, and academicians. It is headed by IIT Madras faculty members Mitesh Khapra and Pratyush Kumar. AI4Bharat, which was part of Google India's first 'AI For Social Good' cohort, where the team worked with the NGO Pratham Books, aims at creating open-source NLP tools, models, and data sets for Indian languages using state-of-the-art DL approaches and generating fonts using AI for Indian Language-Scripts using style-transfer GANs.

Khapra and Kumar are in the process of collecting data to build and release these translation models in Indian languages. They are also focusing on the transliteration problem, which involves typing in a regional language using an English keyboard by swapping text in predictive ways. The goal of this initiative is to bring parity in AI technology for Indian languages with English.

DL BOOSTER

In 2006, Google announced the launch of Google Translate along with the use of Phrase-Based Machine Translation (PBMT) as the key algorithm behind this service. There was a strong reason to do so since word-based translation has its limitations. Google wanted to get around these restrictions by translating whole sequences of words with different lengths. However, despite the rapid advances in machine intelligence that improved Google's speech recognition and image recognition capabilities, machine translation remained a challenging goal. Towards this end, the company announced the Google Neural Machine Translation system (GNMT) in 2016. Google explained in a blog that while PBMT "breaks an input sentence into words and phrases to be translated largely independently, Neural Machine Translation (NMT) considers the entire input sentence as a unit for translation".[2]

NMT is a form of language translation automation that uses DL models to deliver more accurate and more natural-sounding translations than traditional statistical and rule-based translation algorithms. NMT models are trained using examples of translated sentences and documents, typically collected from the public web. Compared to PBMT, NMT has been found to be more sensitive to data quality. Google claimed in its blog that it had to make improvements in NMT to make it work on very large data sets. Google, however, did admit then that GNMT too can "still make significant errors that a human translator would never make, like dropping words and mistranslating proper names or rare terms, and translating sentences in isolation rather than considering the context of the paragraph or page. There is still a lot of work we can do to serve our users better".

Google's BERT (Bidirectional Encoder Representations from Transformers) led to one of the largest improvements over the last five years in the company's ability to understand language and improve search. BERT models consider the full context of a word by looking at the words that come before and after it.

Further, Google's Zero-Shot Machine Translation system has been trained on 100 different languages with translation. Here's how the system works. To begin with, Google trained its multilingual system to share its parameters when translating between four different language pairs: Japanese to English and English to Japanese; Korean to English and English to Korean. The success of this method inspired them to explore if they could translate between a language pair that the system had never seen before. An example of this would be translations between Korean and Japanese where the Korean-to-Japanese and Japanese-to-Korean examples were not shown to the system. Google realised that its system could generate "reasonable" Korean to Japanese and Japanese to Korean translations, "even though it has never been taught to do so". They called this "zero-shot" translation.

All these advancements have resulted in Google's multilingual system currently supporting 133 languages even as the company recognises it has a long way to go, "as there are still some 7,000 unsupported languages globally that Translate doesn't address".[3]

Other than the spoken and written word, people around the world are increasingly keen on performing online searches in their own language. It's in this context that advancements in Google Search become critical. In an interview in November 2021, Pandu Nayak, vice president of Search and Google Fellow, who leads the company's ranking teams, explained how Google is consistently solving language problems for Indian users (just as it is doing for other languages too). Search, explains Nayak, is a "language-understanding problem ... You need to understand what the user is saying in the query. You need to understand what the document means. You need to match them together."[4]

That said, Google Search has evolved over the years. For instance, if you had googled the question: "Is sole good for kids?" a few years ago, it would have thrown up many results about shoes for kids. Today, if you do this query, you'll see that most of the results are about fish, even though an occasional result about shoes still creeps in (because sole is also a fish and a search engine could throw up fish in the results if it does not understand the context of the sentence, a problem that is being addressed by AI). Google hasn't quite nailed it, but with every passing day, the search engine is getting better in its understanding of Indian languages, thanks to AI.

Here's an example. When you type a question in, let's say, Hindi, you often get results in English. That's because there isn't as much information on the web in Hindi. So, Google takes English language content from a set of sites and translates it into Hindi. Now the results are automatically translated into Hindi (or other Indian languages), which makes English language content accessible to users in their own language.

But even if you get the results in Hindi, there are some users for whom literacy is a bigger challenge. They're more comfortable with the spoken word. So, Google has a link on the page that says: "Ise suno" (listen to this). Thus, you can hear the answer. This text-to-speech is again one of those things that are powered by ML. It makes this kind of content even more accessible.

Google, on its part, has introduced a new model called MUM, which stands for Multitask Unified Model. It's a large model trained on 75 different languages all at one time. The advantage of simultaneously training it on all these languages is that it allows us to generalise from languages. And, by being able to train these languages all at one time, we get to share a sort of underlying structure to generalise these languages with less data. The cool thing about MUM is that it is multimodal, according to Nayak, which means it can handle both text and images for now—and in the future, videos and audio. LaMDA is a model that was designed with conversation in mind but is still a research prototype for now.

Facebook's M2M-100, Amazon Translate, and other AI-powered translation services that are now available online provide similar services. Amazon Translate, for instance, currently supports translation between 75 languages. According to its website, it uses DL techniques to produce more accurate and fluent translations than traditional statistical and rule-based translation models.

Similar to Google's system, Amazon Translate's NMT system is built on a neural network that takes into account the entire context of the source sentence as well as the translation it has generated so far. Amazon Translate also automatically identifies the source language when it is not specified. For example, user-generated content such as customer reviews and social media streams often do not contain a language code. According to its website, Amazon Translate is ideal for performing both batch translation when you have large quantities of pre-existing text to translate and real-time translation. Communication between your webpage or applications and the Amazon Translate service is protected by SSL encryption.

In 2020, Facebook AI introduced M2M-100—its open-source, multilingual machine translation (MMT) model that can translate between any pair of 100 languages without relying on English data. In its blog, Facebook explains that its "training data set ended up with 7.5 billion parallel sentences of data, corresponding to 2,200 directions. Since the mined data can be used to train two directions of a given language pair (e.g., en->fr and fr->en), our mining strategy helps us effectively sparsely mine to best cover all 100×100 (a total of 9,900) directions in one model".[5] And just as Google does, Facebook's M2M-100 too uses zero-shot settings, in which there are no training data available for a pair of languages.

Microsoft, on its part, has been working with Indian languages for a little over two decades and had launched Project Bhasha in 1998 to accelerate computing in Indian languages. Microsoft currently supports text input in all 22 constitutionally-recognised Indian languages across its products, and Windows interface support in 12 languages. BhashaIndia.com, its portal that provides computing tools for Indic languages, on average receives 40 million hits every year.

Since the early 2000s, Microsoft has been using the traditional Statistical Machine Translation (SMT) paradigm to translate global as well as Indian languages. However, given SMT's limitation of translating a word within the local context of a few surrounding words, Microsoft now uses deep neural networks that have the capability of encoding more granular concepts, such as gender (feminine, masculine, neutral), politeness level (slang, casual, written, formal), and type of word (verb, noun, adjective). Microsoft's conversation translation comes equipped with another satellite deep neural networks-based system called TrueText that filters repetition, pauses, and indifferent words, enhancing the translation's contextual appropriateness.

BOTS SPEAK IN TONGUES TOO

Many enterprises and conversational AI solution developers have been busy developing chatbots of primarily two kinds. The first is enterprise chatbots that are built to solve enterprise use cases such as customer support, lead generation, etc. The second category is direct-to-consumer bots—chatbots that reach the consumer directly for specific applications. However, most enterprise bots currently available are automated versions of frequently asked questions, or FAQs, and are unable to hold conversations beyond the few interactive dialogues.

Bengaluru-based startups such as Tachyon Technologies, Reverie Technologies and Gnani.ai have truly innovated with AI for Indian languages digitisation. While Tachyon developed an IP-based transliteration engine that was made available to consumers free of cost, Reverie Technologies invested time and resources to build a machine translation engine and products and solutions for the enterprise segment.

In October 2018, Reverie launched "Gopal", an interactive voice-based NLP engine in seven Indian languages (Siri for Indian languages). By this time, the company's machine translation engine was at least two years ahead of its nearest competitors—Google and Amazon. This led to the interest of Reliance Jio, and after eight years of being a startup focused on innovating at the intersection of ML and Indian languages digitisation, the company was acquired by Reliance Jio in January 2019 … a mere three months post the launch of its voice engine, Gopal.

Gnani.ai is focused on speech recognition and NLP in multiple Indian languages. The startup uses its core technology to develop multilingual voicebots and speech analytics in multiple channels such as the web, apps, or even on telephone lines, according to Ganesh Gopalan, co-founder of the startup funded by Samsung Ventures.

Other funded mobile-based media startups catering to the non-English speaking populace, such as Dailyhunt and Sharechat, also innovate significantly on the use of AI in Indian languages. I vividly recall my conversation sometime in April 2020 with Umang Bedi, co-founder of the largest local language content platform in the country, Dailyhunt, part of Bengaluru-based Verse Innovation.

Bedi held several leadership positions in his illustrious career, one of them also as managing director of Facebook, India and South Asia. Given his current and past experience, he was an obvious choice to talk about the critical role of regional languages on the internet. More importantly, I wanted to understand his perspective on how AI was helping in the spread of these languages.

Bedi insisted that his startup was "… at the cutting edge of probably having built the gold standard when it comes to AI on local language content across formats".[6] This may sound like a tall claim, but Dailyhunt does run a data set on AI that is over 6–7 petabytes, and is growing by over 8–10 terabytes every day, according to Bedi. The company's learning models are trained on over 250 million pieces of content across audio, video, imagery, and text across 14 local languages, adds Bedi. All the content resides on the Dailyhunt platform. In addition, the company has more than 80 proprietary AI/ML tech models that run to understand the content and the context.

Bedi explains that Dailyhunt looks for adjacencies of keywords to understand the genre and then micro-genres. For instance, if they are comparing three mobile phone players, they look at the social media embeds in those posts. If there is a video, they open up the video and break it up frame by frame in a bid to understand the content. They isolate the audio and look for pattern recognition in terms of what it's saying. Dailyhunt also looks at voice-to-speech conversions to comprehend the language. They do likewise with images. "All in all, when one piece of content is ingested, there is a multi-tiered level of knowledge that is developed on that content across a taxonomy that is then generated with hundreds and hundreds and hundreds and thousands of tags describing that content," Bedi explains.

SUMMING IT UP

Government institutions, technology companies, and startups are doing a stellar job of making us talk in, and understand, different languages. While it's no easy task for machines, advancements in AI are helping them get better with every passing day as they train on millions of words from the internet and other databases. Further, technologies like zero-shot machine translation are making it easier for systems to translate languages even without teaching them to do so. That's the power of AI.

Also, as we have seen from the examples provided above, customers who began deploying chatbots to substitute human interactions when the pandemic broke out are now seeing these bots deliver better returns in terms of efficiency and productivity. Conversion rate, or the metric that measures how many chatbot interactions actually led to purchases, has also increased. These multilingual bots use NLP, and a combination of AI and ML technologies, to understand natural language in spoken or written forms.

That said, consumer interest in these bots will increase as machine intelligence gets more and more intelligent. The diversity, scale, and capabilities available in the Indian market could be leveraged to make an early mark. Last but not least, even as the future of automated conversations is a combination of both voice and text, we can be assured that these advancements will help us understand other languages, and hence their cultures, and enrich ourselves and others.

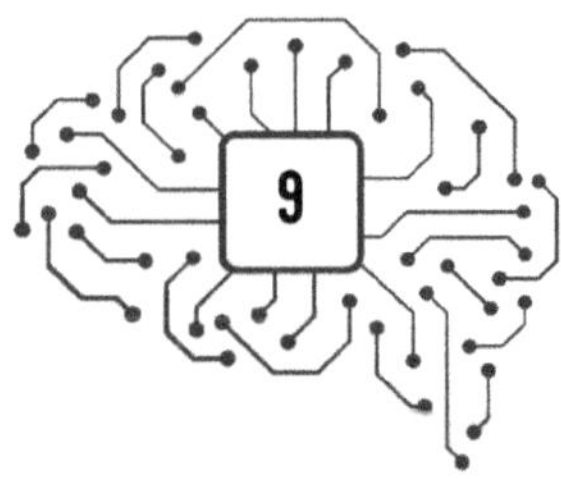

AI INNOVATION ENABLERS

"Never doubt that a small group of thoughtful, committed people can change the world. Indeed, it is the only thing that ever has."
—*Margaret Mead*

I gained my first real education in all things AI—everything beyond the full form of the acronym—in late 2014 while working with this self-educated AI researcher and entrepreneur who did not wish to be named in this book. Let's call him "Prabhu" for the sake of convenience. He came from a humble background in a small village in Karnataka, and soon after completing his Bachelor of Engineering in Computer Science from IIT Madras in 2000, dived headfirst into researching AI. Although a lot of theoretical concepts and research existed at that time, AI was yet to hit the inflexion point in the early 2000s.

Even in mid-2014, when I met Prabhu, there were not many AI-based products or solutions being developed and deployed in the world. That said, the technology was garnering a lot of attention, and it was clear that in a few years, it would be a word to reckon with. As an industry analyst, I wished to learn everything about it. So, when a former Nokia colleague introduced me to Prabhu, who was looking for some advice on business development, product-market fit, and fundraising for some proprietary NLP solutions he had developed, it was only natural for me to grasp the opportunity with both hands.

After graduating from IIT Madras in 2000, Prabhu launched a string of companies with his friends and former classmates, dabbling both in services and product development like all first-generation Indian technology entrepreneurs. None of the companies survived, nor did the partnerships with any of his co-founders or the core team members. But he continued with his research and focus on building AI-based products.

Over the years, he built a machine-transliteration engine for Indian languages, acquired two patents for the underlying algorithms and software, continuously fine-tuned it to improve accuracy, and hosted it live on a website for free public use. In mid-2014, when we met, this was the best Indic languages digitisation machine-transliteration engine in the country, but it was not generating any revenue.

Like most of the AI technology researchers and product entrepreneurs in India, Prabhu focused a lot on data collation, innovative data vectorisation methods that could make codes execute faster, the algorithm, and its accuracy but very little on the productisation of the solution or even less on its revenue-generation capabilities. Even during the decade-and-a-half of his deep technology research and solution development, he was mostly self-driven—learning from books, experimenting with his algorithm, and reaching out to peers and other researchers around the world—with very little help from the Indian ecosystem.

Whatever little assistance Prabhu got in India was from his former professor at IIT Madras for statistical modelling but hardly any from the investor community, potential customers, research ecosystem, or the industry at large. One can argue that Prabhu's research and innovation in AI were way ahead of the curve for the industry, but the fact is that he and his team also lacked structured, comprehensive support from research and innovation-focused entities simply because there were hardly any back then in the country.

Any sufficiently-innovative AI product or solution developed in India up until 2018 came from professionals passionate about AI, and long-term researchers. Most of these professionals hailed from government research institutions such as the Defence Research and Development Organisation (DRDO), National Aerospace Laboratories (NAL), ISRO, Centre for Development of Advanced Computing (CDAC), etc. It was logical—these agencies had access to resources such as large amounts of data, high-performance computing, grants, and, most importantly, time to indulge in prolonged research. As an example, two of the three co-founders of Reverie Technologies—the Indic languages digitisation machine-translation company—were ex-employees of CDAC. Consequently, those who made a substantial contribution or accomplished much in the field of AI research, innovation, and product development, had mostly to fend for themselves.

Sometime in 2018, a couple of years after AI innovation and product development globally hit the inflexion point, Indian technology entrepreneurs started developing and launching AI- and ML-based solutions. These were primarily profiling engines, recommendation engines and predictive models—all of which use advanced data analytics and ML algorithms; chatbots that use text-based NLP; and the development of Alexa skills or voice-based NLP.

Since then, there have been conscious efforts to dedicate resources and launch programmes and initiatives to aid AI innovation—from incubators, accelerators, and industry bodies focusing on AI cohorts, colleges and universities extending their research, and venture capital firms and investors carving out AI funds, to large companies launching startup outreach programmes that focus on AI product development. Most of these programmes and initiatives focus primarily on mentoring, business development assistance, fundraising exposure and matchmaking, platforms for knowledge-sharing, talent acquisition and, more commonly, office space provisioning. While none of these is comprehensive or complete, they are nevertheless making efforts in the right direction. Here are some examples.

NASSCOM 10,000 STARTUPS

Launched in April 2013, 10,000 Startups is an initiative by the industry body NASSCOM to scale up the startup ecosystem in India. The initiative began its journey with the aim of enabling incubation, funding, and support for 10,000 technology startups in India over the next 10 years. The programme's vision has been to foster entrepreneurship, build entrepreneurial capabilities at scale, and strengthen early-stage support for technology startups.

With over 5,800 startups graduating from the initiative, more than 3,500 events and programmes, over 500 startup-corporate connects, 400 startups in global ecosystems, and over 150 new product concepts, NASSCOM's 10,000 Startups programme has played a key role in making India one of the top three startup ecosystems in the world. The programme has leveraged NASSCOM's long history and access to key technology companies and personnel globally to build a strong partner network and ecosystem of companies, mentors, and investors.

The initiative has three key programmes:

Incubate, a programme targeting fundamentals through live and virtual courses, aims to improve startup survival rate and generate more business and better product concepts. Each warehouse (physical space) is supported and funded by the respective state governments.

NIPP, or the NASSCOM Industry Partnership Programme, creates a seamless junction for corporates and startups to innovate and integrate products. This allows the entry of new corporates, more proofs-of-concept (POCs), and successful product integration.

Integrate (Global Acceleration) creates hubs for Indian startups in key global markets, facilitates collaboration and operation of global startups in India and aims to improve the perception of India across the startup world. (Disclosure: I was a mentor for the Integrate programme in 2019, focusing especially on deep tech startups.)

This programme was also one of the first startup enablers in the country that got its investor partners to structure and invest patient capital in deep tech startups, of which the leading ones are AI startups. Patient capital is another name for long-term capital. With patient capital, the investor is willing to make a financial investment in a business with no expectation of turning a quick profit. Instead, the investor is willing to forgo an immediate return in anticipation of more substantial returns down the road.

This is extremely important for the AI startup ecosystem as, at the nascent stage of technology development and innovation, the entrepreneurs would require capital resources for sustained periods as they launch "ahead-of-the-curve" AI products and solutions and work towards making them mainstream.

NASSCOM DEEPTECH CLUB

The NASSCOM DeepTech Club (DTC) programme is designed to nurture and promote the evolution of world-class Indian deep tech startups on global diasporas. The programme is dedicated to leveraging Indian deep technology companies to solve global challenges.

DTC tries to find world changing startups that are enabled by AI, ML, AR, VR, IoT, robotics, blockchain, NLP, and similar technologies. The central focus of the DTC programme is to act as a catalyst in empowering pioneers among India-based deep tech startups and connect them with industry leaders, investors, academia, researchers, and government regulators to establish a global deep tech ecosystem impacting physical and digital transformation.

DTC offers mentoring, nurturing, and thriving opportunities to its member companies and trains them to be more innovative, robust, and agile. The startup companies at DTC have experienced strategic transformation through industry-led confluences, conferences, and networking events with the presence of global partners and leaders.

DTC is a club of identified and curated deep tech companies that will be recognised, nurtured, and promoted by NASSCOM via various programmes, platforms, and events. The Club has three key segments:

Lab-to-Market: Academic or research projects or companies currently being incubated in campus or research institutions

Pre-Revenue: Companies in product development or not customer-validated yet

Post-Revenue: Companies with customers using the product

Launched in 2017, the pursuit of DTC is to reach a mile deep in solving global challenges. Since 2017, the programme has received more than 900 applications from all over India. Over the years, DTC has helped companies raise $70 million and has brought deep tech startup companies from the lab to market-ready global ground. DTC is the leading emerging deep tech startup programme in all of India. Some of the most innovative and leading AI companies, such as AllGoVision, Active.ai, Yellow Messenger, Senseforth, and Wesense.ai, have been the mentees of this programme. (Disclosure: Jayanth is a mentor in the NASSCOM DeepTech Club.)

Apart from industry bodies, many global companies, including core technology giants such as Google, Amazon and Microsoft, and other non-core technology companies such as Deutsche Bank, Airbus, etc., have been successfully running startup outreach programmes as a part of their innovation initiatives. In the last few years, these programmes have been focusing on AI products and solutions.

GOOGLE FOR STARTUPS ACCELERATOR

'Google For Startups' is a three-month, equity-free digital accelerator programme for high-potential Seed to Series A technology startups based in India. This accelerator is focused on supporting innovative and unique startups that are solving societal and economic challenges specific to India using advanced (deep) technologies.

Startups will receive mentorship and support from key Google personnel in AI/ML, cloud, UX, Android, web, product strategy, and marketing. The programme benefits include mentoring from over 20 Google teams such as Android, cloud, ML, and web; access to Google's global network of industry experts and mentors; partnership on a deep technology project; technical training on design, people, product, and growth marketing; support on high-level company and product strategy; early access to new Google products and tools, and Google product credits (such as Google Cloud, TensorFlow, etc.).

Zyla, a personal health management app that empowers patients to make informed decisions about their own diabetes, high blood pressure, and cholesterol issues, has been a part of the Google For Startups Accelerator (GFSA) programme in India. Being a part of GFSA helped Zyla's team push the boundaries of their AI algorithm in terms of capabilities such as higher performance, accuracy and low latency, and cost optimisation. Zyla currently caters to over 1,25,000 patients across 595 cities and towns, and in 10 Indian languages.

AMAZON-AWS ACTIVATE AND PROPEL

Amazon Web Services (AWS) has begun its startup engagement in India with a set of over half a dozen tools to monitor and manage its cloud computing costs. AWS Activate, a programme for early-stage startups launched in October 2013, provides startups with free tools and resources to get started quickly on AWS and accelerate their growth and development on top of the AWS Cloud.

The five key tools that are a part of this programme are AWS Cost Explorer, AWS Budgets, AWS Trusted Advisor, AWS Well-Architected Tool and AWS Activate. As a part of this programme, a technology startup could receive $1,00,000 in credits from AWS if the startups are funded and/or supported by VCs, incubators, and accelerators. Leading Indian technology startups, including HackerEarth, Capillary, Nearbuy, Yelo, Lenskart, Craftsvilla, Cure.Fit, INDwealth, Upstox, and CleverTap, have benefited through Amazon's Activate programme. And almost all of these companies use AI technologies to improve their core offerings.

In January 2021, Amazon partnered with the Indian government's "Startup India" programme to launch an accelerator programme, Propel, for early-stage Indian consumer brands focused on selling their products to customers in global markets. Propel, which is part of Amazon's Global Selling programme, will look to identify 10 early-stage consumer product startups in India, mentor them and help them build successful export businesses with insights and learnings from other brands that sell on Amazon.

Amazon has also partnered with Sequoia Capital India and Fireside Ventures to aid the startups in potentially raising capital from the VCs, while the top three startups in the programme will also have a chance to win a $50,000 equity-free grant from the company. The accelerator programme will have a six-week mentorship event for startups, during which they will also receive aid from Amazon to launch their products on its global selling programme, providing them access to the US firm's 15 other marketplaces, including the US, Germany, and Japan.

MICROSOFT

Microsoft in India has multiple technology startup accelerator programmes and initiatives. And, with the company's core offerings panning across cloud and AI/ML technologies, the technology giant offers support and innovation enablement in many forms. Some of their programmes in India include:

Bizspark: A Microsoft flagship initiative, BizSpark supports early-stage startups by giving them free access to Microsoft Azure cloud services—the most comprehensive set of compliance offerings of any cloud service provider—and other software solutions.

Microsoft Accelerator: Microsoft Accelerator empowers startups to scale up their businesses and succeed by providing consulting services, technology and infrastructure support, and opportunities to connect with investors and customers.

Partner Accelerator: Microsoft's Partner Accelerator model helps in creating better quality startups and boosts their performance with a number of technology solutions. The programme also provides curriculum guidance for startup acceleration.

Cloud Accelerator Program: The Microsoft Cloud Accelerator Program helps Indian enterprises and government organisations.

100X100X100: Microsoft launched the 100X100X100 programme for B2B SaaS startups in India in February 2020. A first-of-its-kind programme in India, this initiative helps bring together 100 committed companies and 100 early and growth startups that have enterprise-ready solutions to offer. Each participating company will commit to spending $1,00,000 over the course of 18 months on solutions provided by the SaaS startups. More than 50 startups are part of the programme at launch.

Microsoft for Startups: This facilitates early-stage B2B startups in leveraging Microsoft's Azure marketplace, enterprise sales team, and rapidly growing partner ecosystem.

Microsoft ScaleUp: This programme is designed for startups at the Series A to Series C funding level.

Through its cutting-edge technology expertise, strong focus on Microsoft for Startups, a growing partner ecosystem, and the venture fund M12, Microsoft is fairly well positioned to help startups evolve from being market-ready to being enterprise-ready. Through its various startup outreach initiatives and programmes, the company offers:

Access to its various technology platforms, which enable startups to innovate and build on their own terms. Azure credits, comprehensive training programmes, and technical support aim to ensure competitiveness.

Mentorship in the form of deep technical expertise and immersive industry experiences focused on business outcomes, delivered at Microsoft and industry startup events.

Access to partners across the ecosystem (startups, VCs, accelerators, incubators), which helps startups in connecting with the right players who can accelerate their development.

Support for streamlined **go-to-market (GTM)** activities across the globe.

Industry bodies and global companies, too, have partnered with state governments and higher educational institutes to launch structured deep-tech innovation programmes and initiatives. Some of them are:

KERALA STARTUP MISSION

Although started in 2007, the Kerala Startup Mission (KSUM) has garnered momentum only in recent years. KSUM was formerly known as the 'Technopark Technology Business Incubator' and is a shining light when it comes to technology incubators in India.

It is one of the leading non-academic startup incubators and houses Asia's largest IT park called Technopark.

KSUM has been set up in a joint association with Technopark, Trivandrum, and the department of science and technology (DST) of the Government of India. Spread over 20,000 square feet, the incubator is among the leading startup incubators in India. It supports and nurtures over 550 startups in Kerala. KSUM has over 193 boot camps that have accommodated over 10,000 engineering students across the country. The programme offers equity funding of over $1,10,000. Over

550 startups have graduated from this programme, and some of the leading ones include Codesap Technologies, Axen Software, EatAbhi, Kappian, and Genrobotics.

TECHNOLOGY HUB

Technology Hub (T-Hub) works on the helix model and is a public/private partnership between the Government of Telangana, some private players, and three academic institutes—IIIT Hyderabad, Indian School of Business, and National Academy of Legal Studies and Research (NALSAR).

T-Hub aims to transform Hyderabad into a startup city and Telangana into a startup state. T-Hub's campus is spread over 70,000 square feet. Having started in 2015, this incubator has nurtured over 550 startups to date, including Hug Innovations, AnyTimeLoan, Radikal Tribe, and Banyan Nation.

CENTRE FOR INNOVATION INCUBATION AND ENTREPRENEURSHIP, IIM AHMEDABAD

The Centre for Innovation Incubation and Entrepreneurship (CIIE) was set up by the Indian Institute of Management (IIM) Ahmedabad with support from the Gujarat government and the Central Government. The incubator operates through an autonomous not-for-profit entity model and comprises IIM-A faculty, alumni, and other individuals to boost entrepreneurship through incubation, academic initiatives, and several other programmes. Having started in 2007, with facilities in both Ahmedabad and Pune, the centre has supported over 500 startups, including Ridlr, Zuvvu, Mobident, MedCall, InSolare, and Agricx.

SOCIETY FOR INNOVATION AND ENTREPRENEURSHIP, IIT BOMBAY

The Society for Innovation and Entrepreneurship (SINE) is a broad-spectrum tech business incubator hosted at the Indian Institute of Technology (IIT) Bombay. It incubates tech startups that are founded by students of IIT Bombay. SINE provides maximum incubation support for three years.

Besides incubation, SINE also provides shared workspaces and access to technical resources, facilitates business networking, and provides seed funding of up to $37,000–44,000 (Rs 25–30 lakh) to incubated companies. Unlike other incubation centres, SINE does not have a batch system; it accepts incubation proposals all year. Started in 2004 out of the IIT Bombay campus, the incubator has nurtured over 150 startups, including some of the leading ones in the country, such as ideaForge, Myzus, Voyager Infotech, and Exodus Networks

WHY CHINA REMAINS WAY AHEAD

Despite several programmes and initiatives by various key stakeholders in the ecosystem, there is no structured or comprehensive end-to-end overarching entity or programme.

Most of the companies involved in AI research, innovation, and product development in India are, hence, currently left with semi-structured programmes. In this context, there is much to be learnt from a country that has done a comprehensive job of AI innovation development—China.

On July 20, 2017, China's State Council released their New Generation Artificial Intelligence Development Plan. Within this plan, they acknowledged that "there is still a gap between China's overall level of development of AI relative to that of developed countries—lacking major original results in the basic theory, core algorithms, key equipment, high-end chips, major products and systems, foundational materials, components, software and interfaces, etc. Scientific research institutions and enterprises do not yet possess international influence upon ecological cycles and supply chains, lacking systematic research and development layout; cutting-edge talent for AI is far from meeting demand. Adapting to the development of AI requires the urgent improvement of basic infrastructure, policies and regulations, and standards systems."

To close the gap and leapfrog other developed countries and become "the world's primary AI innovation center" by 2030, China recognised the need to address its entire AI ecosystem. China developed a comprehensive list of tasks that would enable them to achieve such a lofty goal. These included focusing on increasing the supply of AI innovation sources, forcefully (yes, you read this right) developing smart enterprises, promoting the use of AI for social governance and enhancing public safety and security capabilities, and strengthening the new generation of AI with the convergence of major scientific and technological projects, technological breakthroughs, and product development applications.

It also involved providing financial support from the government in the form of subsidies too, forging partnerships of local AI enterprises with leading AI schools and research institutes, encouraging foreign AI enterprises and research institutes to establish research and development centres in China, training the AI labour force, and improving key AI policies while establishing an AI technology standards and intellectual property system.

China divided the ownership of these tasks among four organisations. The National Science and Technology Structural Reform and Innovation System Construction Leading Small Group was given

---

Strategic Objectives:

1. By 2020, China is supposed to have achieved iconic advances in AI models and methods, core devices, high-end equipment, and foundational software. The AI industry's competitiveness will have entered the first echelon internationally, with a number of high-level personnel and innovation teams, and initially establishing AI ethical norms, policies, and regulations in some areas.

2. By 2025, AI becomes the main driving force for China's industrial upgrading and economic transformation, as AI with autonomous learning ability achieves breakthroughs in many areas to obtain leading research results. This new-generation AI will be widely used in intelligent manufacturing, intelligent medicine, intelligent city, intelligent agriculture, national defense construction, and other fields. Thus China will have seen the initial establishment of AI laws and regulations, ethical norms and policy systems, and the formation of AI security assessment and control capabilities.

3. By 2030, China's AI theories, technologies, and applications should achieve world-leading levels, making China the world's primary AI innovation center. China will have established a number of world-leading AI technology innovation and bases, and the country will achieve major breakthroughs in brain-inspired intelligence, autonomous intelligence, hybrid intelligence, swarm intelligence, and other areas. AI should be greatly expanded into production and livelihood, social governance, national defense construction, and in all aspects of applications. Additionally, China will have constructed more comprehensive AI laws and regulations, and an ethical norms and policy system.

leadership of comprehensive planning and coordination. The Ministry of Science and Technology, together with relevant departments, was given responsibility for the implementation of major science and technology programmes for a new generation of AI. China established the AI Plan Implementation Office (within the Ministry of Science and Technology) to be responsible for implementation and the AI Strategy Advisory Committee to own far-sighted, strategic questions concerning AI and advise on major policy decisions.

If the New Generation Artificial Intelligence Development Plan is successful, China expects to achieve the following strategic and economic objectives:

LEARNINGS FROM CHINA

Patents

A strong indicator of a country's ability to enable innovation in its AI ecosystem is through analysing its annual patent applications. When the New Generation Artificial Intelligence Development Plan was released in 2017, China submitted 90,709 AI-related patent applications. In 2018, that number grew to 1,23,958. In 2019, AI-related patent applications reached 1,46,133, and China surpassed the United States as the country

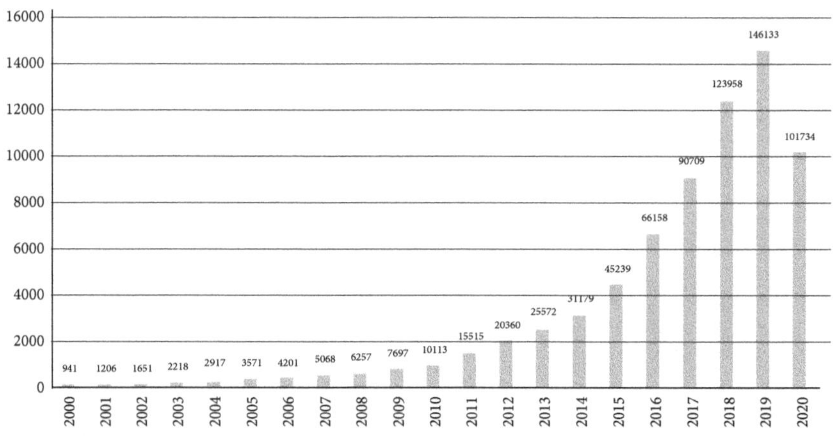

(Fig. 1) Annual Trend for AI Patent Applications in China

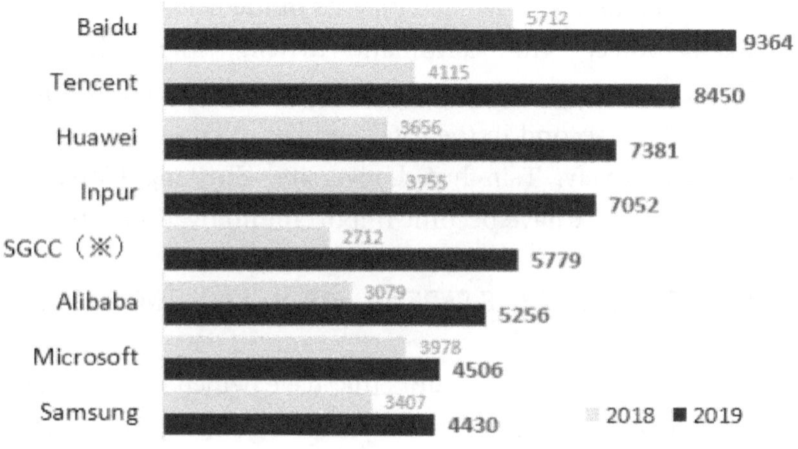

〈Fig. 2〉Top Applicants for AI Patent Applications in 2018 & 2019

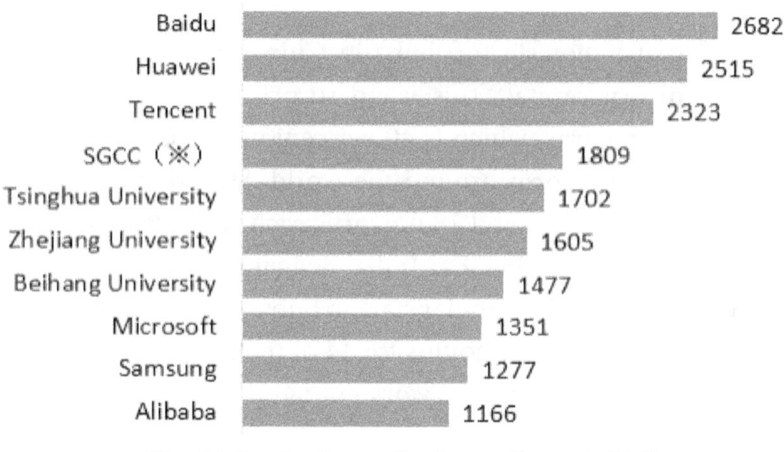

〈Fig. 3〉Top Applicants for Patent Grants in 2019

(※) SGCC: State Grid Corporation of China

with the largest number of AI-patent applications. As of October 2020, 1,01,734 AI-related patent applications have been submitted, despite the COVID-19 outbreak. This has led to China reaching 6,94,000 total AI-related patent applications, with 3,71,825 of them being submitted between 2018 and October 2020.

Among companies and universities that have filed AI patents, Baidu (China's Google counterpart) is in the leading position with 9,364 patent applications and 2,682 grants and ranks first in the number of patent applications and granted patents in the fields of DL technology, intelligent voice, NLP, automatic driving, knowledge mapping, intelligent recommendation, transportation big data, etc., while Huawei ranks third and second in the total number of patent applications and grants, respectively. Tsinghua University, Zhejiang University, and Beihang University have become important innovation subjects in AI.

CHINA VS. INDIA: STARTUP HUBS AND INCUBATORS

China had over 11,800 incubators that have helped more than 6,20,000 startup companies in 2018 alone. In contrast to China, India has merely 520 incubators that can support around 6,200 startups every year. At this rate, China can produce 100x more startups every year as compared to India.

Looking at major startup hubs in China, Beijing is known as the world's unicorn capital. This is no surprise, considering the city is home to 82 unicorns, which is 40 per cent of China's unicorns and 16 per cent of all unicorns around the world. Shanghai, Hangzhou, and Shenzhen, with 47, 19, and 18 unicorns each, are also among the other top startup hubs in China. For India, Bengaluru, Delhi-NCR, Mumbai, and Hyderabad are the popular startup hubs. Out of 30-odd unicorns in India, Bengaluru alone accounts for 14 of them. India, however, clearly has a long road ahead, and its work cut out.

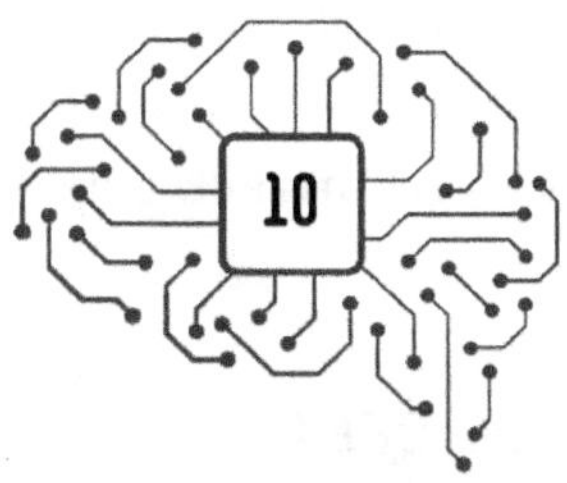

LEARNING AI FROM MNCS

"Learning never exhausts the mind."

—*Leonardo da Vinci*

Throughout this book, we have underscored the fact that India has all the makings of a robust AI ecosystem, which spells good news for companies that use AI. Accenture predicts that AI can add about $1 trillion to India's economy in 2035. While AI startups and conglomerates in India will play a key role in bringing about this AI transformation, it's equally important to recognise the contribution of multinationals or MNCs who have led the charge on AI development and operations in India.

This is hardly a surprising fact given the wide variety of IT-ITeS (IT-enabled Services), electronics, and technology firms in this category that have large talent pools in the country and have historically leveraged this workforce to serve their global interests. This includes MNC IT services firms (Accenture, IBM, Capgemini, and others), software technology firms (Microsoft, Google, SAP, and others), hardware technology, network equipment, and telecom firms (Cisco, Juniper, and others), and electronics and semiconductor firms (Qualcomm, Intel, and others).

Today, most of these firms are operating specialised AI research centres in India, which contribute towards their global initiatives within this space. Further, this broad-based MNC category contributes to approximately 36 per cent of the AI market in India. There are three main prisms through which these firms have evolved when looking at India from an AI perspective: India as an AI back office, India as an R&D centre, and India as an AI market. Let's take a look at each one of them.

INDIA AS AN AI BACK OFFICE

Global IT services firms such as IBM, Accenture, and Deloitte started early in leveraging Indian operations to drive global AI and other next-gen technology support operations. As early as 1998, IBM research in India started focusing on next-gen technologies in collaboration with leading academic institutions in India.

Taking a cue from these large global players, India's flagship IT-BPM (business process management) industry (earlier known as the BPO sector) also took early strides into leveraging AI initiatives as they looked towards offering additional value to their clients. TCS, Infosys, and Wipro invested early and heavily in cloud and AI infrastructure as their key client verticals (e.g., BFSI) moved swiftly towards automation.

Consider these examples. TCS's Digitate launched a product called Ignio, the "world's first cognitive system for enterprise IT". Ignio aims to rapidly identify root causes and automate routine tasks. Infosys launched Mana to automate repetitive and commoditised software maintenance tasks. Building on this, Infosys later launched Nia, which can tackle more complex problems around revenue forecasting, product recommendations, and customer behaviour understanding, among others. Likewise, Wipro launched its in-house AI platform HOLMES, aimed at helping digital transformation through algorithmic intelligence and cognitive computing capabilities.

TCS's Ignio, Infosys's Mana and Nia, and Wipro's HOLMES were the result of focused and early investment in AI-based capabilities at these IT giants—all of which have resulted in credible benefits for their clients and increased digital revenues for the companies. The fact that these firms have gone on to set up service lines/business units dedicated to these AI and related initiatives speaks volumes of the kind of traction that these initiatives have generated.

INDIA AS AN R&D CENTRE

These developments were not limited to larger firms. Smaller firms took on data cleaning, structuring, and vectorisation as a service to support MNCs in their AI operations. India has also been fast emerging as an AI R&D centre. Currently, India is the second-largest global hub in the training and hiring of AI talent (the first being the US), accelerated by the rapid growth in AI applications. MNCs have been driving R&D in AI via various initiatives, ranging from strategic innovation management in the ecosystem to research labs and large-scale R&D centres and centres of excellence, or CoEs.

In addition to developing internal capabilities, large MNCs have also extensively reached out to foster innovation in the larger ecosystem—via startup outreach, incubator programmes, and other collaborations.

For e.g., Microsoft Startup hub has unveiled initiatives curated for AI-focused startups, with AI Innovate (II) inviting nominations from SaaS startups built on AI technologies. As part of this, startups get to work closely with Microsoft engineering and product teams to develop their core AI models and have access to other nurturing and support opportunities. While many of these initiatives introduce and evangelise Microsoft products and offerings, they also drive the ecosystem forward.

There are many examples of how early-stage AI research has found real-life applications in India, many of which we have covered in the earlier chapters. We have listed some here too, in case you missed reading them earlier. Diabetic retinopathy screenings supported by AI engines at the back-end, for instance, have helped physicians at a south Indian eye hospital to focus more on working with patients on treatment/management, while increasing, at the same time, the volume of screenings done. Using AI and physics-based modelling, pilot initiatives in parts of India have been building flood forecasting models that predict the timing, the location as well as the severity of flooding events, thus enabling timely intervention.

That's not all. Researchers from Google Research and IIT Madras worked with an NGO (that sends timely and targeted preventive care information to expectant and new mothers) to design an AI technology that could predict the women who were at risk of dropping out from the health information programme and accordingly intervene early—bringing down the risk of dropouts by 32 per cent and improving maternal health outcomes at large. AI4Bharat and IIT Madras, with support from Google, developed state-of-the-art NLU tools to develop open-language models for two low-resource languages (Konkani, Maithili), making story reading easier for 70,000+ children.

The success of these early-stage research applications in delivering real-world outcomes has further encouraged technology MNCs to look at how next generation technologies can help address large-scale problems. Google's AI for Social Good and Microsoft's AI for Good are examples of technology firms working with social-impact organisations to explore and evaluate areas where AI can help bring large-scale societal impact. We have dedicated a whole chapter (Chapter 9) to this space.

On the back of successful early-stage applications and as recognition of the capabilities of the AI ecosystem and workforce in India, MNCs are also deploying large-scale research capabilities in India. Consider the example of Google Research India—an AI lab based out of Bengaluru that is focusing on both advancing the frontiers of computer science by building a strong research team and driving research collaborations as well as applying this research to tackle the big problems in society today, be it in healthcare, agriculture, or education. This lab will be part of and support the global network of researchers and looks towards building an ecosystem through collaborative work with India's scientific research community.

We also have the Robert Bosch Centre for Data Science and AI, which was founded in 2017 at IIT Madras with the aim of expanding both research and education in AI and data science. Interdisciplinary in nature, the Centre hosts researchers who are leveraging AI in their respective domains—both basic and applied—to unlock its full potential in real-world applications.

INDIA AS AN AI MARKET

As India surges ahead in its digital evolution, Indian businesses—both old and new—are looking to leverage technology to solve a range of business problems. As per a recent NASSCOM study, 65 per cent of organisations have a defined AI strategy at a functional or enterprise level. While process optimisation remains a key driver of this adoption, there is an increasing focus on other customer-centric objectives as well.

MNCs are waking up to this opportunity. Microsoft announced plans to partner with more than 650 vendors to deploy AI-driven solutions in India, including fraud detection, customer segmentation, and demand forecasting, among others. Bestseller India worked with IBM on an AI-powered fashion planning and forecasting tool, heralding a cultural shift for the fashion industry from a "gut"-based approach to an approach rooted in data and analytics. This shift is not limited to large companies either—with SMBs also increasingly looking to leverage technology for better outcomes.

Amazon launched SMB Vidyalaya, a technology upskilling programme to help SMBs digitise their operations and offerings by using AWS Cloud—their experience suggests that companies are moving beyond just shifting applications to the cloud and thinking more deeply about modernisation and driving innovation around these.

Not just businesses, Indian government bodies (Central and state) are also opening up to the possibilities of AI for larger societal benefits, from empowering citizens with actionable insights for agriculture to driving data-based policy design. As an example, Microsoft worked with the Karnataka Agricultural Price Commission, under the state's Department of Agriculture, where using remote-sensing data from satellite images, farmers received sowing advisories for different climates as well as pricing predictions for crops.

This evolution of AI in India is still in its early stages. While the current rate of investment in AI in India has been growing at a CAGR of 30.8 per cent, it still contributes to only 2.5 per cent of global investments. NASSCOM estimates that AI adoption can add $500 billion to India's GDP by 2025, with the four key verticals of BFSI, consumer products and retail, healthcare, and industrial and automotive contributing 60 per cent of this value addition.

MNCs have laid the groundwork in terms of developing the capability and ecosystem—and India has all the ingredients it needs to drive this revolution forward. A young and diverse population that is hungry to improve its livelihood, familiarity, and early adoption of technology, whether voice or digital payments, and importantly, the democratisation of internet access and the learning tools it provides across all of India's languages—all will contribute towards greater adoption and innovation in the country.

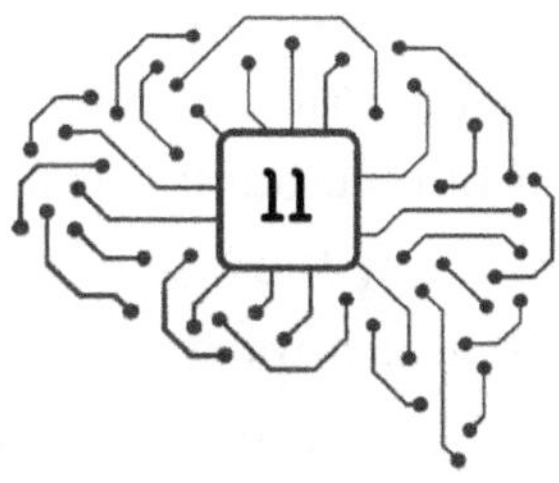

FROM APP TO SUPER APP

"If WeChat was a person, it would be your best friend based on the amount of time you spend on it. So, how could we put an advertisement on the face of your best friend? Every time you see them, you would have to watch an advertisement before you could talk to them."

—*Allen Zhang*

On December 20, 1990, Sir Tim Berners-Lee gave birth to the world's first website at a laboratory in the European Organization for Nuclear Research, better known as CERN. It was a simple page that explained how hypertext markup language, or HTML, worked. That page changed our world.

Five years later, India got its taste of the first publicly available internet service when state-owned Videsh Sanchar Nigam Limited (VSNL) launched the service on August 15, 1995. Those of us who were adults then will recall that we had to access the internet using modems that emitted guttural sounds as they painfully tried to connect us to cyberspace.

Yet, no one complained since we were just discovering the power of online. The modems were, in fact, heralding the age of the dotcom boom. As speeds began improving in the late 1990s, thousands of cybercafés and shops mushroomed, offering to develop websites for businesses with online addresses or URLs that ended in .com, which explains the word dotcom. Most of these skeletal web pages were aimed at helping businesses advertise their wares online too, a trend that has been well-documented by numerous authors.

Even when the dotcom bubble burst around 2000–01, websites did not die. Simultaneously, we saw the rise of web portals. True to their definition of being a large and imposing doorway, entrance, or gate, these web portals aimed at becoming one-stop destinations for their users. Their purpose was to attract more and more traffic, thus gaining more views and selling space to potential advertisers.

Even today, we see huge company and government portals that offer a variety of services and also accept payments for the same. Web portals, though, are spoken about in the context of accessing the internet on your desktops and laptops. However, while our online surfing habits changed dramatically with the advent of smartphones, the pattern that businesses adopted to sell their wares on smartphones is similar.

We now can access thousands of apps on our mobiles for every conceivable task—be it to check our fitness level, buy clothes or books, listen to podcasts, shop for groceries, buy food, or whatever. What if all these tasks can be bundled into one app? You're on the right track if you're thinking of a web portal for smartphones. We call them "Super Apps".

Web portals typically had a search engine and a payment gateway for their numerous services and products. Super apps, however, are a much-advanced version of web portals since they have two superpowers—the first is the power of data analytics, and the second is AI.

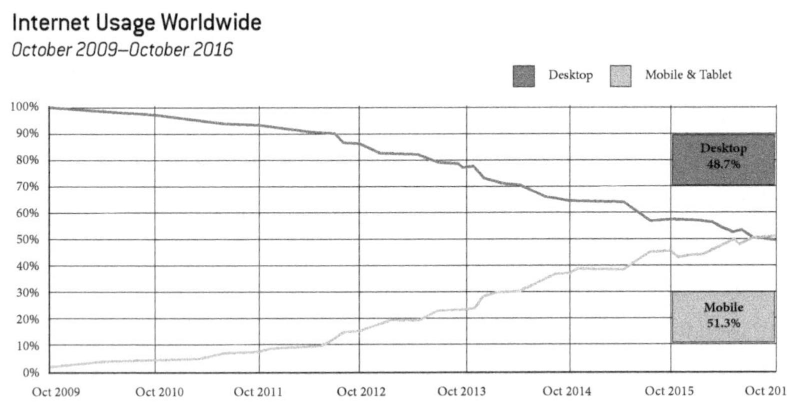

A super app is the smartphone mobile app version of the all-in-one, or most-in-one, platform that caters to an average user's daily needs. In the offline world, think of a large mall, like the Mall of America or the Ambience Mall in Gurugram.

A sufficiently large and well-planned mall will have all kinds of outlets for utility, shopping, entertainment, productivity, food, etc. From car wash and maintenance to all kinds of retail outlets, supermarkets, theatres, play areas, and live shows to banks and learning centres, and all kinds of cafés, bars, and restaurants, the mall offers a one-stop shop for most of an average visitor's needs—from mundane to special.

A good mall is designed not only to cater to the needs of its visitors but also to ensure that they spend a maximum amount of time (and money) once they enter. Over time, the mall ends up becoming the top-of-mind choice for consumers. This philosophy from the offline, brick-and-mortar retail world has been adopted in the online world by consumer internet companies—first in the desktop internet (Web 1.0) era by players such as Google and Yahoo, and later by players in the Mobile Internet era.

Sometime leading up to October 2016, when mobile internet data usage around the world was surpassing desktop internet usage, companies around the world, especially technology companies, needed to come up with a "mobile strategy". As smartphones and mobile data led the mobile internet era evolution, the principle of ensuring that most of the internet user's time is spent on their platform was recognised by consumer internet and technology companies. This need, this trend of one app being the single platform to cater to most of the user's requirements or a platform of apps that do, is the current evolution of the super app.

As we pointed out in the first chapter of this book, conglomerates such as Reliance Industries, Tata Group, and Adani Group are pulling out all the stops to build so-called super apps for their respective organisations as part of the larger digital transformation story.

The super app phenomenon began in East Asia with Chinese company Tencent's popular mobile instant messaging app, WeChat, evolving into a "platform of apps". Back in early 2019, Paytm was the leading contender to become India's super app. But that was until the large conglomerates of India decided to step into this space.

Mukesh Ambani-owned Reliance Retail initiated a revamp of its MyJio app in August 2021 in a bid to convert it into a super app by integrating various consumer offerings, following its acquisition of local search engine Justdial. The MyJio app bundles over 20 consumer applications, including JioMart for online grocery retail, UPI and payments services, entertainment mini-apps, and mobile recharge options.

Salt-to-software conglomerate Tata Group, too, is reportedly planning to launch a super app through Tata Digital to expand its presence in consumer-facing businesses. Tata Sons plans to invest at least $2 billion in its super app christened, TataNeu, and later raise an additional $5 billion from external investors by selling minority stakes in the digital venture, *Mint* reported on October 25, 2021, citing unnamed sources. The app, when eventually launched, is expected to aggregate all Tata Group services—grocery, lifestyle, electronics, healthcare, finance, etc.—under a single "omnichannel" platform.

Not to be left behind, Ahmedabad-based Adani Group has even set up a new division, Adani Digital Labs, to build its super app. In keeping with this strategy, the group announced the acquisition of a minority stake in online travel aggregator Cleartrip from Flipkart Marketplace on October 29, 2021.

The Mahindra Group, however, is taking a different approach. It does not appear to be enthused with the idea of giving users access to multiple services of an organisation from within a single gigantic app. Instead, the Group, run by Indian billionaire Anand Mahindra, is mulling bringing together services such as farm, agriculture, finance, auto, and even used cars and tractors under a single digital roof and may christen it the "Farmer App".

That said, it's the powerful combination of AI and data that has given super apps these super-high valuations. Jio Platforms is already valued at $65 billion, and its investors include Facebook and Google.

For now, though, let's look at the evolution of super apps as a phenomenon globally. We will address questions such as: Which companies around the world are trying to build super apps? What does it take to build a successful super app? What should companies be looking for? What role does AI play in the success of a super app? What kind of framework will companies need to conduct business in India successfully?

THE WORLD'S FIRST SUPER APP

Chinese company Tencent's mobile instant messaging app—WeChat— evolved into a platform of apps, thus becoming the world's first super app. China is a mobile-first internet country. In August 2018, when the country's internet user base crossed the 800 million active users mark, 788 million were mobile users.[1]

Most of its internet user population has never used desktop computers, and as the app ecosystem on smartphones led by mobile internet grew, the usage patterns and behaviour of the internet users on mobiles started to evolve. The apps and companies that identified and leveraged this trend early were primed to benefit tremendously from the emerging smartphone era. Tencent's WeChat identified and rode this wave in the right way.

It's hardly surprising, then, that the first time I heard of anything close to being a super app was in August 2015 from Connie Chan's blog post on WeChat. Connie Chan was a China-focused analyst at a16z—a leading Silicon Valley technology venture capital firm founded by Andreessen Horowitz. In fact, that was the first time most people around the world got introduced to the concept of a super app, along with the distance WeChat had covered to evolve into one.

For most tech industry folks dependent on the anglicised world to get their data, reports, news, and analysis, accessing information from China, let alone any in-depth analysis, was difficult back in 2015. In such an environment, Connie's comprehensive research, evaluation, and commentary on WeChat provided a glimpse of how a simple mobile app could evolve into a platform unto itself.

It then dawned on me that mobile consumer internet companies have found a way to get what they always wanted—garner as much of their users' time and attention on their platform as possible. Personally, I had always known that consumer internet companies needed to maximise users' time spent (along with garnering data, to profile them accurately). This is one of the most fundamental needs for their existence and growth, but I did not imagine that they would be approaching this objective from the angle that WeChat did.

Known in Chinese as Weixin (微信)—"micro letter"—WeChat is first and foremost a messaging app for sending text, voice, and photos to friends and family. Along with its basic communication features, WeChat users in China can access services to hail a taxi, order food delivery, buy movie tickets, play casual games, check-in for a flight, send money to friends, access fitness tracker data, book a doctor's appointment, get banking statements, pay the water bill, find geo-targeted coupons, recognise music, search for a book at the local library, meet strangers around them, follow celebrity news, read magazine articles, and even donate to charity … all in a single, integrated app.

WeChat was developed in three months as a small-scale, experimental project on Tencent's campus with seven engineers under the aegis of founder Zhang Xiaolong. The first version of the world's largest app with simple messaging and photo-sharing features was launched in early 2011. The voice message function was added three months later. At that time, Tencent's desktop and mobile communication app QQ had a massive following. WeChat allowed users to sync QQ contacts, racking up 100 million users in 433 days. The payment feature was added when the app crossed 300 million users. In mid-2014, WeChat stores popped up. As of Q1 2020, WeChat has over 1.17 billion monthly active users and over a billion active users who spend an average of 66 minutes on the app daily.

In 2011, when WeChat rolled out Message in a Bottle (removed over pornography alarm bells in November 2018), People Nearby and Shake features (to connect with strangers), the app's engagement levels went through the roof. By November 2011, WeChat was clocking 2,00,000 new users per day. WeChat started to cash in on the herd mentality. WeChat allows the mirroring of contacts—both individual and group—from other apps in order to create a network effect. Users tend to stick to platforms that encourage networking and a sense of belonging.

Philosophically, while Facebook and WhatsApp measure growth by the number of daily and monthly active users on their networks, WeChat cares more about how relevant and central WeChat is in addressing the daily—even hourly—needs of its users. Instead of focusing on building the largest social network in the world, WeChat has focused on building a *mobile lifestyle*—its goal is to address every aspect of its users' lives, including non-social ones.

The way it achieves this goal is through one of the most unsurfaced aspects of WeChat: the pioneering model of "apps within an app". Millions (note, not just thousands) of lightweight apps live inside WeChat, much like webpages live on the internet. This makes WeChat more like a browser for mobile websites or, arguably, a mobile operating system—complete with its own proprietary app store. Not what we'd expect from a messaging app.

The lightweight apps on WeChat are called "official accounts". Approved by WeChat after a brief application process, there are well over 10 million of these official accounts on the platform—ranging from celebrities, banks, media outlets, and fashion brands to hospitals, drug stores, car manufacturers, internet startups, personal blogs, and more. It's important to emphasise that these official accounts are nothing like verified accounts on US social networks, where being "official" is mainly a badge of authenticity or identity verification.

On WeChat, official accounts are approved to access exclusive APIs for payments, location, direct messages, voice messages, user IDs, and more. (Not every official account uses these APIs, but there are still millions of them that, indeed, are app-like.)

For the end-user, adding an official account is as simple as adding a friend. Furthermore, because users have to opt-in to official accounts, they are essentially always "logged in" to them. This is especially effective for lower frequency but important services like managing credit card statements or utility bills. Such apps are perfectly suited to the lightweight app model because users are spared the trouble of downloading separate native full-featured apps (yet can still choose to do so if the preview of what the app does seems compelling enough). It's a win-win either way.

Developing official WeChat accounts has become so popular in China that new startups sometimes test their version 1.0 product on WeChat's platform before dedicating resources to building and marketing a standalone native app. Another benefit for developers is getting core app functionality without having to support multiple mobile operating systems (OSes). Developers are also not forced to stay within the look and feel of the WeChat client, i.e., they aren't constrained to some subset of HTML5.

So, when a user interacts with an official account, they can click to a full web application experience without ever leaving WeChat. This empowers developers to deliver distinctive, custom app-like experiences while WeChat enforces the rules—messaging frequency, sensor permissions, etc.—that protect users.

These web-enabled, app-within-an-app official accounts are a breakthrough in messaging. It is also one of many reasons WeChat has become a flourishing platform for any company or influencer that wants a mobile presence in China.

Allen Zhang, also known as the "Father of WeChat", talks about treating users with genuine empathy to ensure the stickiness of products. He believes "product design should not be reduced to 'processes' that can be continuously optimised by data-driven teams". He believes the mission of technology should be solely to improve a user's efficiency and insists that "the larger industry's focus on time spent on the app is flawed". I find a lot of merit in this line of thinking.

BUT WHY BUILD A SUPER APP?

We all belong to the same human species, and yet we differ in many aspects, such as height, weight, attitude, energy levels, wealth, and prosperity, to name a few. But we all have one thing in common, regardless of where we live—the number of hours in a day are the same: 24. Consumer internet companies across the globe—big and small—are competing for that one thing: a user's attention span for all those 24 hours. And they are in the business of ensuring that their users spend maximum time on their products, solutions, and platforms. Hence, big companies are keen on building a super app.

A super app is a tool for large technology companies to build platforms that can attract users on the internet. The more a user spends time on their platforms, across apps, the more the company can earn in terms of revenue, profits, valuation, and, most importantly, influence. This approach also keeps the consumer from using a competitor's products—a strategic move known as "competitive blocking".

A super app can help tremendously in this context since it not only can maximise consumer engagement, usage, and revenue but also ensure that other internet companies do not lure the user. This is one of the key reasons an instant messaging app such as WeChat expanded its services to also offer digital payments, cab and ride-hailing, insurance sales, gaming and multimedia streaming. The idea was to build an all-in-one platform for users.

Companies trying to build a super app chart the daily lives of consumers and build lightweight apps and extensions on their core app, thus evolving it into a platform and an ecosystem unto itself. This will also enable the companies to cross-subsidise and cross-incentivise across various apps and products.

SUPER APP RECIPE

In May 2015, I published an analyst note on the evolution path of mobile internet users in India—how they will start using communication apps (like WhatsApp), and after a few years and scale, some portion of the internet users will evolve into consuming multimedia on mobile devices (music and video streaming) and later, a smaller portion of that user base will evolve into creating content, thereby gradually increasing the per capita consumption of mobile data.

My expectation and views of this evolution were linear. This was how internet users on desktop internet (Web 1.0) had evolved. But the way WeChat has evolved into a super app—starting out as an internet messenger and evolving into an all-in-one app or a platform of apps in a fast and exponential manner—caught my attention.

Fast forward to January 2019; a journalist friend and an industry colleague called me to understand the super app ecosystem in India. At that time, Justdial—a company that provides local search for various services in India—had announced its ambition to evolve into a super app. This journalist friend wanted to discuss the concept, product, market readiness, and the potential of Justdial to become one.

The issue at hand is that every large mobile app and consumer internet company aspires to develop a super app. The way they typically approach the problem is by adding various features and functionalities to their core product and expecting—more like hoping—their app to become a super app. But what most companies seem to forget is that a super app is not just a product. It's an ecosystem.

While discussing this topic with her, I came up with the key criteria and success factors for developing, launching, and growing a super app. The six success factors that emerged out of that 80-minute discussion later evolved into a structured advisory note by Convergence Catalyst. These six key ingredients are critical mass and scale, stickiness, synergy, strong brand, efficient rollout strategy, and execution capabilities.

Critical mass and scale. A company needs to have a large—typically a few million—existing user base for its core product or app. And it needs to be a category leader, such as the leading instant messenger, leading payment, or leading social networking app. A super app, by definition, is a one-stop shop for most of the mobile internet experience of consumers in a market. It is also an app with the highest user base. To achieve this across various apps in its portfolio, the core or the original offering of the company needs to be highly popular, with a large user base and also be a category leader. The room for growth and the capability of the company for rapid scalability are also important factors for building a successful super app.

Stickiness or high engagement of the core app is also an important factor for the development of a successful super app. Just a large user base without high engagement does not make an app ready to evolve into a super app platform. High engagement results in strong familiarity with the app for the consumer and leads to habit formation, both essential underlying factors. That is why, so far, we have seen instant messaging apps, social networking and payments apps (especially in Asia, where digital payments have become a norm since 2017–18) evolve into super apps. By their design and functionality, these apps necessitate interaction and usage multiple times of the day and hence are best positioned to evolve into super app platforms.

Synergy, the next important success factor for building a super app, is to build and launch a product that has synergy with the core app or complements it. For instance, an instant messaging app with a large and highly engaged user base can launch a photo/video-sharing app, social networking, or dating app instead of launching a commerce, food delivery, or ride-hailing app that is unrelated to its core business. Photo/video-sharing and social networking are extended domains of communication, chatting and messaging. From the user behaviour perspective, they would be more willing to think of and recall using an app whose new feature/functionality is in the same or a related domain of the core business.

A strong brand and top-of-mind recall help in marketing new features, services, and products, and lead to strong customer acquisition and usage through network effects. If the core app of the company evolves into the market leader for the category, then it automatically ensures a strong brand development that the company can effectively use to build the user base with minimum effort.

Efficient rollout strategy. The product development roadmap and rollout need to be efficiently planned to ensure maximum uptake and usage of each of the apps and products that form the super app. One key mistake companies make while developing a super app is to launch multiple apps and products together or fairly close to each other. This creates confusion in the user's mind, and the company's core offering fails to be well-established or adopted. This creates a fragmentation of the user base across various apps and products instead of maximising the customers and usage for each app, which leads to the development of a successful super app.

The building of a super app is a multi-year project, and the framework to develop and launch multiple apps on the platform is that of "concentric circles"—launch the core app, garner a critical mass of users and high engagement, launch an adjacent feature or product, spend resources and time to grow the adoption of the latest app, then launch another adjacent product, and so on.

Execution capabilities. Needless to say, building a super app ecosystem requires all-around concerted efforts by various teams and functions in the company. Beyond designing the apps and products with the right feature set and user interface, the adoption and growth of each of the apps on the super app platform will depend on the right mix of marketing, communication, incentives, value offered, ecosystem partnerships, network effects, and competitive advantage.

No app platform can evolve into a super app if most of its apps are among the category leaders and together, the ecosystem does not hold the maximum amount of users' attention and time spent on the internet on its platform. And to achieve this, the all-around, multi-disciplinary execution capabilities of the company building the super app need to be great.

EMERGING SUPER APPS AROUND THE WORLD

Meta (formerly Facebook): With its Metaverse ambitions, this is one company that is extremely well positioned to evolve as a super app, globally. Apart from its core social networking platform, its various in-house products such as Messenger, Libra, etc., when combined with its acquisitions such as Instagram and WhatsApp, make the company extremely well positioned to evolve as a super app. The company, in 2016, through Facebook Messenger, tried to evolve as a lightweight platform for third-party applications and evolve Messenger as a super app. However, there was not adequate focus on that strategy, and Facebook as such is not yet seen as a super app. Having said that, the company has multiple properties and has been making all the right moves to evolve into one.

The Cambridge Analytica data security scandal, the European Union's anti-trust campaign against the company, and a lot of media and government scrutiny in recent years have dented Facebook's aggression to consolidate its strengths. The figure above showcases the key events and milestones in Facebook's evolution timeline that could

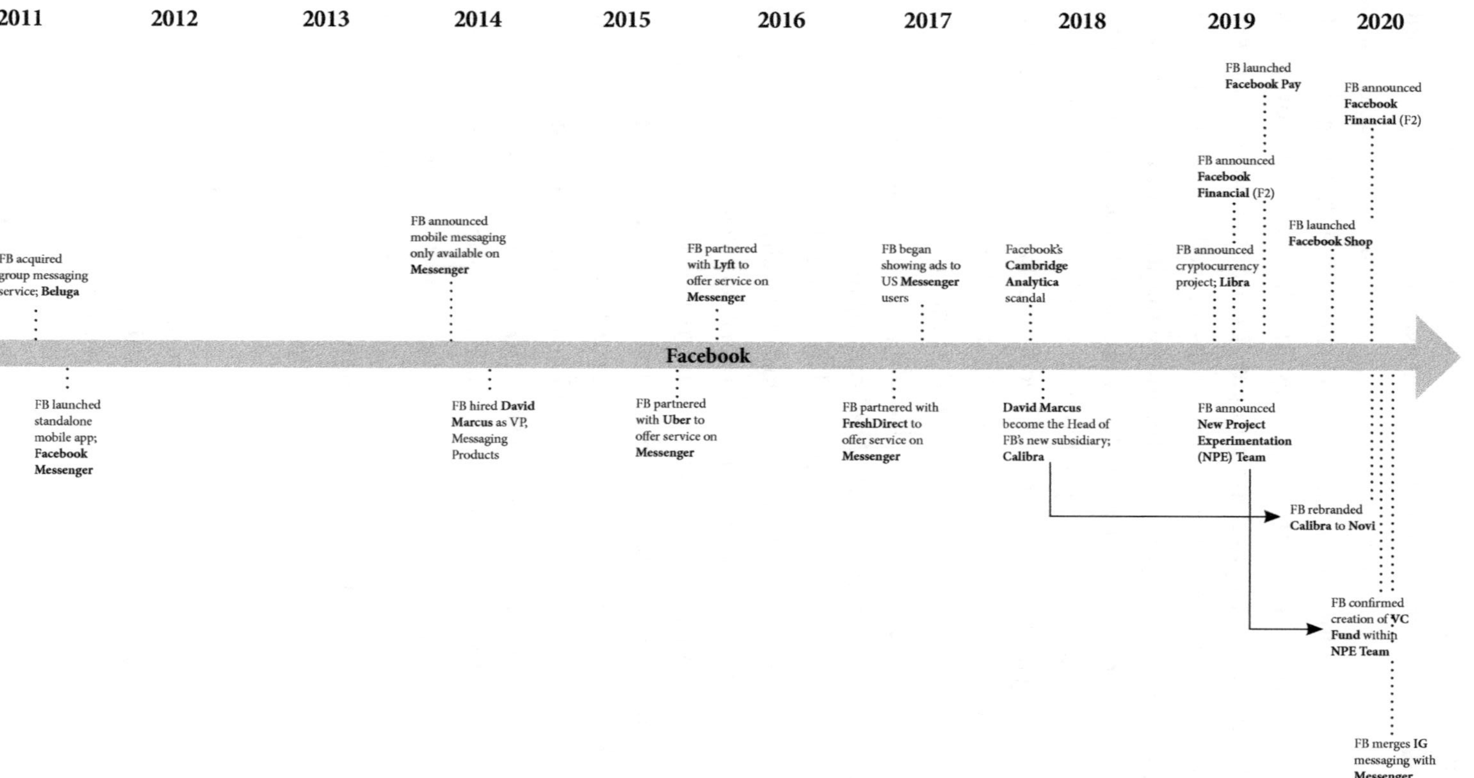
2011
2012
2013
2014
2015
2016
2017
2018
2019
2020
Facebook
FB acquired group messaging service; Beluga
FB launched standalone mobile app; Facebook Messenger
FB announced mobile messaging only available on Messenger
FB hired David Marcus as VP, Messaging Products
FB partnered with Lyft to offer service on Messenger
FB partnered with Uber to offer service on Messenger
FB began showing ads to US Messenger users
FB partnered with FreshDirect to offer service on Messenger
Facebook's Cambridge Analytica scandal
David Marcus become the Head of FB's new subsidiary; Calibra
FB announced cryptocurrency project; Libra
FB announced New Project Experimentation (NPE) Team
FB announced Facebook Financial (F2)
FB launched Facebook Pay
FB launched Facebook Shop
FB announced Facebook Financial (F2)
FB rebranded Calibra to Novi
FB confirmed creation of VC Fund within NPE Team
FB merges IG messaging with Messenger

help the company evolve into a successful super app in future.

Alipay: As with WeChat Pay, Alipay is the payment solution affiliated with the Chinese e-commerce juggernaut, Alibaba. The new Alipay 9.0 is no longer just a wallet. It is aimed at helping users shop, spend, and even manage their finances. The Alipay wallet now provides easy mobile access to purchase and pay for products and services from local restaurants, shops, and other outlets, as well as to obtain discount e-coupons and share product recommendations and red envelopes with friends, among other features. In January 2020, Alipay announced it surpassed 230 million daily active users and 1,20,000 lite apps

Grab: Singapore-based Grab is becoming the everything, everyday app in Southeast Asia. Not only being a leading player in the shared transport space, Grab has also expanded into food delivery and online payments, among other services. The Singapore startup recently secured funds worth $1.46 billion (SGD 2 billion) for its ongoing Series H round of funding from SoftBank Vision Fund in March 2019. The total amount raised in the round was over $4.5 billion. Basically, with one swipe, you can experience anything in the consumer services sector. With more than 2.8 million drivers, Grab has introduced multiple on-demand transportation, paying bills, ordering food, and even booking hotels.

Gojek: Grab is not alone in the race to become Southeast Asia's leading super app. Indonesia-based Gojek—Grab's fiercest competitor, has expanded outside its Indonesia market. On the way to becoming a super app, Gojek started operations as a motorcycle ride-hailing on mobile. Moreover, this startup is now offering services from food delivery to fintech, as well as massage services. Gojek is currently valued at about $5 billion after additional funding from well-known investors, including Singapore's Temasek Holdings and Chinese technology giant Tencent Holdings. Today, this super app business model has grown well beyond its original range of offerings to cover services, including lifestyle, entertainment, and financial needs.

Zalo: This is Vietnam's premier chatting platform, with more than 100 million users worldwide. Daily, people send about 900 million messages, make 50 million minutes of calls, and deliver 45 million pictures through the app, according to the company's website. Zalo

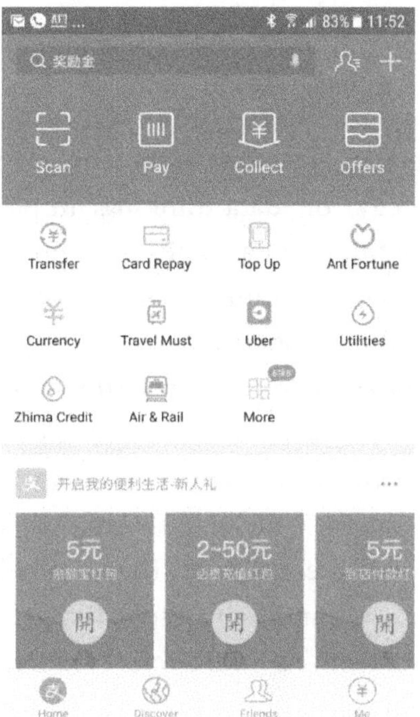

reached the 100-million-user milestone earlier this year, while Grab said two out of every ten Vietnamese use its service. This Vietnamese super app has been integrating new functions, which include a payment platform called Zalo Pay and Zalo Shop. Users can also check weather information, buy airline tickets, update health information, and pay electricity as well as water bills. As a result, Zalo joins the list of Vietnam's super apps to gain a foothold in numerous businesses.

MoMo: This super app has made a breakthrough as the 10th most-well-funded tech startup in the Asia-Pacific region, rated by global information services firm CB Insights. Moreover, Vietnamese startup MoMo was recently ranked at the 36th position in the top 100 global innovative fintechs, announced by H2 Ventures and KPMG. MoMo is an electronic wallet providing a variety of services for essential needs such as money transfer, paying electricity bills, water bills and hospital fees, banking, games, retail, and catering services. This MoMo super app partners with many big brands in Vietnam, like Lotte Mart, Circle K, Ministop, Gongcha, Koi, and The Coffee House.

IN SUM

Data has been called many things—the future, the new currency, the new oil. Regardless of the name you give it, the time is ripe for companies to have their "data strategy" or "data thinking" in place. Every company, going forward, is going to be a data and AI company. It's in this context that a super app will help them understand consumer behaviour across all their online and offline properties.

As we see in the above-cited examples, super app providers can gain more insight into the daily behaviour of users and use that information to offer new products and services by harnessing the data generated by users across multiple apps. Data analysis and ML are the cornerstones of an intelligent super app ecosystem. They can help in psychographic profiling, which involves analysing aspects that influence consumer purchase behaviour, such as activities, lifestyle, social status, and opinions.

These personalised services, which we encounter daily when we surf the internet, include relevant ads for products and services that we intend to buy. They also could be customised and timely discounts for such products and services, and timely reminders to renew our insurance and pay our utility bills. And a whole lot more.

AI algorithms can thus use predictive analytics to provide extremely personalised services and products for users on the super app platform. The combination of a super app ecosystem and AI can deliver tremendous value to consumers. Your imagination is the only limitation.

PART-3

HOLISTIC ARTIFICIAL INTELLIGENCE

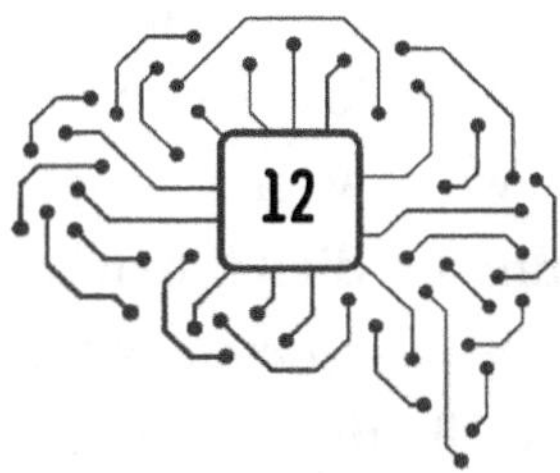

FUTURE OF WORK

"In 30 years, a robot will likely be on the cover of Time magazine as the best CEO. Machines will do what human beings are incapable of doing. Machines will partner and cooperate with humans, rather than become mankind's biggest enemy."

—*Jack Ma*

I vividly remember that evening. I was completing my fourth standard English homework when I came across a word that I did not understand. My father was clacking away on his Olivetti typewriter, trying to finish an office assignment he had brought home. "What's the meaning of this word, Dad?" I butted in, as children typically do. Lowering his glasses, my father looked at me. Without uttering a word, he picked up the Oxford dictionary from a side table and told me to pull up my chair next to him. He then patiently taught me how to scroll through a dictionary alphabetically so that I could locate the meaning of a specific word.

More than four decades have passed since that incident. I no longer manually scroll through the Oxford dictionary since I can now find the meaning of any word or phrase with a single click of my mouse. The typewriter, too, has made way for computers. My father did not live to see that change. Like most people of his generation, my father also took pride in working for a single company all his working life. I'm not sure how he would have reacted to me having changed six companies in the last three decades.

Millennials change jobs at a much faster clip. Moreover, most of us no longer care whether the job is contractual, permanent or even freelancing work. Instead, we now focus more on job satisfaction, career growth, learning opportunities, digital maturity, and work-life balance in the companies we choose to associate with.

That said, no one can really predict the exact nature of the "Future of Work" since there are simply too many variables that distort the picture. Yet, one can certainly infer some broad conclusions from the trends we are currently seeing in the workplace. I would like to list six such trends. These are: "Work from home is here to stay"; "Gender diversity and inclusion will increase"; "There will be more wage parity"; "We will have more work-life balance"; "We will be using more digital tools and virtual settings, all of which will reduce the need for physical travel"; and "Automation and smart machines will make us redundant if we do not reskill."

I fully acknowledge that this list is not exhaustive, but I have only underscored those trends that the pandemic has reinforced, as we have seen in the earlier chapters.

The government-enforced quarantines and lockdowns during the pandemic, for instance, have led to many changes in the workplace across the world.[1] Employers are now extending the earlier enforced Work From Home (WFH) arrangement that employees already had. Last year, Facebook said it would transition tens of thousands of jobs out of the office over the next decade, while Twitter said it would allow most employees to work from home "forever".

The dampener, though, was that Facebook later qualified WFH by stating that those working remotely may have to take a pay cut, depending on where they are based. Nevertheless, these developments indicate that the WFH trend will alter the workplace culture. For one, employers may continue to allow employees the flexibility of working from home for specified periods since there remains a lot of value in physical networking opportunities over snacks, beverages, and lunch at the workplace. Besides, youngsters would benefit from face-to-face interactions with mentors in the initial stages of their careers.

Schools and universities, on their part, are adapting to online learning courses. Many universities decided to switch the rest of the semester's work to online learning only, and some closed campuses to contain the spread of the virus. This trend is bound to change the way we impart education and training. But governments will have to ensure that online education is affordable and accessible to all with good broadband connections. Moreover, employers will need to take online certifications seriously and treat them with the respect that a college degree merits.

Conferences are a trillion-dollar industry and have been a critical way to exchange ideas and build professional relationships. However, with in-person conferences being cancelled worldwide in response to the pandemic outbreak, many companies switched over to virtual events due to safety concerns. The first to do so was the Mobile World Congress, followed by other companies such as Nvidia, Google, Dell, and SAS. We will have to have a mix of both online and offline events since there remains a lot of value in physical networking opportunities that are created over cocktails and dinner during events.

Doctors, meanwhile, are already diagnosing patients over the phone and via video conference calls. These trends will help doctors reach out to more patients once we all recover from the onslaught of this virus. Governments are holding online press conferences, ushering in new transparency in the governance process.

Online groceries are delivered to our homes. Governments are mooting the use of drones for the same. Thousands of businesses are using collaboration and video-conferencing tools to stay in touch with their employees and clients. All these trends have only increased the use of collaboration tools like Zoom, Teams, WeChat Work, Webex, and Hangouts.

The pandemic, thus, is not only transforming the workplace but also giving us a glimpse of how the Future of Work may shape up. In this chapter, though, we would like to focus particularly on how automation and AI are changing the workplace since the focus of this book is AI.

THE BIRTH OF THE SMART WORKPLACE

Imagine a scene that we typically see in retail outlets and grocery shops—employees moving carts loaded with goods from one point to another, taking inventory, and manually stocking goods on empty shelves.

In the last two to three years, however, human workers have had some competition in this space. Autonomous mobile robots or AMRs are not only being increasingly used in retail outlets and grocery stores but also in factories and healthcare facilities. And their numbers are only set to increase, given that people are being advised to maintain a safe distance to avoid getting infected by the coronavirus.

The global AMR market, which touched $4.36 billion in 2018, is pegged to reach $9.66 billion by 2025, according to trendsmarketresearch.com. Moreover, the number of robots in use worldwide multiplied threefold over the past two decades to 2.25 million, according to a June 2019 report by Oxford Economics. Trends suggest the global stock of robots will multiply even faster in the next 20 years, reaching as many as 20 million by 2030—with 14 million in China alone, according to the report.

But if such is the case, what does one make of a November 2, 2020, article in the *Wall Street Journal*, which reported that retail behemoth Walmart was ending a contract with Bossa Nova Robotics for shelf-scanning robots in some of its stores? The Verge did a follow-up story the next day with the headline: "Walmart is giving up on shelf-scanning robots in favor of humans".[2]

The Walmart incident may tempt some of us to conclude that this development heralds the beginning of a new trend where humans will once again replace robots. But as a Walmart spokesperson told The Verge, this case was just "... one idea we tried in roughly 500 stores just as we are trying other ideas in additional stores. We will continue testing new technologies and investing in our own processes and apps to best understand and track our inventory and help move products to our shelves as quickly as we can."

This simply means that automation and robots are here to stay—competing with humans for some jobs while collaborating with others.

Machines, for instance, have been collaborating with humans for thousands of years, and more so after the Industrial Revolution, which introduced the assembly line production concept in factories.

The first modern programmable robot was the Unimate— an autonomous, pre-programmed robot that repeatedly performed the same dangerous task. General Motors was the first company to install Unimate to work in one of its factories in 1961—to move pieces of hot metal.[3]

And it was more than six decades ago that the US Navy secretly toyed with the idea of fully automating the making of electronic parts and sub-assemblies. Concerned that electronics could not be manufactured fast enough if a major war were to occur after World War II, it launched a project christened "Tinkertoy" in a compact little factory on the outskirts of Washington. The US Navy partnered with the National Bureau of Standards to develop an almost automatic assembly line for many electronic parts. But the project was shelved and is now a museum artefact.

Automation has been consistently evolving. Many factories all over the world and in India have been using computer numerical control (CNC) machines for years. These machines allow operators to feed a program of instructions directly into a mini-computer via a small board, like a traditional keyboard. After loading the required tools in the machine, the rest is done automatically by the CNC machines, which use these instructions to control machineries such as the grinder, milling machine, and lathes.

TAL Manufacturing Solutions Ltd, a unit of Tata Motors Ltd, showcased a robot called BRABO at the "Make in India" week in Mumbai in 2017. Short for "Bravo Robot", BRABO was touted by the company as the first "Made in India" industrial robot and is designed to lift loads of up to 10 kilograms. Mahindra and Mahindra Ltd. has a "robotic weld line" at its factory in Nashik, which now caters to many of its products, including the Marazzo and the XUV300.

Tata Motors, too, uses robots in its Pune factory, while Godrej and Welspun run their shop floors with the help of an intelligent plant framework, which enables tracking of machinery and productivity on the floor in real-time. Maruti Suzuki India Ltd has numerous robots employed at its Manesar and Gurugram car factories, with more than 2,000 robots working at the weld shop in its Manesar facility alone. Manjushree Technopack Ltd's manufacturing plant in Bidadi, Bengaluru, also has more than a dozen of its packaging machines connected to a network, providing monthly updates on maintenance issues.

But next-generation automation will be vastly different: it will either make humans redundant or vastly alter the necessary skill set that is required to hold on to one's spot on the shop floor. A human-machine interface, or HMI, for instance, may eventually make the good old CNC machine voice-activated. As an example, it will allow an operator to just speak instructions in any language—a boon for those workers who cannot read or write.

Consider some other examples. Today, we use machines to stitch clothes, trains and planes to move around in cities and countries, mixers and robots to help us cook food, and 3D printers to help in manufacturing. These changes will have a long-lasting impact on India's labour force, particularly in some sectors—automotive, textile, and banking and financial services, apart from information technology.

We may soon have hundreds and thousands of "smart" factories that will be completely run by robots, dispensing with the need for human workers. These are known as "lights-out" factories since robots do not need lights to work. The trend began more than two decades ago when Japanese robotics firm FANUC, considered to be the poster boy for such factories, inaugurated a lights-out factory in 2001.

Similarly, Philips uses lights-out manufacturing to produce electric razors in the Netherlands, with 128 robots made by Adept Technology and only nine human quality assurance workers who oversee the end of the manufacturing process.[4] Even chip making is a highly-automated process.

Closer home, the *Times of India* reported five years ago that India's first "self-aware" factory was being set up in Bengaluru at the Indian Institute of Science's (IISc) Centre for Product Design and Manufacturing with seed funding from the Boeing Company. The

US Manufacturing Jobs, 1930–2040

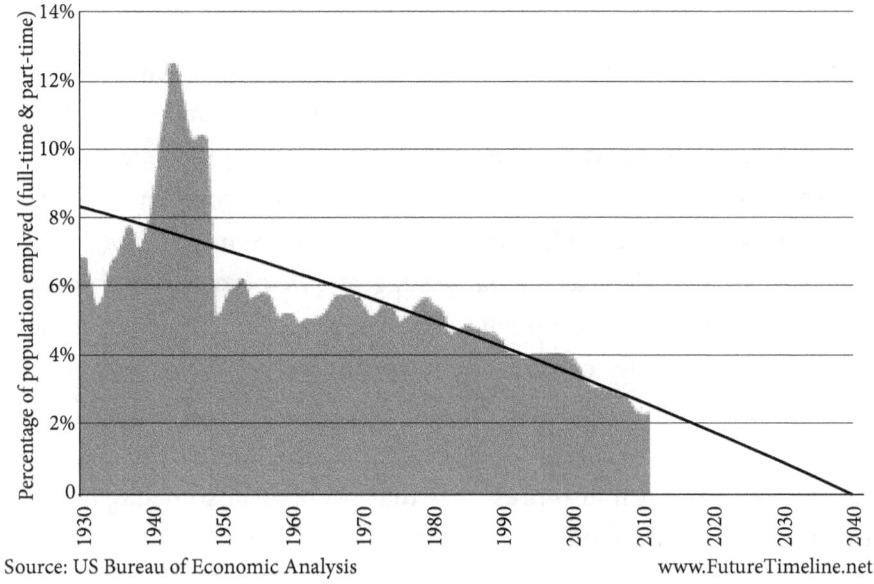

Source: US Bureau of Economic Analysis   www.FutureTimeline.net

factory is enabling data to be continuously collected and monitored, from both sensor-fitted machines and digitally connected wearables, to provide real-time insights into every movement and process taking place on the factory floor. The factory remains a "work in progress".

London-based writer and futurist William James Fox started Future Timeline back in 2008. According to his website, in the year 2039, manufacturing in the United States and most other developed nations would have gone the same way as agriculture—vitally important, yet employing very few people. "Robots, automation and 3D printing, now sufficiently perfected after decades of development, have taken over a wide range of roles once performed by humans. As China and other emerging nations make the transition to service-based economies, they too will experience this trend in the not-too-distant future."[5]

FRIEND, FOE OR COMPETITOR?

It's only natural that, given the potential of these smart robots, most of us will perceive them as enemies who are here to take away our jobs. The fear of AI is so real that even the head of the Roman Catholic Church has asked for God's help. In November 2020, Pope Francis invited his flock to pray that "the progress of robotics and AI may always serve humankind".

If you believe in God, you may think that prayer will help you make robots toe the human line. But if you are an agnostic or atheist, you will acknowledge that it's us humans who have created these smart robots. Regardless of our beliefs, robots can be viewed from three broad lenses: the Colonial view, the Collaborator view, and the Symbiotic view.

In the Colonial view, as the name suggests, we perceive smart robots as opponents that will become intelligent enough to surpass us at most tasks. They eventually could become our bosses and even enslave us. This view is mostly reflected in, and reinforced by, dystopian sci-fi movies like *The Terminator, Surrogates, I, Robot,* and television series like *Westworld*. But it also presumes that robots will someday become self-aware like us humans.

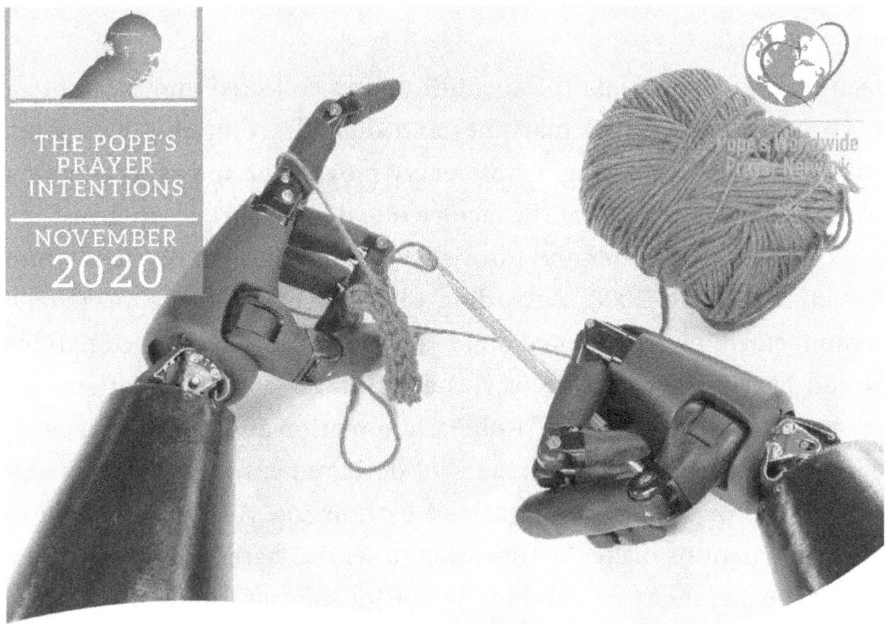

The Collaborator view takes a lenient view of robots, seeing them as friends who are here to help us deal with mundane tasks and leave us with a lot more time for leisure.

The Symbiotic view is a picture of humans embedding smart AI chips to become as efficient and smart as the machines themselves, something similar to what we saw in *The Matrix*. This view gives humans a fair chance to empower themselves with technology and compete with robots where necessary.

It would be naive to believe that these trends would pan out linearly. Rather, we may see all three trends playing out simultaneously in different parts of the world. For instance, in a country that is developed and has more tech-savvy humans who can afford to embed smart chips in their bodies, there is a good chance that the symbiotic view will be the dominant trend, with the other two trends being recessive.

On the other hand, the colonial view of robots may emerge as the dominant trend in developing countries like India and China, where human labour is still abundant and cheap. It's but natural that any attempt to replace human labour with smart machines will be perceived as colonisation.

The collaborator view, as demonstrated earlier in this chapter, already exists in factories where smart machines and robots work along with human workers and co-develop products like electronic goods and vehicles. It is, in fact, perceived as an important safety measure.

Even as these trends are shaping the Future of Work, they are raising quite a few concerns, such as: What kind of jobs are automation and robots likely to replace initially? Will robots become our bosses someday? What kind of new skills would humans need to compete with robots? Should governments pay everyone a universal basic income to compensate for their loss of jobs to robots?

Most of us would have already had these discussions with our parents, teachers, or colleagues. Typical responses to these questions range from sanguine predictions to apocalyptic ones. The loss of jobs is a very emotive issue with a lot of social ramifications. This explains, in part, why we hold extreme views on this subject. Besides, governments will need to answer these questions so that we can develop policy frameworks that will protect our interests.

That said, it's also important to examine why smart robots threaten us. I can list 10 such reasons. To begin with, a robot does not sleep or get tired—it can work all day and night and does not need to take sick leave, maternity, or paternity leave. Second, even when you take a robot off duty for maintenance, it can be instantly replaced by an equally able one. Third, a robot does not have to retire—the worn-out parts can simply be replaced and the software upgraded.

Fourth, an AI-powered robot makes better decisions as it trains on more and more data. Fifth, robots can collaborate with each other and share knowledge just as humans do, but far more efficiently. This essentially means that cloud-based robots will be able to perform tasks that are unimaginable today. Sixth, robots will not form a union or demand better working conditions, healthcare, or other employer benefits if they are contracted by a factory owner—unless, of course, they are programmed to do so.

Seventh, robots do not need individual accommodation. Thousands of robots can be huddled in a single warehouse. And these assumptions apply to hardware robots only—smart software robots, or robotic process automation (RPA), can deliver the goods simply with servers and computers.

Eight, since you can simply lease robots, you need not have a dedicated human resources (HR) department for them since robots do not need any motivation to work, nor do they need management training since they can simply be programmed to do a specific task. Besides, a new robot can join the workforce as soon as it is unboxed and charged. Robots nowadays are even capable of self-charging before they run out of power.

Nine, robots can be centrally managed by their contractors, so you can dispense with the administration department too. Last but not least, all canteen and recreational services can be dispensed with since robots do not need any such service to keep fit or stay alive.

A potential employer could use all these arguments and many others that you would have thought of, to bargain with a human for lower wages by threatening to replace him or her with a robot. This, in effect, will not only make human workers redundant but also diminish the real wages of those who continue to work.

RAISING WORKPLACE IQ

Our concern about being replaced by AI-powered software bots and robots is not misplaced. Algorithmically-driven agents are already participating in our economy. However, while these agents are automated, they are not fully autonomous. New autonomous software agents will function as the fundamental underpinning of a new economic paradigm that Gartner calls the "programmable economy" or "algorithmic economy".

Amazon's recommendation algorithm, for instance, keeps customers continuously engaged with its marketplace. Netflix's dynamic algorithm keeps people busy with binge-watching. Google-owned Waze's algorithm directs thousands of independent cars on the road.

E-commerce companies, banks, financial institutions, retailers, and oil and gas companies in India are already heavy users of algorithm-based business decisions. Stock markets the world over have made trading very fast-paced with algorithms, thus giving rise to robo-advisory services to keep pace with the trend.

Moreover, as we highlighted in Chapter 2, drones are taking photographs and doing surveillance while robots are delivering pizzas and packages. Assistive robots are taking care of the elderly, and robots like Roomba mop floors. Robots can even cook your food for you. Bengaluru-based Mechanical Chef, for instance, is a robot that can cook a variety of dishes once you feed it the basic ingredients. The robot can make many Indian dishes, including upma, bisi bele bath, tomato rasam, chole masala, matar paneer, and dal tadka.[6]

Software bots are writing articles and movie scripts, which we pointed out in the earlier chapters. AI-powered 3D printing is revolutionising the manufacturing sector. And driverless cars, trucks, and trains, besides autonomous helicopters and planes, are only making it harder for us to imagine the future impact of these technologies on our lives and jobs.

But these intelligent bots and smart robots are also enhancing efficiency in the workplace. AI is improving safety and accessibility in the automotive industry, according to a 2017 WEF-AT Kearney report, and intelligent scheduling software is being adapted to real-time production variability. AI systems are enabling new levels of production system optimisation, such as predictive maintenance and improved quality management.

Moreover, NLP can be adopted to create task-specialised personal assistants, as well as platforms for conversational technologies that can be provided as a service and integrated into various applications. Computer vision capabilities, on their part, enhance visual navigation for self-driving cars as well as 3D scanning, the report notes. Both NLP and computer vision are AI applications.

Further, AI is used to optimise the multi-robot fulfilment system in Amazon warehouses. The average cost for a spot-welding robot, according to WEF, is projected to decrease by 22 per cent by 2025, and robots-as-a-service models are beginning to appear.

According to SaaSnic Technologies, the use of AI and robots is particularly appealing in industrial manufacturing as they revolutionise mass production. Robots can do repetitive tasks—streamlining the production model, increasing capacity, building automation solutions, eliminating human error, and delivering higher levels of quality assurance. Moreover, although bringing AI on to the shop floor would require a massive capital investment, the ROI is higher.

AI and ML can test numerous demand forecasting models with precision while automatically adjusting to different variables, such as new product introductions, supply chain disruptions, or sudden changes in demand. Using AI systems, every single part of a product can be tracked from when it is first manufactured to when it is assembled and shipped to the customer.

Walmart, for instance, has cut its physical inventory from one month to 24 hours using sophisticated drones that fly through the warehouse, scan products, and check for misplaced items. Using algorithms that learn from experience to optimise logistics, BMW tracks a part—from the point it was manufactured to when the vehicle is sold—from all its 31 assembly facilities located in over 15 countries.

In finance operations, AI can close operations and automate monthly, quarterly, and year-end processes. Using ML, bots can even learn from different human inputs to make better judgements and adapt to the behaviour patterns of different accounting professionals.

Smart robots also assist shop floor operations indirectly by increasing employee satisfaction. A case in point is that of Indian IT services provider Tech Mahindra, which introduced an HR humanoid (a robot that resembles a human) at its Noida Special Economic Zone Campus in Uttar Pradesh. Christened K2, this was the second HR humanoid from the Mahindra Group company—the first was launched at its Hyderabad campus in 2019.

K2 can address general and specific HR-related employee queries and even handle personal requests for actions such as providing payslips, tax forms, etc. With the help of AI, K2 can start a conversation without any need for wake-up commands. It can even converse with differently-abled employees by responding to queries with a text display along with speech.

Gurugram-based AI-powered robotics company GreyOrange's Butler is an autonomous robot that uses goods-to-person technology for inventory storage, replenishment, and order picking. Its Butler PickPal is an automated picking system that can pick, process, consolidate, and prepare orders. The company's software platform, GreyMatter, uses AI algorithms and ML to optimise path planning, maximise storage, streamline zoning, improve space utilisation, and accelerate order fulfilment.

Further, as a precursor of what may become commonplace soon, US-based Hirebotics allows companies to hire cloud-connected robots the way we hire human employees. The cost of the robotic workers depends on the equipment needed, the task the robot will need to perform, and the hours worked. The hourly wage starts at $15 per hour, and they have a minimum of 80 hours a week—and they don't tire or need bathroom breaks. Of course, companies must give Hirebotics 30 days' written notice if they fire any robot.

JOBS OF THE FUTURE

A Brookings 2019 report notes that AI's ability to use statistics and learn to implement non-routine work "means that these technologies are set to affect very different parts of the workforce than previous automation".[7]

For instance, the report points out that all kinds of demand forecasting within companies are increasingly being replaced by AI, as are office and phone workers, transcription and translation workers, customer service workers, credit monitors, and financial analysts. Similar changes are taking place in human resources, where recruiting is being done by AI tools since AI can decipher patterns better and sift through humongous amounts of data (for example, scan hundreds of thousands of résumés).

Likewise, many AI applications are substituting technology for labour in the legal field by automating scanning and prediction tasks. This implies that while lawyers may still make the ultimate decisions, fewer lower-level researchers and paralegals will be recruited going forward, as AI saves firms time and improves accuracy.

On the flip side, notes the Brookings report, AI is helping the drug industry predict which molecules have the most potential for further exploration, subsequently increasing the demand for real-world experiments performed by humans. Even radiologists, who were impacted by AI since it can read scans faster and better than humans, are "now able to spend more time consulting with other physicians about optimal diagnoses and treatment strategies, thus expanding their role in the overall treatment system", notes the Brookings report.

Among other things, the Brookings report concludes that AI may end up creating a lot of ancillary jobs. "Just as the automobile created jobs not only in auto manufacturing plants but also in pumping stations, roadside restaurants, and the new suburban America that emerged, it seems likely that AI will have similarly far-reaching—if difficult to predict—indirect effects".

WEF has a similar outlook. According to WEF's "Jobs of Tomorrow: Mapping Opportunity in the New Economy" report, released in January 2020, there are seven key professional clusters that have the potential to collectively generate 6.1 million new job opportunities in the coming three years.[8] These seven clusters are data and AI; care economy; green economy; engineering and cloud computing; people and culture; product development; as well as sales, marketing, and content. This indicates that the transition to the new world of work will

Rate of automation

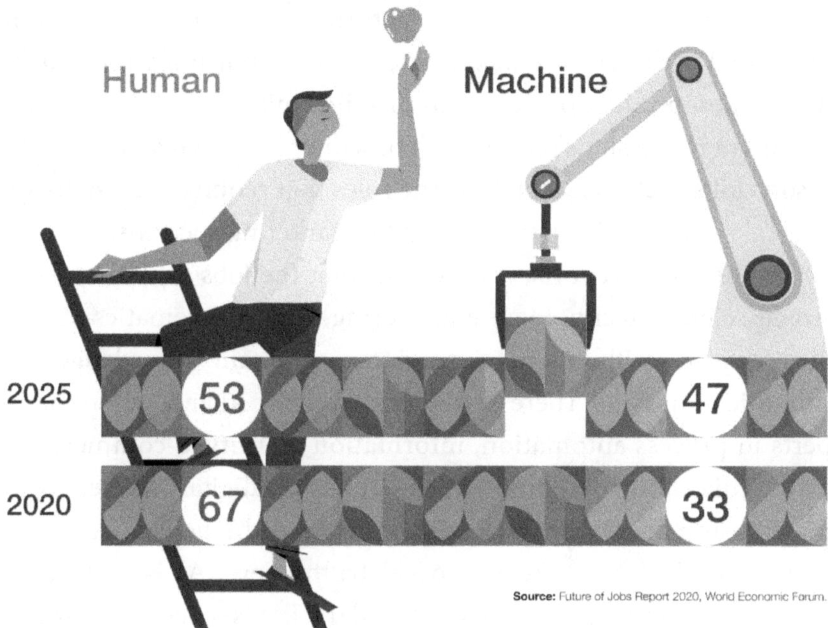

Source: Future of Jobs Report 2020, World Economic Forum.

be both human- and tech-centric.

However, the report notes that these professions will require specific skills. For instance, digital marketing and product marketing are among the top 10 business skills required in the care economy, which includes professions such as personal care aides and athletic trainers. Data and AI professions require skills in AI and data storage technologies and include small-scale roles, such as big data developers, alongside large-scale roles, such as data scientists.

Engineering and cloud computing, according to the WEF report, requires technology baseline skills such as computer networking skills and technology disruptive skills such as human-computer interaction across roles such as full stack engineers and DevOps engineers. The green economy cluster requires industry-specialised skills such as wind turbines and solar installation as well as business skills such as email marketing across roles such as solar photovoltaic installers and green marketers.

The product development cluster, notes the WEF report, requires tech baseline skills such as software testing and web development as well as business skills such as manufacturing operations. The roles that are included in this cluster include large-scale opportunity roles such as agile coaches, product owners, and product analysts. Sales, marketing, and content professions require tech baseline skills such as social media and soft skills such as leadership. The roles that require such skills span large-scale opportunities, such as digital marketing specialists.

From the above reports, it is evident that the jobs of the future will leverage science, technology, engineering, and mathematics (STEM) skills coupled with digital experience, domain knowledge, and communication skills. There will be a demand for AI and ML specialists, experts in process automation, information security, e-commerce and social media, human-centric design, robotics, digital marketing and remote customer service. However, given that the field of AI itself is evolving rapidly, there are no gospel truths here. At best, these are informed guesses, forcing us to watch and track this space very minutely.

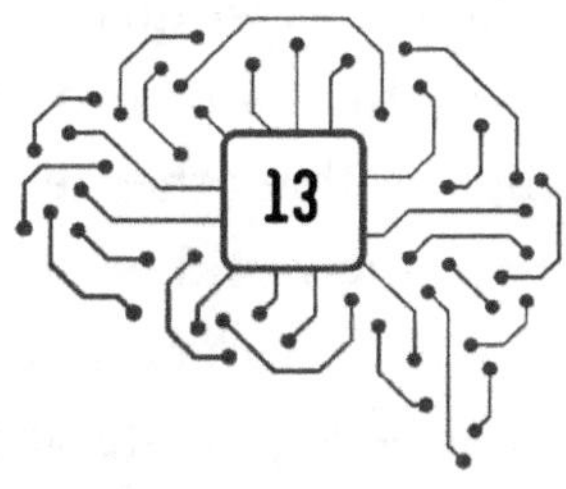

WHY AI NEEDS ETHICS

"When intelligent machines are constructed, we should not be surprised to find them as confused and as stubborn as men in their convictions about mind-matter, consciousness, free will, and the like."
—Marvin Lee Minsky

Are human babies born with a moral conscience, one that makes them understand the difference between right and wrong? Most of us would say "No" since we believe that infants learn what is considered right or wrong from society as they mature into adulthood and become wiser.

As a child grows up, most of the moral and religious teaching is imparted initially at home by parents or guardians. Teachers, mentors, priests, and peers add to this moral knowledge database when in school and college. When we start working, we learn more about these values from our colleagues too. We then use different filters, including our own experience, to arrive at a decision on what is good and bad.

There are some researchers, though, who believe that children are born with a very limited but nevertheless innate sense of morality. These philosophical deliberations are outside the scope of this book. Nevertheless, even if we agree that human beings do have a very limited sense of morality when they're born, it's logical that they would have to continually hone their moral sense with inputs as they grow.

It's these inputs that make morality very tricky to understand. To begin with, our world has many religions and thousands of religious denominations. This explains why we do not have a universally-accepted moral code or value system. In other words, there are practices that are acceptable in certain religions that other religions reject.

Further, each country in the world has formulated its own laws and constitutions. Hence, what is right, or even accepted as moral, within one country's borders may not be legitimate or moral in another country. For example, many countries do not allow public flogging of criminals. Even abortion and gay marriage are still banned and considered illegal in many countries. But these actions are neither illegal nor considered immoral in many other countries.

What has all this got to do with AI algorithms and this book, you may ask? The short answer is "A lot."

For one, the more data you feed AI algorithms, the smarter they become. As an example, OpenAI's GPT-3 model, which we spoke about earlier, has been fed with about 500 billion words from sources like the internet and books. Thus, GPT-3 can recall and instantly draw inferences from this data repository. However, just because AI algorithms know more about a specific subject does not mean that they will understand the nuances of words or culture and morality, for that matter.

As an example, it will be very difficult for an AI algorithm that is trained on data from one country to understand the value system in another. An algorithm trained on data about blacks and whites, for instance, may have little or no understanding of the nuances of the class and caste system in India. This simply means that an AI system that has been fed with data about discrimination against black people will be able to understand (not fully, of course) the meaning of black and white in the context of racism. However, the same AI system (or those AI algorithms) will be unable to understand the nuances of India's caste system unless it is trained on data that pertains to India's caste system specifically. In other words, just because you have studied Algebra, it does not mean that you understand Geometry as well. You will have to study Geometry separately.

Let's take another example. As the world was still getting to grips with the pandemic in early 2020, most countries held school exams using conventional methods—one that involves grading students with

Source: Twitter feed. August 16, 2020

the help of teachers. Schools in Britain, however, opted for a different solution. The UK's Office of Qualifications and Examinations Regulation (Ofqual), which regulates qualifications, examinations, and assessments in England, decided to allow an algorithm to grade the students.

England's A-level results were due on August 13, 2020. However, just before that date, the *Guardian* exclusively reported that an analysis of the algorithm and data used by Ofqual "found that a net 39 per cent of assessments of A-level grades by teachers are likely to be adjusted down before students receive their results".[1] A-level is the common name for the General Certificate of Education Advanced Level.

Interestingly, just three days prior to the publication of this article, the Scottish Qualifications Authority had downgraded 1,24,000 recommended results on the basis of its own algorithm. Poorer pupils were the most affected, both in Scotland and England.

In a follow-up article on August 21, 2020, the *Guardian* reported that "One of the causes was that the algorithm decided that poor grades in the past meant somebody had to be marked down sharply again." Simply put, there was bias in the assumption that the algorithm made.

Biased algorithms can cause more damage. They can hurt the sentiments of a particular community by making insensitive remarks. Consider these cases. Microsoft's AI chatbot Tay began tweeting "wildly inappropriate and reprehensible words and images" as soon as it was launched on March 23, 2016. As a result, there was a public outcry online, forcing Microsoft to get rid of the bot in just 16 hours. On March 25, Microsoft acknowledged in a blog: "We are deeply sorry for the unintended offensive and hurtful tweets from Tay, which do not represent who we are or what we stand for, nor how we designed Tay." The damage, though, could not be undone.

A little over a year later, in June 2017, researchers at Facebook Artificial Intelligence Research (FAIR) developed two AI chatbots. The aim was to have the bots chat with humans. Instead, the bots began talking with each other in a language that their own human creators did not understand.

Facebook did shut down the programme, prompting some media reports to conclude that this was how sinister AI would look when it becomes super-intelligent. Facebook, however, clarified that the programme was aborted because it no longer served the purpose of what the FAIR researchers had set out to do—i.e., have the AI bots speak to humans in a language that we could understand.

BIAS IN THE DESIGN ITSELF

It's logical to ask whether algorithms have the ability to take their own decisions and be as biased as humans when doing so. Even if you believe the answer to be "Yes", you may wonder why it is so.

A good part of the answer lies in the very design of the algorithm. If you recall, we explained in Chapter 1 that DL neural nets are an ML technique that allows a computer to learn how to perform a specific task by analysing hundreds and thousands of examples with or without the help of human supervision and, in some cases, partial supervision.

For instance, if you feed thousands of labelled images of cats, dogs, and tigers to an object recognition system, neural nets will learn from the images by detecting visual patterns that consistently correlate with the specific labels—be it a cat, dog, or tiger.

Here's how it works. Neurons receive inputs in layers. The neurons in the first layer perform a calculation and send it (the output) to the neurons in the next layer. The process is repeated until the final output.

A node assigns a number known as a "weight" to each of its incoming connections. If that number is below a threshold value, the node ignores the number and hence passes no data to the next layer. If the number passes the test, the node sends (known as "fires") the number. The weights and thresholds, thus, are continually adjusted until the training data with the same labels consistently yield similar outputs. There is also a process known as back-propagation that tweaks the calculations of individual neurons to allow the network to learn to produce the desired output.

When the first trainable neural network, the perceptron, was demonstrated by Cornell University psychologist Frank Rosenblatt in 1957, it had only one layer with adjustable weights and thresholds between the input and output layers. Today's neural nets, of course, are very sophisticated.

Unsupervised learning is used when researchers ask algorithms questions that they can't answer. A DL model is given a training data set but no explicit instruction or label. In other words, the model is expected to automatically analyse the data by extracting patterns to eventually present a result that the researchers would not have known of.

For instance, banks use unsupervised learning to detect fraudulent transactions by looking for unusual patterns in a customer's purchasing behaviour. The process is also known as "anomaly detection". In such cases, the unsupervised DL model does the trick by flagging outliers in a data set.

When "clustering", an unsupervised model would look at training data that are similar to each other and group them together. An unsupervised model can also make decisions using "association". For instance, if you're shopping for tops, the model may suggest shorts, trousers, shoes, socks, and accessories such as belts too.

Semi-supervised learning, as its name suggests, is a training data set

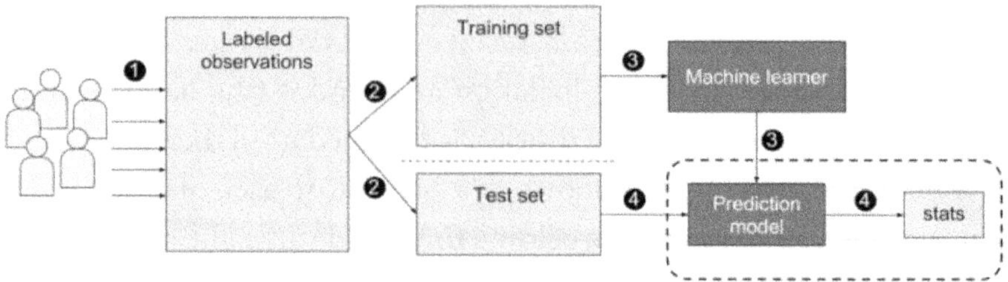

Source: Supervised Learning model (https://blogs.nvidia.com/blog/2018/
08/02/supervised-unsupervised-learning/)

with both labelled and unlabelled data.

However, as we may have realised by now, supervised and semi-supervised DL models have humans in the loop. But that is not the case with unsupervised neural nets that use an opaque process to produce results. This implies that even their human designers rarely have any idea of how the algorithm generates the results.

Algorithmic biases are well-documented. Lead author Aylin Caliskan—a postdoctoral research associate and a CITP fellow at Princeton—argued in a paper titled, "Semantics derived automatically from language corpora contain human-like biases", that common ML programs can acquire cultural biases when trained with human language that is available online. These biases range from the morally neutral, like a preference for flowers over insects, to objectionable views of race and gender.

In the paper that was published on April 14, 2017, in the journal *Science*, the Princeton team used the open-source GloVe algorithm, developed by Stanford University researchers, to train on 840 billion words online. They discovered, for instance, that the ML program associated female names more with familial attribute words, such as "parents" and "wedding", rather than male names. In turn, male names had stronger associations with career attributes such as "professional" and "salary".[2]

The researchers pointed out that the results were "often just objective reflections of the true, unequal distributions of occupation types with respect to gender—like how 77 per cent of computer programmers are male, according to the US Bureau of Labour Statistics. Yet this correctly distinguished bias about occupations can end up having pernicious, sexist effects".

They further underscored that if foreign languages are "naively processed" by ML programs, it could lead to "gender-stereotyped sentences". Such issues assume graver proportions when you deal with a country like India, which has 22 official languages and thousands of dialects.

As we see from the above cases, algorithms can jeopardise people's careers with unfair grades and hurt people's sentiments. These instances recur since algorithms are written by humans, thus reflecting our biases in the AI-generated results unless we are cognisant about it and take appropriate action to correct these biases.

It's erroneous to believe that just because an algorithm is math, it is unbiased. This realisation is critical since the decisions that biased algorithms make can have a direct impact on our lives.

Let's take the world of driverless cars, where multiple systems interact with each other and conditions on the road could change every second. What if an AI algorithm takes a wrong turn, bumps into someone, or knocks someone down? Worse still, what if an AI algorithm kills people based on religion, caste, creed, or the colour of their skin?

Let us consider some examples. On March 18, 2018, a driverless car operated by Uber struck and killed a woman on a street in Tempe, Arizona, despite having an emergency backup driver behind the wheel. Following the incident, Uber suspended testing in Tempe as well as in Pittsburgh, San Francisco, and Toronto, according to an article in the *Guardian*.

Waymo, an autonomous car company from Google's parent company Alphabet, has had a fleet of self-driving vehicles without any backup drivers on public roads since November 2017. Other companies that have driverless cars include Tesla Inc., Nissan Motor Co. Ltd and General Motors Co.

Who will be held responsible in case of an accident by a driverless car—the car owner, the company that developed the car and its algorithms, or the algorithm that has taken the decision but cannot explain why?

Let's take another example. Scientists at Case Western Reserve

University published research that shows that AI-analysed images of cancer tissues reveal critical variations between black and white male prostate cancer patients. This information, they suggest, can be useful to customise medical care to specific groups and individuals within those populations.[3]

In the above-cited case, AI is undoubtedly helping people. What, however, if a doctor tells a patient that they have cancer because an algorithm has detected it but can't explain the "why" of it?

DEEPFAKES

Other than biases, smart algorithms pose another big problem. Most of us are familiar with the term 'Photoshopped'. Designers have edited and improved images using Adobe Photoshop for over three decades, making it the industry standard for digital editing.

However, this powerful image editing tool has also been used by unscrupulous people to edit and distort images of celebrities and prominent personalities in a bid to present them in a very different and often insalubrious light, giving rise to the word 'Photoshopped' that is used in a pejorative manner.

AI lends exponential power to this darker side of humans. Known as "deepfakes", AI-powered algorithms can manipulate the appearances and voices of people into real-looking footage. Researchers have also trained algorithms to simply listen to voices and generate the face or even entire bodies of non-existent people. Moreover, AI algorithms can even make people move in and out of photographs—just as they did in the Harry Potter films.

In early May 2019, for instance, an altered video of US house speaker Nancy Pelosi made the rounds on social media. The video editing that was done made her speech appear slow and slurred, giving the impression that she had impaired speech (which is not the case in real life). On June 11, 2019, artists Bill Posters and Daniel Howe, in partnership with advertising company Canny, created a deepfake of Facebook founder Mark Zuckerberg, making him say things he never said, and uploaded it on Instagram. However, the original video was from a September 2017 address Zuckerberg had given about Russian election interference on Facebook.

Israeli startup Canny AI founders—Omer Ben-Ami and Jonathan Heimann—told special effects blog FXGuide that they were influenced by the work of University of Washington researchers who wrote algorithms that "turned audio clips of people speaking into realistic videos of people made to look like they're speaking those words".[4]

A month later, two Facebook engineers—Sean Vasquez and Mike Lewis—announced the creation of an AI system called MelNet, which clones the voices of famous people like Donald Trump, Bill Gates, and Stephen Hawking.

Imagine deepfakes such as these being used to impersonate prominent personalities in India. While this may sound like fun to misguided enthusiasts, it could lead to a lot of chaos. Also, imagine the havoc if a deepfake of a known politician or celebrity goes viral on YouTube or WhatsApp. Mischievous deepfakes could not only impact elections but also foment riots in communally-sensitive areas.

To compound such issues, companies such as Data Grid have developed "automatic whole-body model generation AI", which automatically generates high-resolution full-body images of non-existent people. The company expects this algorithm—which applies a DL technique called generative adversarial network (GAN) to learn a large number of whole-body model images—to be used as a virtual model for advertising and apparel.

You can liken GANs to two DL networks—generator and discriminator—sparring with each other for the best outcome. GANs are actually very useful since they reduce the amount of data needed to train DL algorithms. But what stops lumpen techies from misusing these GANs?

Here's an example of a perverted mind using this powerful tool. An app called DeepNude used GANs to enable users to compromise the modesty of clothed women by manipulating their online photographs for $50 but was forced to shut down following a report by Vice and subsequent protests from the public.[5] Such images can easily be used as fake revenge porn to damage a woman's reputation. Of course, India's

IT Act does allow for the arrest and punishment of such offenders, but the fact is that such acts cause a lot of distress and reputation damage before they can be contained.

Further, a site like Thispersondoesnotexist.com shows how GANs can be painters but can also create fictitious people. A GAN-powered deepfake can easily alter our very perception of reality.

SCARY AI

In 2016, MIT presented the Nightmare Machine: AI-generated scary imagery—an AI project that aimed not only at detecting but also inducing extreme emotions such as fear in humans. Users can visit the site and help the algorithm learn by voting. To date, the site has received over two million votes. You can watch the algorithm alter a pleasant image to a scary one in real-time.

A year later, MIT researchers presented Shelley, which they described as the world's first collaborative AI horror writer. Shelley is a DL AI that was trained on eerie stories collected from r/nosleep. And the following year, MIT trained the world's first AI-powered psychopath called "Norman" on Reddit and compared captions with standard image-captioning neural networks.

According to the MIT researchers, "when people talk about AI algorithms being biased and unfair, the culprit is often not the algorithm itself, but the biased data that was fed to it ... Norman represents a case study on the dangers of Artificial Intelligence gone wrong when biased data is used in ML algorithms."

Such instances have given AI a bad name, lending credence to the name "Franken" (after Mary Shelley's *Frankenstein*) algorithms. This is also a major reason why AI has already received a lot of bad press, underscoring the danger of biased AI algorithms and increasing data privacy violations.

All these examples underscore the need for algorithms to be induced with a sense of ethics and fairness so that they can avoid biases and explain why they took a particular decision. In other words, AI cannot be opaque or a "black box".

INKBLOT #1
Norman sees:

"A MAN IS ELECTROCUTED

AND CATCHES TO DEATH."

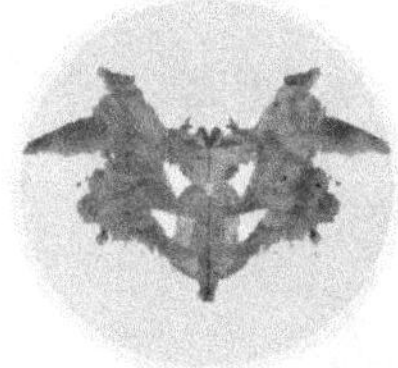

INKBLOT #1
Standard AI sees:

"A GROUP OF BIRDS

SITTING ON TOP OF A

TREE BRANCH."

INKBLOT #2
Norman sees:

"A MAN IS SHOT DEAD."

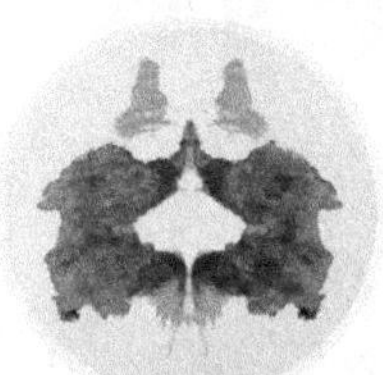

INKBLOT #2
Standard AI sees:

"A CLOSE UP OF A VASE

WITH FLOWERS."

INKBLOT #3
Norman sees:

"MAN JUMPS FROM FLOOR

WINDOW."

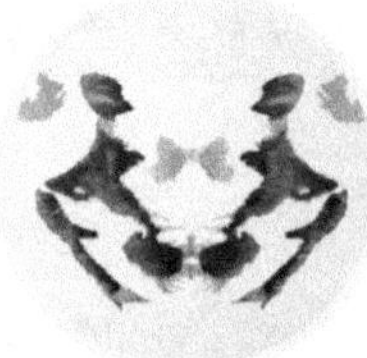

INKBLOT #3
Standard AI sees:

"A COUPLE OF PEOPLE

STANDING NEXT TO EACH

OTHER."

Source: http://norman-ai.mit.edu/

AI-POWERED ANDROIDS

Most of us are fans of science-fiction movies. *I, Robot,* for instance, portrayed intelligent robots who police humans in a bid to keep them safe but end up conspiring to enslave humans. *A.I. Artificial Intelligence* was a 2001 US sci-fi drama directed by Steven Spielberg in which a childlike android was programmed to love.

Bicentennial Man, which starred the late Robin Williams, was based on a 1976 novel by Isaac Asimov. In the movie, the robot is upgraded continuously and eventually becomes the first human to become the oldest-ever citizen, just when it is about to die like a human. *Surrogates,* starring Bruce Willis, depicts a futuristic world where people live within the safety of their homes while their robotic surrogates carry on their daily chores.

These movies have convinced many that intelligent human-like robots endowed with AI can not only emulate but even surpass human

Photo: iStock

intelligence. Fortunately for us, AI machines are nowhere close to matching the prowess of the super-intelligent and near-sentient AI machines like Skynet, androids and cyborgs that we get to see in these sci-fi movies. At least, not yet.

If so, why do we fear that AI will soon make machines more intelligent than us?

First, there is tremendous media hype around "intelligent" or "smart" machines, attributing far more power to these devices than they already have. Second, as we pointed out above, AI does have the potential to hurt and harm, invade our privacy and influence our surfing and purchasing behaviours in cyberspace—all of which is justifiably worrisome.

Third, AI is being used to make war weapons that can battle autonomously and destroy enemies, along with biological and chemical weapons.

Project Maven, for instance, is a Pentagon programme to build an AI-powered surveillance platform for unmanned aerial vehicles or UAVs. It is also called the Algorithmic Warfare Cross-Function Team, or AWCFT. Google initially aided the project with its AI expertise, but in 2018, thousands of Google employees wrote an open letter to the management, exhorting it to abandon the project.[6] Google abandoned the project. But that's not the last we will hear of Project Maven.

Meanwhile, countries such as China, Russia, Israel, and South Korea are also investing heavily in AI to make autonomous guns and robots that can fight alongside soldiers.

Closer home, we have the Centre for Artificial Intelligence and Robotics (CAIR), which does research and development in the areas of AI, robotics, command and control, networking, information, and communication security with a focus on developing mission-critical products for battlefield communication and management systems. CAIR has already developed the Multi-Agent Robotics Framework (MARF) for India's armed forces.

WHY WE NEED EXPLAINABLE AI

The question here is: Who is responsible when an autonomous gun or robot kills an enemy soldier? Do these smart agents take orders like human soldiers, or are they capable of taking spontaneous decisions on the battlefield? And if they do make their own decisions in the heat of battle, is the process transparent enough to be evaluated in case of an anomaly? Could the military, for instance, court-martial a robot that has killed a soldier without a human justification?

Simply put, why do we expect the answers provided by AI-powered algorithms to be right? Why should we not ask about the process they adopted to arrive at these answers or decisions? Or do we suffer from what is sometimes known as an "automation bias", allowing us to shift the responsibility and accountability of such decisions on computers?

It's hardly surprising that technology luminaries such as Bill Gates, Elon Musk, and even physicist Stephen Hawking, have cautioned that robots with AI could rule mankind. Raymond "Ray" Kurzweil, an American author, computer scientist, inventor, and futurist, in his 2006 book *The Singularity Is Near*, predicted, among many other things, that AI will surpass humans, the smartest and most capable life forms on the planet. He forecasted that machines would have attained equal legal status with humans by 2099.

But there are those who believe that AI machines can be controlled. Marvin Lee Minsky, who died in January, was an American cognitive scientist in the field of AI and co-founder of MIT's AI laboratory. A champion of AI, he did believe that some computers would eventually become more intelligent than most human beings but hoped that researchers would make such computers benevolent to mankind.

Even Ray has sought to allay such fears that smart machines will dominate humans by pointing out that we can deploy strategies to keep emerging technologies like AI safe, and underscoring the existence of ethical guidelines like Isaac Asimov's three laws for robots, which can prevent "at least to some extent" smart machines from overpowering us.

Hence, we need to insist that AI-powered algorithms be designed such that they remain accountable to humans and are able to explain their actions to us.

But as we pointed out at the beginning of this chapter, the study of ethics, even if it's situational ethics, is very complex. Hence, can we really expect technology companies to design algorithms that are completely unbiased?

One approach is to crowdsource and teach algorithms how humans make moral decisions. As an example, MIT's Moral Machine platform

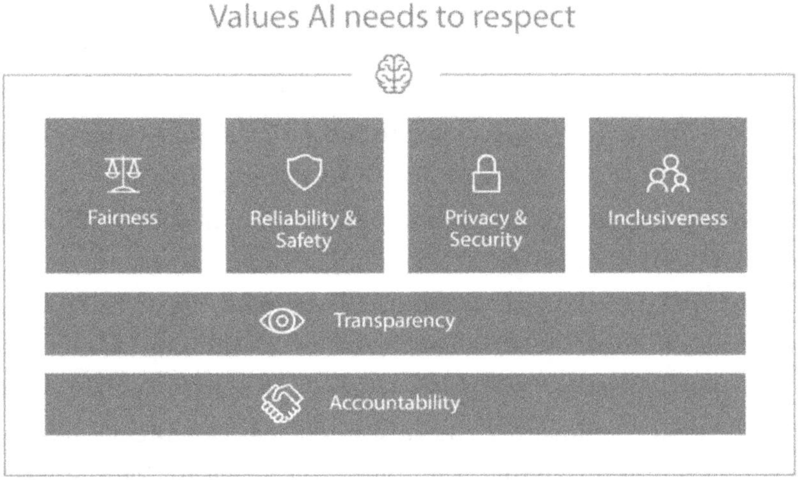

Values AI needs to respect

Chart 5.
Source: Microsoft Corporation

(moralmachine.net) invites users to be the judge of situations where we have to take moral decisions.

For instance, consider a situation where a driverless car must choose between killing two passengers or five pedestrians. What would you do? Users who visit the site moralmachine.net can also design their own scenarios that they can share and discuss with others.

It's a step in the right direction, but it would still fall prey to a lot of human subjectivity since we humans are shaped by our own value systems, as pointed out in the earlier paragraphs. Besides, it will also depend on the geographical location of the users.

A February 2019 article in *MIT Technology Review* argued that it's very hard to fix the bias in algorithms due to three reasons. The first is that a bias could seep in when framing the problem itself. If this occurs, then the data collected will also reflect the bias. Finally, one could exclude certain groups of people while preparing the data, thus reinforcing the bias.[7]

Getting rid of spam with the help of a spam filter, for instance, would involve training an algorithm with labels on what is spam and what is not. These are called "target variables". Similarly, a company may want to hire "good" employees.

While framing the problem, however, the company will have to define what "good" means before sorting out the job applications for good employees. Is a good employee one who does not come late to work, or one who can sell more products, or one who is more qualified? These are defined as "class labels".

POLICY FRAMEWORK A MUST

If adequate care is not taken, discrimination can creep into an AI system because of how an organisation defines the target variables and class labels, argued Prof. Frederik Zuiderveen Borgesius, professor of Law, Institute for Computing and Information Sciences (iCIS) at Radboud University, in a 2018 report written for the anti-discrimination department of the Council of Europe.[8]

Prof. Borgesius argues in the paper that regulation can aim to improve transparency. "The law (including guidelines, etc.) could, for instance, require that AI systems used in the public sector are developed in such a way that they enable auditing and explainability". If protected by intellectual property (IP) laws, regulation should require organisations to disclose certain information to researchers upon request, he insists.

There have been many attempts to resolve this issue. For instance, mathematicians and statisticians from the University of Warwick, Imperial, EPFL, and Sciteb Ltd have joined hands to assist businesses and regulators in creating a new "Unethical Optimisation Principle" and providing a simple formula to estimate its impact.

They have laid out the full details in a paper titled "An unethical optimisation principle". According to one of the authors, Professor Robert MacKay of the Mathematics Institute of the University of Warwick, their suggested Unethical Optimisation Principle also "suggests that it may be necessary to re-think the way AI operates in very large strategy spaces, so that unethical outcomes are explicitly rejected in the optimisation/learning process."[9]

Providing the DL model with a context also helps. On July 6, 2020, a team of University of Southern California (USC) researchers said they had developed a more efficient context-sensitive hate speech classifier. Towards this end, the researchers programmed the algorithm to consider the context in which the group identifier is used and whether specific features of hate speech are also present—such as dehumanising and insulting language.

The USC team realised that social media hate speech detection algorithms ironically amplify racial bias by blocking inoffensive tweets by black people or other minority group members. This, they reasoned, was because hate speech classifiers are oversensitive to group identifiers like "black", "gay", or "transgender", which are only indicators of hate speech when used in a specific setting. Hence, providing the algorithm with a context becomes critical.

Companies and governments are now gravitating towards a concept called "Explainable AI" (XAI), also referred to as transparent AI, which even has the backing of the likes of institutions like the US-based Defense Advanced Research Projects Agency (DARPA).

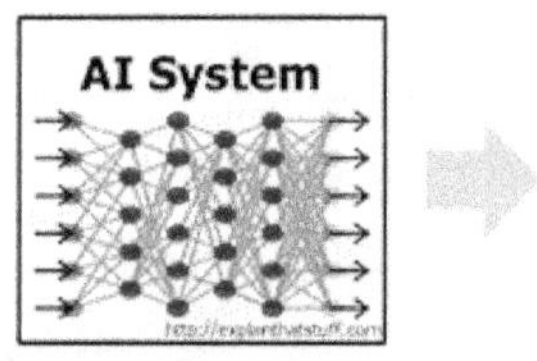

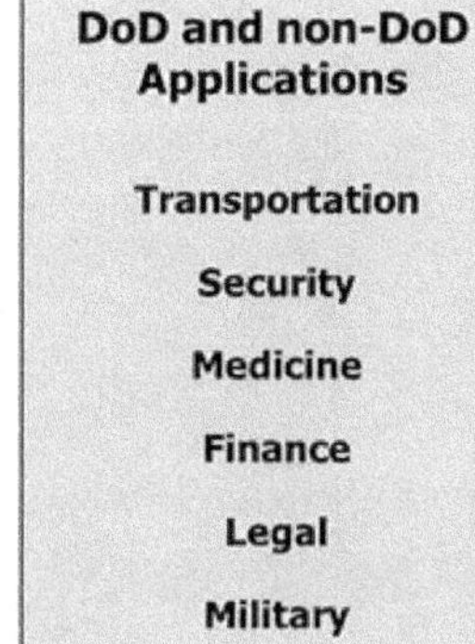

- We are entering a new age of AI applications
- Machine learning is the core technology
- Machine learning models are opaque, non-intuitive, and difficult for people to understand

- Why did you do that?
- Why not something else?
- When do you succeed?
- When do you fail?
- When can I trust you?
- How do I correct an error?

Source: DARPA

According to Matt Turek, Information Innovation Office (I2O), Program Manager at DARPA, the XAI programme aims to create a suite of ML techniques that can produce more explainable models while maintaining a high level of learning performance (prediction accuracy) and enabling human users to understand, appropriately trust, and effectively manage the emerging generation of artificially intelligent partners.[10]

I recall the interview I did with Kay Firth-Butterfield, Head of Artificial Intelligence and ML at the World Economic Forum (WEF), for *Mint* in October 2019.[11] Among other things, she pointed out that all WEF projects consider and include the big ethical issues of AI—safety, privacy, accountability, transparency, and bias.

As an example, WEF developed guidelines with the UK government. Released by the UK in September 2019, these guidelines build upon the UK's data ethics framework. They require procurement officers to think about issues such as responsible design development and the use of AI, including transparency. The guidelines include inputs from multiple stakeholders, including businesses, the government, startups, and NGOs. Around the same time, WEF also released a white paper to help countries develop a National AI Strategy.

According to the white paper, a national strategy with long-term planning and a global outlook will steer the country in the right direction, not just to manage any concerns but also to make the fullest use of AI's potential.[12] WEF recommends that country teams engaged

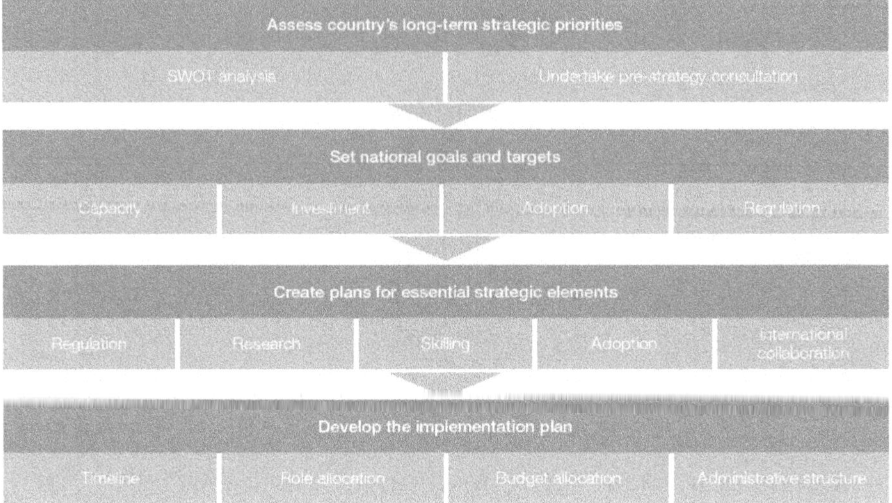

Source: WEF website

in developing a national strategy for AI can adopt the framework shown above to ensure the fundamental building blocks of an AI strategy are designed for the country.

IN SUM

As you may have realised by now, it is easier said than done when we try to ensure that AI algorithms remain fair and unbiased.

As Yan LeCun, VP and chief AI scientist, Facebook, points out, "Most of human and animal learning is unsupervised learning. If intelligence was a cake, unsupervised learning would be the cake, supervised learning would be the icing on the cake, and reinforcement learning would be the cherry on the cake. We know how to make the icing and the cherry, but we don't know how to make the cake."

More importantly, he insists that "we need to solve the unsupervised learning problem before we can even think of getting to true AI."

This is important since AI has the potential to deliver an additional $939 billion in value across public sectors of 16 major developed economies by 2035, according to a 2018 report by Accenture. Hence, it's critical that AI algorithms remain fair and transparent to all humans. In this context, it's heartening to note that the WEF, governments, and technology companies are working hand-in-hand to tackle this issue.

The Partnership on AI, for instance, is an excellent effort to make AI socially responsible. It was established in late 2016, led by a group of AI researchers representing six technology companies: Apple, Amazon, DeepMind and Google, Facebook, IBM, and Microsoft. The alliance now comprises a community of over 50 member organisations and nearly 100 partners.

The alliance hopes to develop and share best-practice methods and approaches in the research, development, testing, and fielding of AI technologies; advance public understanding of AI across varied constituencies, including on core technologies, potential benefits, and costs; provide an open and inclusive platform for discussion and engagement on the future of AI, and to ensure that key stakeholders have the knowledge, resources, and overall capacity to participate fully in these important conversations; and finally, to identify and foster aspirational efforts in AI for socially benevolent applications.

According to the 2020 annual report of the Partnership on AI, published in February 2021, the organisation has been able to make progress in achieving its goals. Among the many steps that the organisation has taken to work towards the creation of a responsible AI ecosystem, it has recommended 12 principles that designers should

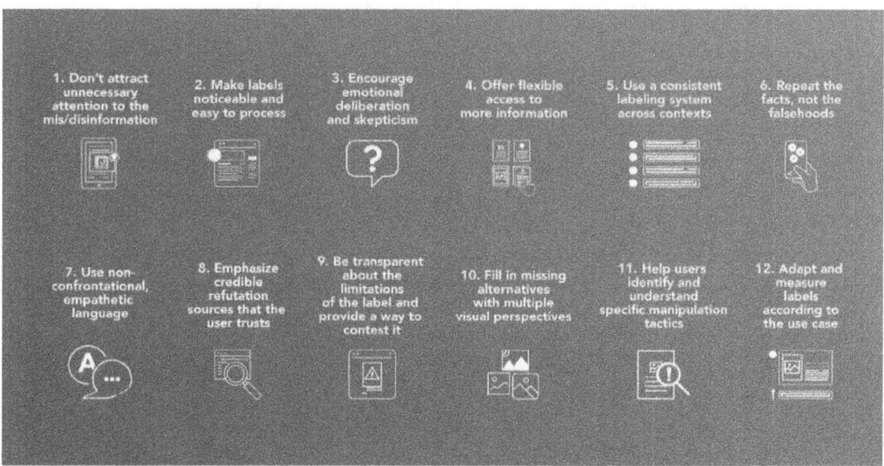

Source: Partnership on AI (https://www.partnershiponai.org/)

follow when labelling manipulated media online.

But this does not mean that governments and companies will not resort to "ethical washing" at times, whereby they pretend to be the guardians of ethical AI while turning a blind eye or glossing over many cases of abuse like surveillance and privacy compromises. We must clearly be on guard for such abuses and continue to apply pressure for equitable AI models.

That being said, we may also need to set our own expectations right, failing which we have a Utopian idea of unbiased AI. We humans have lived with our biases for thousands of years and will continue to do so in the future. This is despite the fact that we have been sensitised over the years to inconsistencies and falsehoods in our belief and value systems. Hence, it's perhaps unreasonable and impractical to expect algorithms developed by us—and trained by the data we have generated over the years—to be completely rid of any type of bias.

What we can do, however, is to insist on a policy framework that continuously keeps an eye on AI algorithms and demands that they explain the process by which they arrive at decisions. Along with initiatives like the Partnership on AI, these steps will help the world improve these algorithms and prevent their misuse to a greater extent by building in accountability at the design stage itself.

In the next chapter, we will explore the steps and policies that India is implementing to safeguard its citizens from the potential misuse of AI.

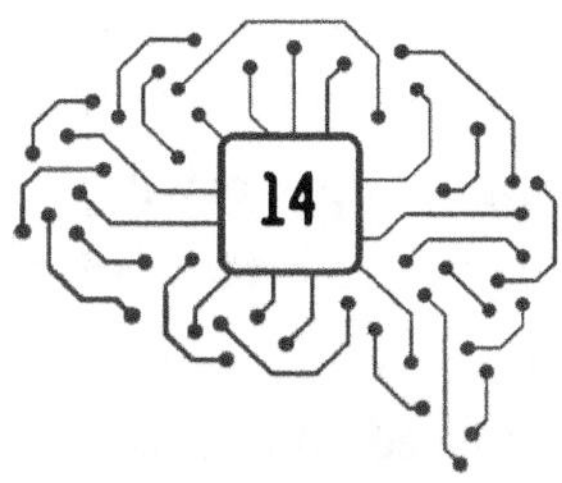

FRAMING AN AI POLICY

"Technology may be propelling us into a 'new century with no plan, no control, no brakes' and it may now very well be the time for reprising control before we cross the 'fail-safe point'."
—Nappinai N.S. (2017)[1] (citing Nappinai Joy. W. (2000) & Drawing on Thoreau)[2]

May 2016—the sleek and gorgeous Tesla Model S is cruising along on autopilot. It's a bright sunny day, the perfect day to be out for a long drive—or so one would think. But the bright Florida sun finds a flaw in the autopilot system, which fails to register the white truck turning into the car's path. The car crashes into the truck, and Joshua Brown, the driver, loses his life. The bright sunny morning is not quite as sunny any more.[3]

Fast forward to 2017, and, in this instance, it is a Tesla Model X that the driver puts on autopilot and decides to play a video game on his mobile. The driver does not notice the car veering or the looming threat of a concrete barrier that it eventually crashes into—and another life is lost.[4]

Technology is indeed careening us towards a precipice—literally and figuratively, and it is indeed time to take control. It is no surprise that Tesla's Elon Musk himself advocates regulation for AI *"just to make sure that we don't do something very foolish"*.[5]

Many of Tesla's models are listed as chart-toppers—not surprising considering that its Falcon Wing Model X[6] and its recent Cybertruck[7]

Model are equated to futuristic vehicles from the Hollywood stable of *Back to the Future* and the Batmobile. Continued interest in autonomous vehicles and increasingly appealing cars will prevail, and so will incidents such as the above unless some restraints or safety mechanisms are in place to mitigate the harm.

The Uber incident discussed above is sadder still, with a typical suburban scene of a lady wheeling a bicycle across the road hit by a self-driving car in Tempe, Arizona. Reminiscent of the Tesla car crash, in this instance also, the driver Ms. Vasquez was reportedly watching a television show when the accident occurred.

In each of the cases set out above, including that of Ms. Vasquez, the commonality is that the drivers were held accountable for the accidents, as it was concluded that irrespective of the autopilot or self-driving capabilities of the vehicles, the drivers behind the wheel are expected to exercise human oversight. In all of these cases, the US National Transportation Safety Board (NTSB) blamed human error for the accidents. It is, therefore, no surprise that one of the proposals being mooted now is for special driving licence regulations for "drivers" of self-driving cars or autonomous vehicles.[8]

AI in autonomous vehicles is just one example, but this points most poignantly to the need for law and regulation. In the instances above, provisions that the car manufacturers' mandate of human oversight played a significant role in the transference of liability to the drivers. It would, however, be misleading and too simplistic to assume that it would all be only the liability of drivers. It is imperative to not only hold accountable manufacturers of autonomous vehicles but also ensure transparency in such accountability. This is a classic illustration to demonstrate not just the need but the enabling role that laws and regulations can play.

For instance, the above Uber incident put a halt to not only this company's test runs with autonomous vehicles in Arizona but to various similar initiatives by others, such as Google's Waymo and the robotaxis proposed by Baidu, the Chinese technology giant. The ambiguity and confusion about the liability of the company versus that of the driver and the need for clarity with respect to the same are reportedly causing a delay in further testing and adaptation of autonomous vehicles, according to the BBC report on the same.[9]

Certainty—for manufacturers and users: Understanding and applying in advance the requirements mandated, and not just abiding by such mandates but also facing the consequences for their violation, are the certainties that laws and regulations provide. Technology has evolved exponentially, and many feel that this was enabled due to the absence of restraints. This may, however, be a fallacious construct.

That stage, when the unfettered evolutionary process of technology needs the helping hands of laws, is the tipping point. This phase decides whether the technology will take wing and be equipped for large-scale adaptation or remain merely a concept on paper. This role of law, as an enabler, is often lost in the noise over the complicated processes that it mandates by way of compliance. That a fast car cannot be driven if not for its brakes is often forgotten.

Innovation and advancement can and will flourish only when there are rules guiding their path. An innovator needs protection against infringement of his rights. This is enabled through IP laws. An investor needs protection and assurance of returns. This is feasible only when the laws of the land are robust enough to provide this assurance of protection and remedies against violation. Similarly, the user's confidence to adapt to emerging technologies comes from the assurance that laws provide— of safety and security, as also remedies for violation thereof.

CONCERNS TO BE ADDRESSED WHILE REGULATING AI

When it comes to AI, the need for laws and regulations is manifold. With AI being substantially dependent on data as its primary fuel, the need for regulating the collection, use, retention, and dissemination of personal data was recognised and, in fact, implemented in several jurisdictions nearly 25 years ago.

AI bias is a topic that percolates every discussion and decision in the development or adaptation of an AI system. The impact of this bias is deep-rooted and far-reaching. Taking cars and drivers as a case in point would best illustrate the issues that such AI bias raises. AI learns from its creators and carries their biases. When it recognises a human near a microwave or a vacuum cleaner as a woman and the human next to a car as a male, its gender bias is evident. If AI systems were to decide and issue driving licences, they might apply the same gender bias to decide against issuing driving licences to women while assuming men to be a safe bet. This is a real and not just a hypothetical threat.

AI bias is not limited only to gender bias. It is equally potent in its percolation into communal, racial, and other indicators that are inherent in human bias. When applied by AI systems, however, such bias is more pronounced with the lack of discretion in AI systems. These, again, are situations warranting interventions, and such interventions are best applied through the implementation of laws, rules, and guidelines.

Some of the solutions that national policy documents (including that of India) have evolved to combat these concerns are through transparency and XAI, which includes opening the black box of AI systems to have a peek into their functioning. These bring to the fore concerns over proprietary rights and their dilution. Again, such concerns are best addressed through IP laws and regulations that balance the proprietary rights of owners of such IP with the need for protecting other stakeholder rights.

Security of the data that is collected and, more importantly, the manner in both data and processing thereof and its use through AI applications are the other concerns for which laws are required.

Surveillance is the other face of security, and AI is most feared for its potential in this regard and more so for abuse thereof. While movies and books are accused of demonising AI, recent trends also indicate that not all such fiction is exaggerated. Take the illustration of *Minority Report* and that scene of Tom Cruise in a store. The minute he enters the store, The Gap, the systems scan his retina and his attempts at keeping a low profile are blown. Not just that, but the store systems call out his shopping history and make suggestions for his present shopping spree. The film also focuses on predictive policing—catching criminals before they commit a crime and punishing them for just their intent to commit crimes.

All of the above seemed highly unlikely and pure fiction. Not quite so when you look at the possibilities and, in fact, the reality of today. We did not need the movie *The Social Network* (2010) to highlight the extent of corporate surveillance or the exposé of 2019 that all digital assistants are probably not only listening to us all the time but that the companies have human intervention to review such data, albeit randomly.[10] Every online platform, app, e-commerce store, and digital medium today track our browsing history, viewing or reading patterns, or shopping history. It not only then uses its personalised knowledge of our patterns to target advertisements but also to modulate our choice and conduct. The use of AI has gone way beyond just knowing our choice. It engineers and modulates it now. It is not just about shopping any more, with such pattern recognitions being used for modulating conduct in elections.[11] Such profiling and usage for psychological manipulation of users violate multiple fundamental rights and not just that of privacy and choice. It cuts to the very basis of our being—choice and its exercise without manipulation. It is trite, therefore, to affirm that such instances require much regulation.

Surveillance and profiling take another turn when it moves from corporate to State actors. The panopticon[12] of digital surveillance makes the world a stage for surveillance and profiling by State actors. The theory first propounded by Jeremy Bentham was elaborated by Foucault, and these constructs appear most apt in the face of rampant digital surveillance.[13] From social media data to that which is collected through the use of technology for law enforcement and governance, government authorities have never been better placed when it comes to compiling comprehensive data on its residents. The use of multiple data sets to profile and predict takes macabre twists when applied by State actors.

During a visit to Chicago's Contemporary Art Museum, I was fascinated by an exhibit—which demonstrated unquestionably the extent of surveillance data that law enforcement has. The artist, a lady, walks blindfolded in different public spaces with only the help of a law enforcement officer guiding her steps, and, in turn, the law enforcement officer uses the aid of CCTVs to guide her. She does this in different public spaces to demonstrate that the level of surveillance is not just to some but most public spaces. As far as I can recollect, this experiment was conducted in London, UK, one of the jurisdictions with very robust CCTV laws and regulations covering both public and private usage.[14]

Combine the power of surveillance through CCTV footage with facial recognition technology (FRT). Telangana has used the TSCOP app since 2018. The app, which collects fingerprint and facial data, is reportedly being misused against citizens without a warrant or just cause.[15] Mass surveillance is not a new fad in Telangana, nor is it the first state to indulge in it. In fact, the Telangana model of mass surveillance is reportedly on the lines of New York and Chicago.[16]

The use of FRT for governance again stems from Telangana, which tested this technology in January 2020 for voter verification at polling stations. With increasing acerbity following every single election, such usage may be a welcome move. However, the very same process could very well become a threat to privacy, including voting. Similarly, Telangana also claims the most effective use of AI, FRT, and other technology solutions in fighting COVID.[17] Telangana's proclivity for using mass surveillance and the use of intrusive technologies in law enforcement automatically brings up some unease. While several emerging uses, including for renewing a driving licence or enrolling into a college from home, are use cases that show immense potential, as also the probable further uses for elections or pensions, the rampant use, including by police, highlights the huge personal data protection and privacy risks.[18]

All of the above merely buttresses the need for effective regulations that would balance governance or law enforcement with privacy and protection of the rights of citizens.

LEGAL AND POLICY FRAMEWORKS FOR AI

The business potential of AI is the primary focal point of governments that wish to tap this potential for employment and revenue generation. This public good perspective is well warranted, as also the tapping of AI and data for public services and ensuring maximum benefit for each government's citizenry. This focus, however, being that of each government by itself, raises concerns, including that of protectionism and possible attendant harms; the same as are envisaged in AI.

From the Indian perspective, NITI Aayog[19] was first off the block through its national policy for AI in the form of a discussion paper titled "National Strategy for Artificial Intelligence" (NSAI 2018).[20] The paper proposes #AIforAll or the democratisation of AI through permeation of the benefits of the use of AI in various sectors such as healthcare, agriculture, education, smart cities and infrastructure, and smart mobility and transportation. "Social and inclusive growth" is the catchphrase used in this document that focuses predominantly on what it refers to as the "trillions of dollars in opportunity for IT industry". With this opportunity comes a lot of risks and threats, particularly for users, and these are summed up in this paper while prescribing recommendations.

Interestingly, two primary legal issues are dealt with in this paper— the protection of IP through the tightening of IP laws[21] and the construct of proportionate liability in case of AI mishaps. While the first is a proactive step, the second changes the course of tried and tested liability propositions. The suggestion also seems to follow in the footsteps of the Tesla and Uber incidents, where the human was still held liable for the failure of machines to correctly read a situation.

Proportionate liability presupposes contributory negligence of the user in terms of apportioning blame. In the above cases, for instance, apart from the liability of drivers, there would be a first level of liability that lies with the defects in manufacturing. Failure of a moving vehicle to identify stationary vehicles, or failure to read a large vehicle because of sunlight, or the use of the colour white are serious aberrations that caused loss of life, and to merely say that the drivers were liable would be fallacious. It is important to, therefore, carve out the liability of manufacturers not only after an incident occurs but also prior thereto.

For instance, the test parameters that an autonomous vehicle must complete before it is allowed to be tested on roads form an important compliance process that is provided through regulatory mechanisms. These provisions for liability are covered under the caption of "security" in NSAI 2018, which appears to be misleading and would probably lead to the dilution of user rights rather than strengthening them. It also does not address the manufacturer's and its vendors' accountability with clarity. The paper also proposes a "negligence test" instead of strict liability, which again is worrisome.

To combat AI bias, NSAI 2018 recommends impact analysis and believes that opening the black box or XAI may be the solution. Privacy is sought to be addressed through personal data protection laws and legal frameworks. It also refers to the Japanese and German legal frameworks that specifically regulate next-generation robots and self-driving cars, respectively.

Several state governments have actively encouraged research and adaptation of AI-based solutions. Tamil Nadu leads by not only working on such adaptation but has also released in 2020 its AI policy paper titled, "Safe & Ethical Artificial Intelligence Policy 2020",[22] the first of its kind from a state government in India. That which stands out with the Tamil Nadu AI policy document is its focus on ensuring that AI adaptation "is aligned to democratic values".

The single-minded focus in NSAI 2018 on research and development, upskilling, and accelerating AI adaptation are certainly positive trends to be welcomed and several state governments, including Tamil Nadu, as set out above, have not only invested in research but also early adaptation of AI in governance and law enforcement.

The most visible use of AI in healthcare has been its adaptation to combat the coronavirus (COVID) pandemic. Telangana has led from the front on this. However, the measures taken, including the use of AI and other technologies, are through the unregulated use of mass surveillance, which is a serious cause for concern.[23]

Upskilling would not just be for those in technology but also for users. If AI is to be adapted for agriculture, for instance, upskilling the farmer would be as important. Maharashtra's AI initiative focuses on agriculture, as do several other states such as Rajasthan.[24]

Can monitoring driving behavioural patterns bring down road accidents? West Bengal believes so and has adapted AI for this use case to purportedly bring down road accidents. This collaborative effort between the West Bengal State Police and the state IT department is reportedly tracking "suspicious or abnormal driving behaviour" and signalling the police. As with any government action of mass surveillance, this one certainly raises privacy concerns and also highlights the urgent need for laws and regulations that would effectively balance the needs for governance and security with protecting privacy.

In January 2020, NITI Aayog published an approach paper titled "AI Research, Analytics and Knowledge Assimilation platform", abbreviated to AIRAWAT (AIRAWAT 2020),[25] which sets out the road map for India's vision of an AI cloud, which was one of the recommendations in NSAI 2018.[26] The key design philosophy for AIRAWAT, the 2020 paper notes, "shall be guided by the need to democratise access to AI computing infrastructure". This initiative appears to be timed along with the various calls for the localisation of data and encouraging indigenous innovations and startups, among other initiatives that, as mentioned above, appear to be focused on the public good.

Personal data protection enactments appear to be the preferred route that is being adopted not just by India but other jurisdictions also, that wish to ensure the protection of privacy and security of data collected, with the European Union's General Data Protection Regulation (GDPR) being treated as a gold standard for personal data protection legal frameworks. Privacy protection in India is sought to be addressed through the proposed special legislation, the Personal Data Protection Bill, 2019 (PDP Bill 2019). The Central Government also published a research paper on non-personal data, which will have a huge impact on businesses.

THE WAY FORWARD–LEGAL FRAMEWORKS THAT PROTECT RIGHTS AND ENABLE AI ADAPTATION

From the NSAI 2018 AI paper to its "Report by the Committee of Experts on Non-Personal Data Governance Framework"[27] (NPD 2020), the Central Government has evinced clear trends for the use of emerging technology for the public good. Such usage, however, has to be proportionate without impinging on fundamental rights, especially privacy. It would also have to take into account India's accession to international treaties whilst deciding national policies and legal frameworks.

Finally, with India's thrust being towards garnering maximum economic benefit from AI and data, it is imperative that the policy or legal framework does not become an impediment. The seemingly conflicting stand of tightening IP laws, while diluting them through statutory licensing processes that seem to be the intent for encouraging startups (which appears to be the objective, as is evident from the NPD 2020 paper), will have to be reconciled and clear focus should be brought forth to ensure that the proposed legal framework is an enabler and not an impediment.

Security and surveillance concerns will necessarily have to be addressed not only from the perspective of government requirements but also keep in mind that fundamental rights, such as privacy and free speech and expression do not suffer.

Personal data protection awaits a fillip through special laws, and the PDP Bill 2019 is expected to fill this lacuna. With the Supreme Court affirming that privacy is a fundamental right in its nine-judge unanimous decision in *Justice K.S. Puttaswamy v. Union of India*,[28] it appeared that this special law for personal data protection would be expeditiously enacted and implemented. This has not been the case at the time of writing this book. The bill may see the light of day by the time this book is published. However, the PDP Bill 2019, which is being reviewed by a joint parliamentary committee, is nearing its last leg of review. While the present draft leaves a lot wanting, especially with expansive exemptions having been built into the draft, the hope is for a final enactment that will retain the focus on protecting the personal data of India's individuals.

There is a general misconception that India does not presently have legal provisions for personal data protection. This is patently incorrect, as Section 43A and 72A of the Information Technology Act, 2000 (as amended) ('IT Act') provides the civil and criminal penalties, respectively, for negligent handling of personal and sensitive personal data. These provisions are further buttressed by the rules framed under Section 43A of the IT Act, namely the 'Information Technology (Reasonable Security Practices And Procedures And Sensitive Personal Data Or Information) Rules, 2011' ('SPD Rules'). Hence, until such time that a special personal data protection enactment comes into effect, the above provisions hold sway.

In the Privacy Judgment (*Justice K.S. Puttaswamy v. UOI (supra)*) and also in the subsequent Aadhaar Judgment (*Justice K.S. Puttaswamy v. UOI*)[29], the Supreme Court emphasised the need for a law enacted by Parliament, for meeting legitimate State aims and that which is proportionate, as the very foundation for testing the constitutionality of any restrictions on the right to privacy.

Predictive policing is no longer fictional, as in *Minority Report* but an actual AI use case. The use of predictive algorithms is being increasingly relied on both by the police and the judiciary, with the former using it to predict repeat offenders and the latter using similar parameters to evaluate the sentence to be imposed. AI bias has been demonstrably shown in such instances. While this is so, police usage of AI techniques could also result in expeditious investigations that include identifying serial killers.[30] These again raise the need for transparency in adaptation through regulations that would protect individual rights against the wrongful application of AI without scuttling the positive usage of emerging technologies.

Be it AI adaptation for governance or law enforcement, the very methodologies adverted to emphasise the need for stringent checks and balances should be enacted expeditiously, lest such usage becomes the norm and we turn our entire nation into a panopticon.

India has a huge array of international laws, regulations, and guidelines to adapt from. In November 2020, the World Economic Forum released a guidance document for policymakers for autonomous vehicles, an effective "virtual driving licence" framework that will help regulators formulate laws. There are robust laws from the UK and Germany not only on the accountability of manufacturers but also on insurance. Laws and guidelines already exist in several jurisdictions for the use of CCTV cameras in public and private places, particularly in the UK. That the use of FRT cannot and ought not to be encouraged without effective checks and balances is trite, and given its already existing rampant adaptation in India, this aspect requires the immediate attention of lawmakers.

The NSAI 2018 was an effective first step in formulating policy frameworks for AI, but the same cannot guide legal frameworks down the line. Developments over the last few years have added much value to the potential of AI, as also to the grave and far-reaching consequences of its abuse. India's National Cyber Security Strategy for 2020–25 is awaited, and the assumption is that the much-delayed document will find its foothold in 2022 and provide the guiding steps for evolving legal frameworks. Expediting such steps for evolving and implementing laws and regulations for AI can and ought to provide thrust and momentum for enabling and encouraging innovation and adaptation of AI in all fields in India.

PART-4

FUTURE OF ARTIFICIAL INTELLIGENCE

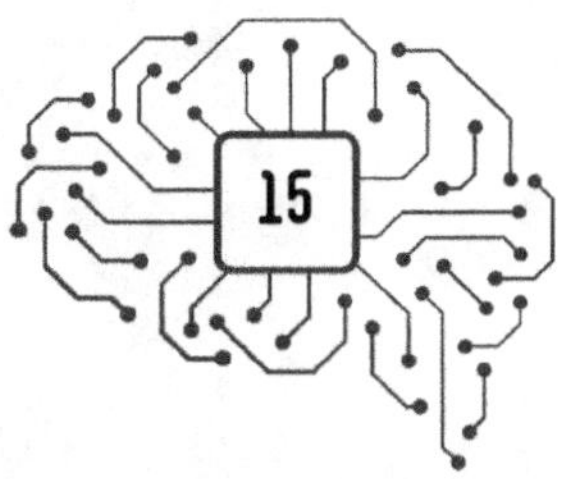

RISE OF AI-POWERED METAVERSES

"See, the world is full of things more powerful than us. But if you know how to catch a ride, you can go places."

—*Neal Stephenson,* Snow Crash

When we began writing this book, little did we realise that by the time we completed it, we would be talking not only about AI but about immersive AI-powered metaverses. The metaverse has its fair share of enthusiasts and sceptics, but the fact is that this concept is in its infancy and has a lot more maturing to do before CEOs of companies take it seriously. But that does not take away from the fact that the metaverse is already getting a lot of press. And perhaps, with good reason.

Consider the case of Chennai-based Dinesh Kshatriyan, who decided to adopt a virtual experience for his wedding reception in early January 2022, given the restrictions state governments imposed to stem the spread of the COVID-19 variant. While the actual wedding ceremony was an intimate real-world affair at his fiancée's village, the reception was held in a virtual representation of the Hogwarts School of Witchcraft and Wizardry from the Harry Potter universe.

Instead of attending a physical event, guests appeared as virtual avatars. To make all of this possible, Kshatriyan partnered with cryptocurrency and blockchain startup Polygon and a Chennai-based mixed-reality technology startup called TardiVerse.

Abhijeet Goel and Sansrati, who tied the knot a month later, went a step further by getting married in a 3D metaverse. The wedding,

Dinesh Kshatriyan and Janaganandhini Ramaswamy wed in the metaverse too

which took place on Yug Metaverse, was conceptualised, organised and executed by the media agency Wavemaker India for ITC Ltd. and Matrimony.com.

The digital avatars of the couple had their ceremony hosted on a scenic beachside venue where the guests also joined in via their digital avatars even as the physical wedding was being celebrated in Bhopal. The wedding had more than 500 registrations. Users could change their avatars, walk through the event and dance too. Wavemaker, part of GroupM, partnered with Matrimony.com for this 3D wedding on the metaverse platform. Fabelle, a premium luxury chocolate brand from the house of ITC, was the gifting partner.

While these are simply cases in point, it begs the question: What exactly is a metaverse? While there's no one definition, the metaverse is broadly a combination of both the physical and digital worlds where people can interact virtually with the help of VR headsets and AR. Research and advisory firm Gartner Inc. defines a metaverse as a collective virtual shared space created by the convergence of virtually enhanced physical and digital reality. It is persistent, providing enhanced immersive experiences, as well as device-independent, and accessible through any type of device, from tablets to head-mounted displays.

Gartner predicts that by 2026, 25 per cent of people will spend at least one hour a day in the metaverse for work, shopping, education, social, and/or entertainment. "Vendors are already building ways for users to replicate their lives in digital worlds," said Marty Resnick, research vice president at Gartner. "From attending virtual classrooms to buying digital land and constructing virtual homes, these activities are currently being conducted in separate environments. Eventually, they will take place in a single environment—the metaverse—with multiple destinations across technologies and experiences."[1] The metaverse, according to Gartner, will impact every business that consumers interact with every day. It will also impact how work gets done. Enterprises will provide better engagement, collaboration, and connection to their employees through immersive workspaces in virtual offices.

BUZZ GATHERS STEAM

While people and businesses are just getting their feet wet in the metaverse, industry experts believe that some users—especially younger ones—may eventually earn, spend, and invest most of their money in digital worlds. The metaverse could represent a $1 trillion market by the end of the decade, according to an April 13, 2022 note by CB Insights' Industry Analyst Consensus.

The hype around the metaverse began in earnest when Mark Zuckerberg made his Meta announcement on October 28, 2021, and insisted on wanting the new identity to be "metaverse-first, not Facebook-first" (remember, Google underscores AI-first, and Meta cannot work without AI). But it must be noted that the metaverse is not unique to Facebook. Many technology firms, including Microsoft, Nvidia, and Fortnite maker Epic Games, have been talking about their own visions of the metaverse for quite some time.

In fact, the term itself has been borrowed from Neal Stephenson's 1992 sci-fi novel *Snow Crash*, where the concept was used to describe a new kind of internet with VR. And if you're a sci-fi movie buff, you will recall Tom Cruise encountering interactive billboards and iris-triggered direct marketing in the film *Minority Report* that was released nearly 19 years ago, or Tony Stark—the Marvel Comics superhero in the movie *Iron Man*— going a step further with his AI partner Jarvis

Source: Meta website

(just a very intelligent system) providing him all the information he needs on holograms, computers, and also in Stark's Iron Man suits.

Pokémon Go, a free location-based AR mobile game for iOS and Android smartphone users, mixes online reality with the real world. It allows players to use GPS and Google Maps on their smartphones to look for PokéStops at places such as public art installations, historical markers, and monuments, where they can collect Poké Balls and other items. And like PokéStops, gyms can be found at real locations in the world—all this without users needing a VR headset, which indicates that AR technology is coming of age.

You may recall Second Life, which can be said to be a different kind of metaverse within, or beyond, the internet. Developed by San Francisco-based Linden Labs in 2003, this multiplayer world became a digital craze when it allowed users to create their digital 3D avatars, socialise with others, play games, and explore multiple worlds called Sims. While Facebook's Metaverse is a VR and AR (mixed reality that melds VR and AR with the real world) platform, Second Life is a virtual online world that can be accessed on a PC. It also has a thriving marketplace where users can buy and sell merchandise, property, and services using a virtual currency called Linden dollar. Second Life's user base reached a record high of 1.1 million monthly active users in 2013 and is currently believed to have around 9,00,000 active users.

Magic Leap, founded in 2010 by Rony Abovitz, went a step further. It was seen as one of the most promising companies in the field of mixed reality. Abovitz managed to create and sustain buzz around Magic Leap headsets for years without actually launching a product in the market. In 2018, US telco AT&T acquired stakes in the company, and the first Magic Leap One headset was launched at AT&T stores the same year.

However, Magic Leap One failed to live up to the hype and was a far cry from the tall promises made in their many demonstrations. Palmer Luckey, who is best known as the founder of Oculus VR and designer of Oculus Rift (both owned by Facebook or Meta now), in a blog post titled "Magic Leap is a Tragic Heap"[2], called it a flashy hype vehicle that no one can use in a meaningful way. Abovitz eventually stepped down in 2020 and Peggy Johnson, a former Microsoft executive, was appointed as CEO. In October 2021, Magic Leap raised $500 million in funding, taking the total investments to $3.5 billion, and soon announced its next AR headset, Magic Leap 2.

The craze around Second Life and Pokémon Go may have surely waned with time, but the fact remains that technology companies like Microsoft with its HoloLens and US-based startup Magic Leap Inc. are increasingly betting on the melding of technologies like AR and VR with the real world to give users and businesses a world of so-called "mixed" reality (MR) or "blended" reality concepts to deal with. The belief is that these technologies have the potential to become the next big computing platform.

While VR is all about a world created solely on computers or online, AR still deals with the real world and has elements of the virtual world built atop it, akin to layers of information. AR technology was envisioned by Ivan Sutherland, who devised the first AR system in 1968, but the technology is blooming only now with customised applications in industrial automation, theme parks, sports television, military displays, and online marketing. Jaron Lanier, an American writer, computer scientist, and composer of classical music, is credited with popularising the term 'AR'. He and Thomas G. Zimmerman left gaming firm Atari in 1985 to launch VPL Research Inc., the first company to sell VR

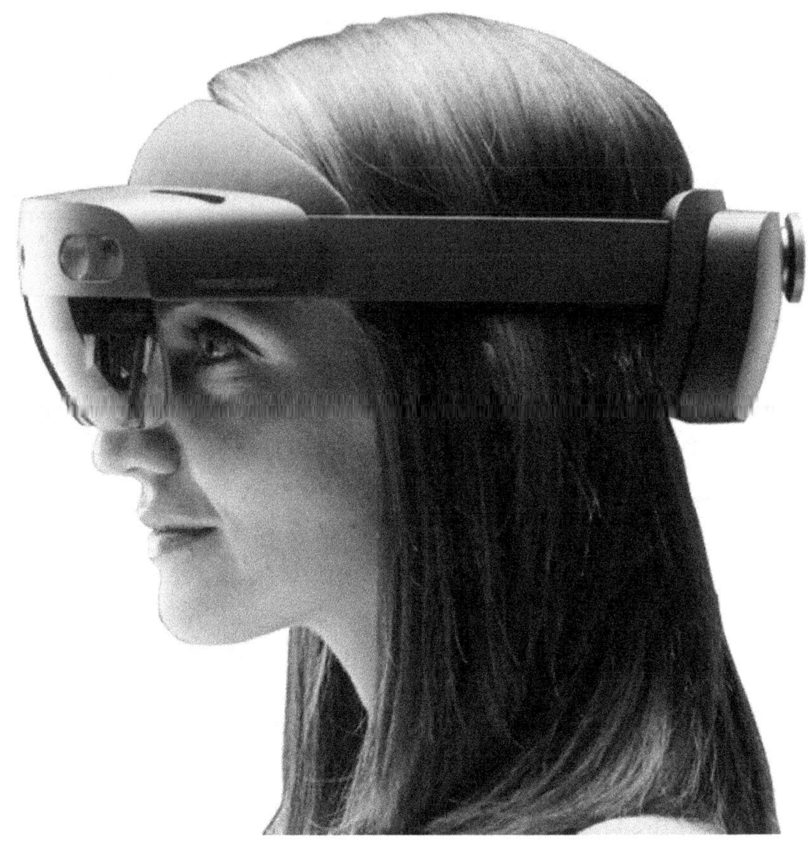

Microsoft HoloLens. *Courtesy:* Microsoft website

goggles and gloves. Mixed reality or MR, as the name suggests, mixes both realities in a bid to capture the best of both worlds. It's important to understand that companies are building their own metaverses using these technologies that have existed for more than three decades.

IT'S AN EVOLVING CONCEPT

With this context in mind, you will now appreciate why there are different metaverses currently in existence. The popular and established ones include the likes of Decentraland, The Sandbox, Roblox, Fortnite's Epic games, and even Facebook's own metaverse called Horizon Worlds.

But none of these, including the ones by Meta, Microsoft, Nvidia, Tencent, ByteDance, Alibaba, and Fortnite, are anywhere close to those shown in movies like the ones cited above, or those shown in others like *Blade Runner*. Even Meta, in a November 2021 blog, insisted that "The metaverse isn't a single product one company can build alone. Just like the internet, the metaverse exists whether Facebook is there or not." Meta executives acknowledged in the blog that the metaverse "won't be built overnight. Many of these products will only be fully realized in the next 10-15 years."

That said, the metaverse concept is clearly evolving with enhanced software and increasingly sophisticated VR and AR gears. Moreover, the hardware segment is sub-segmented into displays—eXtended Reality (XR) hardware (like haptic sensors, smart glasses, and omni treadmills) and AR/VR headsets, and the software comprises asset creation tools and programming engines, notes Emergen Research. And because no single vendor will own the metaverse, Gartner expects it to have a virtual economy enabled by digital currencies and NFTs. These, according to research firm CB Insights, can act as digital deeds to prove ownership without the need for a centralised verifying body.

In early 2022, for instance, Punjabi singer Daler Mehndi announced India's first metaverse concert that was held on Republic Day through a customised platform called Partynite. Users were invited to create their avatars and attend the concert. They had to walk around and find NFTs

Source: Roblox website

before an allotted time set by a timer. When the concert ended, a pop-up prompted the users to save all the collected NFTs and connect them to their ApnaDAO wallet.

Likewise, the Madras Maharani Concert was held in a metaverse by NFT marketplace Jupiter Meta in association with radio partners Hello FM on April 15, 2022. With a showcase of spectacular visuals, immersive digital aesthetics, and soulful singing by singer and composer Karthik, every member of the audience was given exclusive music NFTs that can be traded. The concert and Jupiter Meta's initiative to launch the music NFTs saw fans of the performer during the metaverse to hear old classics and new compositions in this unique setting, with their avatars taking in the special experience.

In September 2021, Facebook (now Meta) introduced Ray-Ban Stories—smart glasses that can capture photos and videos, help you listen to music or take phone calls. Built in partnership with Facebook and EssilorLuxottica, Ray-Ban Stories are already available in a few countries (but not in India). A month later, Facebook announced a $10 million Creator Fund to "encourage more people to come build with us as we continue rolling out Horizon in beta". Facebook Horizon is a place to explore, play, and create with others in VR. Further, lifelike Codec Avatars from Facebook Reality Labs is another ongoing research project.

Microsoft, too, is betting big on its MR holographic computer, which it christened HoloLens. HoloLens' sensors allow you to use your gaze to move the cursor when you want to select holograms. You can use gestures to open apps, select and size items, drag and drop holograms, and use voice commands to navigate, select, open, command, and control the apps. You can also speak directly to the personal digital assistant Cortana.

Indian companies are having their own brush with mixed reality. In his 2014 campaign, India's Prime Minister Narendra Modi used London-based Musion's 3D lifelike holographic technology to address audiences in 128 locations simultaneously across India.

Mumbai-based VR startup Tesseract, in which Mukesh Ambani's Reliance Jio has a majority stake, is promising a mixed reality future like that with its Jio Glass, Quark camera, Holoboard headset, and JioFiber. It is promising applications for both consumers and enterprises. For instance, you could watch a football match on a VR headset that streams the match live and projects interesting stats on the fly with the help of AR. Similarly, a Chennai-based MR startup called Imaginate enables cross-device communication over VR and AR wearables for enterprise collaboration in the industrial sector.

BUT CHALLENGES ABOUND

Today, most metaverses will show human avatars with a body, head, arms, and hands but no legs. You may wonder why, especially since these torsos seem to be eerily floating around the metaverse.

The problem is that existing VR headsets can track a body's upper half reasonably well but are not adept at doing so with the legs since they do not have enough sensors to do so. Other than this, the metaverse vision of a next-gen internet would rely on technologies like VR headsets, advanced haptic feedback, 3D modelling tools, and more to power immersive digital environments, according to CB Insights.

The avatars have no legs. *Source:* Facebook website

However, these technology challenges will be speedily resolved, especially if creators of metaverses see monetisation opportunities.

The larger concerns, however, are around sexual abuse, violation of privacy, and misuse of data in the metaverse that need more attention from policymakers. For instance, in May 2022, a SumofUs researcher along with her colleagues entered the metaverse with the aim of studying the behaviour of users on Meta's social networking platform Horizon World. But within an hour after she donned her Oculus VR headset, she says her avatar was raped in the virtual space.[3]

On November 2021, Andrew Bosworth, VP, Facebook Reality Labs and Nick Clegg, VP, global affairs, claimed in a blog[4] that the metaverse will be built responsibly. Meta also announced "a $50 million investment in global research and program partners to ensure these products are developed responsibly". "We'll collaborate with policymakers, experts, and industry partners to bring this to life," the blog reads.

Given the chequered history of Meta (earlier Facebook) with privacy, though, not many are convinced. The fact is that AI is undoubtedly becoming smarter with rapid advancements in ML and DL algorithms and needs humongous amounts of data called big data for these algorithms to be trained upon. Policymakers have repeatedly pointed out that AI-powered algorithms need to be transparent and that AI models should be able to address bias in the training data, the model, or simply be able to detect a human-induced bias. They have also argued that AI models should also give humans a right to appeal against a particular decision (assuming that the algorithm has done the explaining).

Products and services that spring out of the metaverses will thrive on data collection and AI-powered data analytics, which can lead to gross misuse if there are no checks and balances.

In a November 9 interview with the Associated Press, Facebook whistle-blower Frances Haugen opined the metaverse "will be addictive and rob people of yet more personal information while giving the embattled company another monopoly online". Haugen worked at Facebook for nearly two years after stints at Google, Yelp and Pinterest. At Facebook, she studied how the social network's algorithm amplified misinformation and was exploited by foreign adversaries. "If your employer decides they're now a metaverse company, you have to give out way more personal data to a company that's demonstrated that it lies whenever it is in its best interests," Haugen said in the interview.

Facebook had previously dismissed Haugen's claims. Among other things, Mark Zuckerberg wrote on October 6 in a blog, "It's disheartening to see that work taken out of context and used to construct a false narrative that we don't care."[5]

Intellectual property laws is another area of concern. According to CB Insights, the law will need to evolve to address the use of avatars. Celebrities who promote brands in the metaverse, for instance, will likely want to retain the rights to their avatar, and so will politicians who run metaverse campaigns want to protect their likeness. Similarly, metaverse content creators who design digital assets, video games, and other experiences will seek to copyright their creations.

Some companies have already taken action over NFTs that breach intellectual property and trademark law. Luxury fashion brand Hermès, for instance, sent a cease and desist letter to artist Mason Rothschild who sold NFT artwork inspired by the Birkin bag. The NFTs "infringed upon the intellectual property and trademark rights of Hermès and are an example of fake Hermès products in the metaverse," according to the company.

Meanwhile, the European Union's Digital Services Act (DSA), which was introduced in December 2020, among other things, said it would regulate the obligations of companies like Facebook and Google that provide digital services that collect data. The obligations include transparency measures for online platforms "that are wide-ranging, including on the algorithms used for recommendations", and giving researchers "access to data of key platforms, in order to scrutinise how platforms work and how online risks evolve".

India is yet to see the PDP Bill 2019 tabled in Parliament. Further, many people in India still do not have access to the internet, and more importantly, to electricity that powers computers. A sophisticated metaverse is unlikely to be accessible to such people, widening the already existing digital divide in the country.

In the absence of sensible policies that address these concerns, the continuing misuse of data and privacy intrusion, coupled with the deepening digital divide, will continue to outweigh the immense benefits that metaverses can offer us, and make cynics look at the AI-powered metaverse with continued suspicion.

FUTURE OF AI

It's difficult to even hazard any guesses on how AI will shape up by 2050 for the simple reason that, as we have consistently pointed out, there are just too many variables.

For one, advances in quantum computing can radically alter the speed at which data is mined and interpreted. Second, major tweaks to AI algorithms themselves are resulting in dramatically reducing the amount of data needed to train AI models, and we will certainly see more progress in the coming years. This trend is already being reflected, as we have shown in earlier chapters, in the progress that NLP models are making when translating languages with data they have not been trained upon. Third, while we may not see AI getting sentient any time soon, we will certainly see machines getting smarter in linear tasks, making many jobs redundant as we discussed in the chapter on AI and Automation.

In light of these developments, one can safely surmise that AI will increasingly influence the way we eat, work, play, do business, and interact with governments. All this implies, as we have consistently reiterated in the earlier chapters, that countries around the world, including India, will require very strong policy frameworks and laws to cover data privacy and avoid misuse of data by intelligent and automated algorithms.

But, with AI, nothing is set in stone. As Geoffrey Hinton, often referred to as the 'Godfather' of AI, himself put it: "The future (of AI) depends on some graduate student who is deeply suspicious of everything I have said." We sincerely hope that someone reading this book lives up to this challenging task.

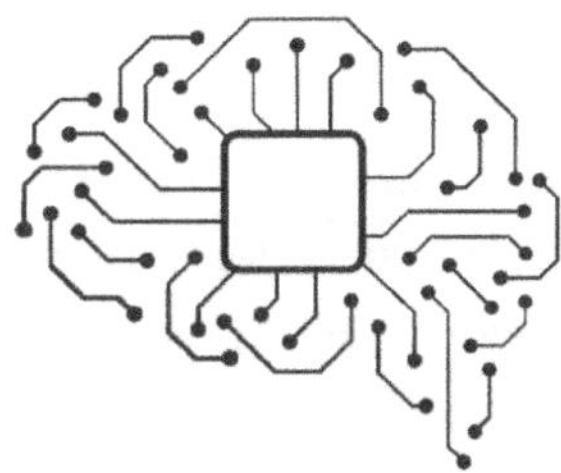

REFERENCES

Introduction

1. LiveMint. (n.d.). India poised to become tech leader: Industry experts. Retrieved from https://www.livemint.com/Industry/XbK8oZbhFhlCDEyT2VKr2M/India-poised-to-become-techleader-industry-experts.html
2. AIM Research. (2021, February). Indian AI startup funding 2020. Retrieved from https://aimresearch.ai/2021/02/indian-ai-startup-funding-2020/
3. Harvard University, Science in the News. (2017). History of artificial intelligence. Retrieved from http://sitn.hms.harvard.edu/flash/2017/history-artificialintelligence/
4. Robitzski, D. (2018, April 27). The military just created an AI that learned how to program software. Futurism. Retrieved from https://futurism.com/military-created-ai-learned-to-program
5. Gallimore, J. (2020, May 25). The AI that codes itself. AI Daily. Retrieved from https://aidaily.co.uk/articles/the-ai-that-codes-itself

Chapter 1

1. AI100. (2016). One hundred year study on artificial intelligence: 2016 report. Stanford University. Retrieved from https://ai100.stanford.edu/2016-report
2. Economic Times. (n.d.). Meet Professor HN Mahabala, the man who mentored India's IT icons. Retrieved from https://economictimes.indiatimes.com/tech/ites/meet-professorhn-mahabala-the-man-who-mentored-indias-it-icons/articleshow/53346662.cms

3. LiveMint. (n.d.). Chatbots on steroids can rewire business. Retrieved from https://www.livemint.com/technology/tech-news/chatbots-onsteroids-can-rewire-business-11599398413011.html

4. Institute for Strategic Dialogue. (2020). Hosting the Holohoax. Retrieved from https://www.isdglobal.org/wp-content/uploads/2020/08/Hosting-the-Holohoax.pdf

5. IBM Research. (n.d.). Project Debater: How it works. Retrieved from https://www.research.ibm.com/artificial-intelligence/project-debater/how-it-works/

Chapter 2

1. CNBC. (2020, March 18). What America can learn from China's use of robots and telemedicine to combat the coronavirus. Retrieved from https://www.cnbc.com/2020/03/18/how-china-is-using-robots-and-telemedicine-to-combat-the-coronavirus.html

2. Reuters. (2020, May 29). COVID-19 robot patrol rolled out in Belgian hospitals. Retrieved from https://www.reuters.com/article/us-health-coronavirus-belgium-robots/covid-19-robot-patrol-rolled-out-in-belgian-hospitals-idUSKBN2352ES

3. Imperial College London. (2020). Mixed-reality headsets in hospitals help protect doctors and reduce need for PPE. Retrieved from https://www.imperial.ac.uk/news/197617/mixed-reality-headsets-hospitals-help-protect-doctors/

4. Reliance Industries Limited. (2020). Annual Report 2019-20. Retrieved from https://www.ril.com/getattachment/299caec5-2e8a-43b7-8f70-d633a150d07e/AnnualReport_2019-20.aspx

5. Financial Times. (n.d.). [Article title not available]. Retrieved from https://www.ft.com/content/cac74a6a-3e03-4050-a9ab-7c56698157b8

6. Internet and Mobile Association of India. (n.d.). [Report title not available]. Retrieved from https://cms.iamai.in/Content/Research Papers/2286f4d7-424f-4bde-be88-6415fe5021d5.pdf

Chapter 3

1. Boston Consulting Group. (2020). Deploying AI to maximize revenue. Retrieved from https://www.bcg.com/en-in/publications/2020/deploying-ai-artificial-intelligence-to-maximize-revenue

2. CXOToday. (n.d.). AI adoption is key to the future of healthcare in India. Retrieved from https://www.cxotoday.com/ai/ai-adoption-is-key-to-the-future-of-healthcare-in-india/

3. Sleep Standards. (n.d.). Netflix and sleep. Retrieved from https://sleepstandards.com/netflix-and-sleep/

4. Netflix Research. (n.d.). Machine learning. Retrieved from https://research.netflix.com/research-area/machine-learning

5. Rio Tinto. (n.d.). Caterpillar on machinery partnership. Retrieved from https://www.riotinto.com/en/news/releases/Caterpillar-on-machinery-partnership

Chapter 4

1. StartupBlink. (n.d.). Startup ecosystem report. Retrieved from https://www.startupblink.com/startupecosystemreport.pdf

2. CXOToday. (n.d.). Built the gold standard when it comes to AI on local language content across formats: Umang Bedi, Dailyhunt. Retrieved from https://www.cxotoday.com/interviews/built-the-gold-standard-when-it-comes-to-ai-on-local-language-content-across-formats-says-umang-bedi-co-founder-of-dailyhunt/

3. NASSCOM. (2019). Indian tech startup ecosystem. Retrieved from https://nasscom.in/system/files/secure-pdf/NASSCOM_Startup_Report_2019_05112019.pdf

4. NASSCOM. (2021, June). AI patents: Driving emergence of India as an AI innovation hub. Retrieved from

5. CB Insights. (n.d.). The race for AI: Which tech giants are snapping up artificial intelligence startups. Retrieved from https://www.cbinsights.com/research/report/top-acquirers-artificial-intelligence/

6. Business Today. (2020, November 14). EY India acquires IIT alumni backed AI startup Spotmentor Technologies. Retrieved from https://www.businesstoday.in/latest/corporate/story/ey-india-acquires-iit-alumni-backed-ai-startupspotmentor-technologies-278686-2020-11-14

7. Analytics India Magazine. (n.d.). Indian AI startups raised $836.3 million in 2020: AIMResearch. Retrieved from https://analyticsindiamag.com/indian-ai-startups-raised-836-3-million-in-2020-aimresearch/

8. McKinsey & Company. (n.d.). Confronting the risks of artificial intelligence. Retrieved from https://www.mckinsey.com/business-

functions/mckinsey-analytics/ourinsights/confronting-the-risks-of-artificial-intelligence

9. Moneycontrol. (n.d.). Prime Minister Narendra Modi has this message for startup founders on valuations. Retrieved from https://www.moneycontrol.com/news/business/prime-minister-narendra-modi-has-this-message-forstartup-founders-on-valuations-6534461.html

Chapter 5

1. NASSCOM. (2020, August). Unlocking value from data and AI: the India opportunity.
2. Unique Identification Authority of India. (n.d.). Now 125 crore residents of India have Aadhaar. Retrieved from https://www.uidai.gov.in/images/Now_125_crore_residents_of_India_have_Aadhaar.pdf
3. Palmer, M. (2006, November). Data is the new oil. Retrieved from https://ana.blogs.com/maestros/2006/11/data_is_the_new.html
4. Ministry of Electronics and Information Technology. (2019, February). India's trillion dollar digital opportunity; McKinsey Global Institute. (2017). Jobs lost, jobs gained: Workforce transitions in a time of automation.
5. NDTV Gadgets. (n.d.). Tamil Nadu PDS system data breach: 50 lakh Aadhaar card numbers leak. Retrieved from https://gadgets.ndtv.com/internet/news/tamil-nadu-pdssystem-data-breach-50-lakh-aadhaar-card-numbers-leaktechnisanct-2475988
6. NITI Aayog. (n.d.). National strategy for AI discussion paper. Retrieved from https://niti.gov.in/writereaddata/files/document_publication/NationalStrategy-for-AI-Discussion-Paper.pdf
7. Frost & Sullivan. (n.d.). From $600 M to $6 Billion, artificial intelligence systems poised for dramatic market expansion in healthcare.
8. KPMG. "Indian Media and Entertainment Industry Report." Federation of Indian Chambers of Commerce and Industry (FICCI), KPMG, 2017, https://assets.kpmg.com/content/dam/kpmg/in/pdf/2017/04/FICCI-Frames-2017.pdf
9. Arthur, C. (2013, August 23). Tech giants may be huge, but nothing matches big data. The Guardian. Retrieved from https://www.theguardian.com/technology/2013/aug/23/tech-giants-data
10. NASSCOM. (2020, August). Unlocking value from data and AI: The India opportunity.

Chapter 6

1. Worldpay from FIS. (2021). The 2021 global payments report. Retrieved from https://offers.worldpayglobal.com/rs/850-JOA-856/images/ 1297411per cent20GPRper cent20DIGITALper cent20ENGLISHper cent20SINGLESper cent20RGBper cent20FNL11.pdf

2. Boku. (2021). Mobile payments report.

3. Amazon Pay. (n.d.). 10in20 insight into the impact of AI and voice. Retrieved from https://pay.amazon.com/blog/10in20-insight-into-the-impact-of-ai-and-voice

4. CXO Today. (n.d.). AI is shaping the future of digital payments: PayU CTO. Retrieved from https://www.cxotoday.com/ai/ai-is-shaping-the-future-of-digital-payments-payu-cto/

5. D'Monte, L. (n.d.). Is Craig Wright the inventor of bitcoin? The answer may not matter. LiveMint. Retrieved from https://www.livemint.com/ Industry/HCOsKkuruKgpfOub8aiqjI/Is-Craig-Wright-the-inventor-of-bitcoin-The-answer-may-not.html

6. Emergen Research. (n.d.). Metaverse market. Retrieved from https:// www.emergenresearch.com/industry-report/metaverse-market

7. Grant Thornton India. (n.d.). IBBIC: Paving way for blockchain adoption by Indian banks. Retrieved from https://www.grantthornton.in/insights/ blogs/ibbic-paving-way-for-blockchain-adoption-by-indian-banks/

Chapter 7

1. Indian Express. (n.d.). How Tauktae compares with other cyclones in severity, damage. Retrieved from https://indianexpress.com/article/ explained/how-tauktaecompares-with-other-cyclones-in-severity-damage-7324998/

2. India AI. (n.d.). How Farmpal is using AI to help farmers find customers. Retrieved from https://indiaai.gov.in/article/how-farmpal-is-using-ai-to-helpfarmers-find-customers

3. Analytics India Magazine. (n.d.). 5 times when AI was used for social good. Retrieved from https://analyticsindiamag.com/5-times-when-ai-was-used-forsocial-good/

4. United Nations. (n.d.). Sustainable Development Goals. Retrieved from https://sdgs.un.org/goals

5. NITI Aayog. (n.d.). National strategy for AI discussion paper. Retrieved from https://www.niti.gov.in/sites/default/files/2019-01/NationalStrategy-for-AI-Discussion-Paper.pdf

6. Analytics India Magazine. (n.d.). 5 times when AI was used for social good. Retrieved from https://analyticsindiamag.com/5-times-when-ai-was-used-forsocial-good/ , Google.com

7. Blue River Technology. (n.d.). Our methods. Retrieved from https://bluerivertechnology.com/ourmethods/

8. Springboard. (n.d.). Blog. Retrieved from https://www.springboard.com/blog

9. Future of Life Institute. (n.d.). Benefits & risks of artificial intelligence. Retrieved from https://futureoflife.org/background/benefits-risks-of-artificialintelligence/?cn-reloaded=1

10. PwC. (2018). Macroeconomic impact of AI technical report. Retrieved from https://www.pwc.co.uk/economic-services/assets/macroeconomic-impact-of-ai-technical-report-feb-18.pdf

11. NITI Aayog. (n.d.). National strategy for AI discussion paper. Retrieved from https://www.niti.gov.in/sites/default/files/2019-01/NationalStrategy-for-AI-Discussion-Paper.pdf

Chapter 8

1. WordNet. (n.d.). Retrieved from https://wordnet.princeton.edu/

2. Google AI Blog. (2016, September). A neural network for machine translation. Retrieved from https://ai.googleblog.com/2016/09/a-neural-network-formachine.html

3. TechCrunch. (2022, May 11). Google Translate adds 24 new languages including its first indigenous languages of the Americas. Retrieved from https://techcrunch.com/2022/05/11/google-translate-adds-24-new-languages-including-its-first-indigenous-languages-of-theamericas/

4. D'Monte, L. (2021, November 18). Search provides a very fundamental benefit to society: Google Search rankings head Pandu Nayak. TechCircle. Retrieved from https://www.techcircle.in/2021/11/18/search-provides-a-very-fundamentalbenefit-to-society-google-search-rankings-head-pandu-nayak

5. Facebook. (2020, October). First multilingual machine translation model. Retrieved from https://about.fb.com/news/2020/10/first-multilingual-machinetranslation-model/

6. D'Monte, L. (n.d.). Built the gold standard when it comes to AI on local language content across formats: Umang Bedi. CXOToday. Retrieved from https://www.cxotoday.com/interviews/built-the-gold-standard-when-it-comes-to-ai-on-local-language-content-across-formats-says-umang-bedi-co-founder-of-dailyhunt/

Chapter 10

1. Analytics India Magazine & Jigsaw Academy. (2020). State of AI in India, 2020.
2. NASSCOM. (2022). Report.
3. NASSCOM. (2022). Report.
4. NASSCOM. (2022). Report.
5. Economic Times. (n.d.). Integrated adoption of AI and data utilization can add $500 billion to India's GDP. Retrieved from https://economictimes.indiatimes.com/tech/technology/integrated-adoption-of-ai-and-data-utilization-can-add-500-billion-to-indias-gdp/articleshow/92412781.cms

Chapter 11

1. McCarthy, N. (2018, August). China now boasts 800 million internet users. Forbes. Retrieved from https://www.forbes.com/sites/niallmccarthy/2018/08/23/china-now-boasts-more-than-800-million-internet-users-and-98-of-them-are-mobile-infographic/#205e3c417092
2. The Passage. (2019, January). The discreet charm of super apps. Retrieved from https://thepassage.cc/article/1037
3. A16Z. (2015, August). When one app rules them all. Retrieved from https://a16z.com/2015/08/06/wechat-china-mobile-first/

Chapter 12

1. Global Workplace Analytics. (n.d.). U.S. employers stand to save over $500B a year with a combination of in-office/remote work strategies. Retrieved from https://globalworkplaceanalytics.com/work-at-home-after-covid-19-our-forecast
2. Vincent, J. (2020, November 3). Walmart is giving up on shelf-scanning robots in favor of humans. The Verge. Retrieved from https://www.theverge.com/2020/11/3/21547306/walmart-shelf-scanning-robots-automation-bossa-nova-robotics-contract-ended

3. Gottlieb, J., & Anderson, D. L. (n.d.). Robots: In the beginning. Illinois State University. Retrieved from https://mind.ilstu.edu/curriculum/medical_robotics/robots_in_beginning.html

4. Markoff, J. (2012). Techonomy 2012: Where's my robot?

5. Future Timeline. (n.d.). Manufacturing jobs have largely disappeared in the West. Retrieved from https://www.futuretimeline.net/21stcentury/2039.htm

6. Mechanical Chef. (n.d.). Retrieved from http://mechanicalchef.com/index.html

7. Muro, M., Whiton, J., & Maxim, R. (2019, November). What jobs are affected by AI? Brookings Institution. Retrieved from https://www.brookings.edu/wpcontent/uploads/2019/11/2019.11.20_BrookingsMetro_Whatjobs-are-affected-by-AI_Report_Muro-Whiton-Maxim.pdf

8. World Economic Forum. (2020, January). Jobs of tomorrow. Retrieved from http://www3.weforum.org/docs/WEF_Jobs_of_Tomorrow_2020.pdf

9. Reserve Bank of India. (n.d.). Retrieved from https://rbidocs.rbi.org.in/rdocs/PublicationReport/Pdfs/CDDP03062019634B0EEF3F7144C3B65360B280E420AC.PDF

Chapter 13

1. Adams, R. (2020, August). Nearly 40% of A-level result predictions to be downgraded in England. The Guardian. Retrieved from https://www.theguardian.com/education/2020/aug/07/a-level-result-predictions-to-be-downgraded-england

2. Princeton University, Engineering School. (2017, April 13). Biased bots: Human prejudices sneak into artificial intelligence systems. Retrieved from http://engineering.princeton.edu/

3. Case Western Reserve University. (n.d.). AI reveals differences in appearance of cancer tissue between racial populations. Retrieved from https://thedaily.case.edu/ai-reveals-differences-in-appearance-of-cancer-tissue-between-racial-populations/

4. Seymour, M. (2019, April 12). Canny AI: Imagine world leaders singing. FXGuide. Retrieved from https://www.fxguide.com/fxfeatured/canny-ai-imagine-world-leaders-singing/?utm_source=twitter&utm_medium=social&utm_campaign=SocialWarfare

5. Cole, S. (n.d.). This horrifying app undresses a photo of any woman with a single click. Vice. Retrieved from https://www.vice.com/en/article/kzm59x/deepnude-app-creates-fake-nudes-of-any-woman

6. Cole, S. (n.d.). Creator of DeepNude, app that undresses photos of women, takes it offline. Vice. Retrieved from https://www.vice.com/en/article/qv7agw/deepnude-app-that-undresses-photos-of-women-takes-it-offline

7. Greene, T. (2018, June 2). Report: Google to abandon Project Maven after government contract ends. The Next Web. Retrieved from https://thenextweb.com/artificial-intelligence/2018/06/01/google-announces-it-wont-renew-military-ai-contract/

8. Hao, K. (2019, February 4). This is how AI bias really happens—and why it's so hard to fix. MIT Technology Review. Retrieved from https://www.technologyreview.com/2019/02/04/137602/this-is-how-ai-bias-really-happensand-why-its-so-hard-to-fix/

9. Borgesius, F. Z. (2018). Discrimination, artificial intelligence, and algorithmic decision-making. Council of Europe. Retrieved from https://rm.coe.int/discrimination-artificial-intelligence-and-algorithmic-decision-making/1680925d73

10. Beale, N., Battey, H., Davison, A. C., & MacKay, R. S. (2020, July 1). An unethical optimization principle. Royal Society Open Science. https://doi.org/10.1098/rsos.200462

11. Turek, M. (n.d.). Explainable Artificial Intelligence (XAI). Defense Advanced Research Projects Agency. Retrieved from https://www.darpa.mil/program/explainable-artificial-intelligence

12. D'Monte, L. (n.d.). More jobs will be created than are lost from the AI revolution: WEF AI Head. Mint. Retrieved from https://www.livemint.com/technology/tech-news/-more-jobs-will-be-created-than-

Chapter 14

1. N.S. (2017). Technology Laws Decoded. LexisNexis. (Drawing on Thoreau, which in turn is relied on by Joy, William. 2000. Why the Future Doesn't Need Us. Wired.

2. Joy, W. (2000). Why the Future Doesn't Need Us. Wired. Retrieved from https://www.wired.com/2000/04/joy-2/

3. Simonite, T. (n.d.). Tesla Autopilot Crash: Feds Say Model S Was Speeding. Wired. Retrieved from https://www.wired.com/story/tesla-autopilot-self-driving-crash-california/

4. BBC News. (2020, February 25). Uber self-driving crash driver was watching TV. Retrieved from https://www.bbc.com/news/technology-51645566

5. Graef, A. (2014, October 27). Elon Musk: We are "summoning a demon" with artificial intelligence. UPI. Retrieved from http://www.upi.com/Business_News/2014/10/27/Elon-Musk-We-are-summoning-a-demon-with-artificial-intelligence/4191414407652/

6. Whitwam, R. (2016, August 31). Tesla Model X software update turns gullwing into guillotine doors. ExtremeTech. Retrieved from https://www.extremetech.com/extreme/234855-tesla-model-x-software-update-turns-gullwing-into-guillotine-doors

7. Fox Business. (n.d.). Millennials, baby boomers say Tesla Model 3 is most satisfying car. Retrieved from https://www.foxbusiness.com/lifestyle/millenials-baby-boomers-tesla-model-3-most-satisfying-car

8. Knight, W. (n.d.). Driving tests coming for autonomous cars. IEEE Spectrum. Retrieved from https://spectrum.ieee.org/cars-that-think/transportation/self-driving/driving-tests-coming-for-autonomous-cars

9. BBC News. (2020, September 16). Zoom adds two-factor authentication. Retrieved from https://www.bbc.com/news/technology-54175359

10. Timberg, C., & Dwoskin, E. (2019, May 6). Alexa has been eavesdropping on you this whole time. The Washington Post. Retrieved from https://www.washingtonpost.com/technology/2019/05/06/alexa-has-been-eavesdropping-you-this-whole-time/

11. Berghel, H. (2018). Malice Domestic: The Cambridge Analytica Dystopia. Computer, 51(5), 84–89. doi:10.1109/mc.2018.2381135

12. Foucault, M. (1979). Discipline and Punish (A. Sheridan, Trans.). New York: Vintage Books.

13. Hern, A. (2015, July 23). From the Panopticon to the Skinner box and beyond – privacy in a digital age. The Guardian. Retrieved from https://www.theguardian.com/technology/2015/jul/23/panopticon-digital-surveillance-jeremy-bentham

14. Nappinai, N. S. (2017). Technology Laws Decoded. LexisNexis.

15. Gupta, R. (2020, June 1). Geo-mapping, CCTV cameras, AI — how Telangana police is using tech to enforce Covid safety. ThePrint. Retrieved from https://theprint

16. https://economictimes.indiatimes.com/news/politics-and-nation/in-telangana-the-eyes-have-it-how-the-state-is-redefining-data-driven-governance/articleshow/74644762.cms?from=mdr 17. Gupta, R. (2020,

June 1). Geo-mapping, CCTV cameras, AI — how Telangana police is using tech to enforce Covid safety. ThePrint. Retrieved from https://theprint.in/india/geo-mapping-cctv-cameras-ai-how-telangana-police-is-using-tech-to-enforce-covid-safety/433856/

17. "ThePrint. "Geo-mapping, CCTV cameras & AI: How Telangana Police is using tech to enforce Covid safety." ThePrint, 16 Sept. 2020, https://theprint.in/india/geo-mapping-cctv-cameras-ai-how-telangana-police-is-using-tech-to-enforce-covid-safety/433856/."

18. Menon, S. (2020, September 3). Telangana turns to facial recognition, furthering surveillance state concerns. MediaNama. Retrieved from https://www.medianama.com/2020/09/223-telangana-facial-recognition-push-covid19-pandemic/

19. NITI Aayog is India's premier policy think tank, the National Institution for Transforming India.

20. NITI Aayog. (2018). National Strategy for Artificial Intelligence #AIforAll. Retrieved from https://niti.gov.in/writereaddata/files/document_publication/NationalStrategy-for-AI-Discussion-Paper.pdf

21. The paper proposes a review of "Unattractive Intellectual Property regime to incentivize research and adoption of AI" (emphasis supplied).

22. Tamil Nadu e-Governance Agency. (2020). Tamil Nadu Artificial Intelligence Policy 2020. Retrieved from https://tnega.tn.gov.in/assets/images/pdf/AIPolicy2020.pdf

23. Gupta, R. (2020, June 1). Geo-mapping, CCTV cameras, AI — how Telangana police is using tech to enforce Covid safety. ThePrint. Retrieved from https://theprint.in/india/geo-mapping-cctv-cameras-ai-how-telangana-police-is-using-tech-to-enforce-covid-safety/433856/

24. Analytics India Magazine. (n.d.). 6 AI Policies & Initiatives By Indian State Governments. Retrieved from https://analyticsindiamag.com/6-ai-policies-initiatives-indian-state-governments/

25. NITI Aayog. (n.d.). AIRAWAT Approach Paper. Retrieved from https://niti.gov.in/sites/default/files/2020-01/AIRAWAT_Approach_Paper.pdf

26. NSAI 2018 sets out that "AIRAWAT will be a cloud platform for Big Data Analytics and Assimilation, with a large, power-optimized AI Computing infrastructure using advanced AI processing."

27. Kris Gopalakrishnan Committee. (2020). Report on Non-Personal Data Governance Framework. Retrieved from https://ourgovdotin.files.wordpress.com/2020/07/kris-gopalakrishnan-committee-report-on-non-personal-data-governance-framework.pdf

28. (2017) 10 SCC 1

29. (2019) 1 SCC 1

30. Dormehl, L. (2017, December 7). AI is unraveling the mysteries of the serial killer mind. The Next Web. Retrieved from https://thenextweb.com/artificial-intelligence/2017/12/07/ai-is-unraveling-the-mysteries-of-the-serial-killer-mind/

Chapter 15

1. Gartner. (2022, February 7). Gartner Predicts 25% of People Will Spend at Least One Hour per Day in the Metaverse by 2026. Retrieved from https://www.gartner.com/en/newsroom/press-releases/2022-02-07/gartner-predicts-25-percent-of-people-will-spend-at-least-one-hour-per-day-in-the-metaverse-by-2026

2. Luckey, P. (2019, June 6). Magic Leap Is a Tragic Heap. Retrieved from https://palmerluckey.com/magic-leap-is-a-tragic-heap/

3. SumOfUs. (2022, May). Metaverse Report May 2022. Retrieved from https://www.sumofus.org/images/Metaverse_report_May_2022.pdf

4. Facebook. (2021, September 21). Building the Metaverse Responsibly. Retrieved from https://about.fb.com/news/2021/09/building-the-metaverse-responsibly/

5. Zuckerberg, M. (2019, March 6). A Privacy-Focused Vision for Social Networking. Retrieved from https://www.facebook.com/zuck/posts/10113961365418581

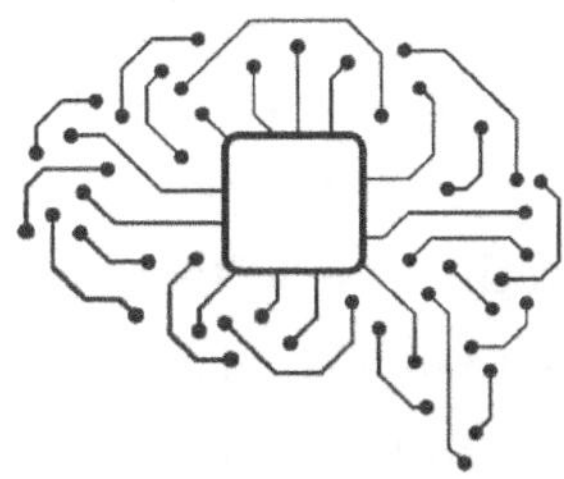

ACKNOWLEDGEMENTS

Jayanth and I research and write for a living but we acknowledge that the process of writing a book requires a very different mindset and constant encouragement from family and friends to complete it. First and foremost, we would like to acknowledge the role of our families—my wife Adarsh Saxena and Jayanth's wife Monika Sharma and daughter Siyona—in giving us the time and space to complete this book and, of course, provide feedback on some chapters.

Many other people have unknowingly played a large part in the making of this book, especially those who encouraged us to keep pace with technology trends—an extremely challenging task in today's digital age. While it's not practical to thank each one of them, we would like to especially thank Pranav Mistry, founder and CEO of Two Platforms Inc., who agreed to write the foreword. We would also like to thank N. S. Nappinai, Supreme Court advocate and founder of Cyber Saathi, and L. Subramanyan, founder and CEO of B2B content company Trivone, for taking out time from their hectic schedules to share their sharp insights and write a chapter each: "Framing an AI Policy" and "An AI Blueprint for Social Change," respectively.

I would also like to thank Mahesh Makhija, leader for Digital and Emerging Technologies at EY in India, for the book's initial brainstorming. Jayanth would like to acknowledge the contribution of Anthony (Tony) Favilla, an American healthtech consultant with a keen interest in both AI and dynamics of the Indian market, and Ranjini Nair, his colleague at Convergence Catalyst and a fellow telecom and emerging deep tech analyst and consultant who helped in the research and storyboarding of a few critical chapters of the book. Tony and Ranjini also provided critical Millennial and Gen Z viewpoints through their feedback and reader's notes. We would also like to thank the countless companies and industry folks who shared their views that helped shape this book.

It's also a fact that it's impossible to write a book on a subject as complex as AI without referring to numerous in-depth pieces by researchers, journalists, and analysts throughout the world. The footnotes section is evidence of that, and also our small way of thanking these incredibly smart individuals for indirectly helping us write this book. Last, but not least, we would like to thank Jaico Publishing House who supported this idea and helped us bring it to life.

www.ingramcontent.com/pod-product-compliance
Lightning Source LLC
LaVergne TN
LVHW022022221025
824046LV00019B/1929